Belfast Battalion
a history of the Belfast I.R.A., 1922-1969

JOHN Ó NÉILL

D1612050

LITTERPRESS

First published in 2018 by
Litter Press
Ballygarran
Wexford

© John Ó Néill 2018

British Library Cataloguing in Publication Data
A CIP catalogue record for this book is available from the British Library

ISBN 978 1 9993008 0 7

Typesetting in Garamond by Litter Press.
Printed by C & R Print, Enniscorthy.

CONTENTS

ILLUSTRATIONS

Page 17: Top: The flag, emblazoned with I.R. (Irish Republic) used on Joe McKelvey's coffin during the reburial in Belfast in 1924 (now in Irish Republican History Museum). Bottom: Joe McKelvey GAA club, 1925-26 with some names suggested (after Quinn 1999).

Page 26: Top left: Hugh Corvin (*Irish Press,* 1970); top right: Dan Turley (Danny Turley); bottom left: Bridie Dolan (*An Phoblacht,* 22nd February 1975); bottom right: Jimmy Steele (1940).

Page 54: Top: Republican election rally, 1933 (*Irish Press,* 28th November 1933). Bottom: R.U.C. guard the gates of Milltown cemetery as republican 1916 commemoration kneels on the road outside (*Irish Independent,* 3rd April 1934).

Page 73: Map of north Belfast showing limits of curfewed district in 1935 (marked in black line).

Page 94: Top left: Charlie McGlade (Quinn 1999); top right: Sean McCaughey (Quinn 1999); bottom left: Hugh McAteer (R.U.C. wanted poster, 1943); bottom right: Chris McLoughlin (courtesy of Chris McLoughlin Jr).

Page 91: Top: Frank Moyna with 200 armed R.U.C. men carrying out evictions in Ardoyne (*Irish Press,* 17th February 1937). Bottom: The after effects of the 1938 bombing of the republican plot at Milltown by the 'Ginger Group' within the Battalion (*Irish Independent,* 12th March 1938).

Page 108: Newspapers: *An Síol* (1933-1938), *Republican News* (1941-1945), *Faoi Glas* (hand drawn in prisons, 1940s, see Ó hUid 1960),

Page 134: I.R.A. Memo, from Chief of Staff to Director of Publicity, Northern Command, 13th June 1942 (P.R.O.N.I.).

Page 141: Top left: Harry White (Quinn 1999); top right: Liam Burke (MacEoin 1997); bottom left: Tom Williams (McVeigh 1999); bottom right: Chrissie Dolan (*An Phoblacht,* 22nd February 1975).

Page 151: Map of curfewed district (lower Falls, Divis, Cullingtree Road, Grosvenor Road), 1942.

Page 160: Top: 1942 *Special Manifesto*; Bottom: Northern Command memo (P.R.O.N.I.).

Page 174: Top left: John Graham (P.R.O.N.I.); top right: Turlach Ó hUid (Ó hUid 1960); bottom left: Madge Burns (McVeigh 1999); bottom right: David Fleming (*Kerryman,* 4th May 1946).

Page 185: Republican newspapers: *Resurgent Ulster* (1951-1955), occasionally as *Ulaidh Ag Aiséirghe.* Republican newspapers, *Glór Uladh* (1955-56).

Page 201: Top: 1962 picket of Crumlin Road over continued detention of political prisoners with Harry Diamond at the front followed by Sean Caughey, Jim O'Kane and Gerry Fitt.

Page 207: Top left: Joe Cahill; top right: Billy McKee (*An Phoblacht,* 29th October 1973); bottom left: Jim Sullivan; bottom right: Billy McMillan (both *United Irishman,* May 1975).

Page 229: Map showing location of barricades in Falls Road, August 1969 (*United Irshman,* September 1969).

Introduction

Belfast, as the second largest city in Ireland, barely needs an introduction to its particular historical complexities. Partition, which made it the largest city in the north-eastern region of Ireland left under unionist control in 1921, merely amplified many of its existing anxieties and lengthy history of violent conflict. By the middle of 1922, around 25% of all fatalities in the violent conflict around Irish independence since 1919 had occurred within the city.

Today we are no further removed, in time, from that steep intensification of violent conflict in the late 1960s, than those who were involved in the late 1960s were from 1920-22. In that light, there is a puzzling absence of detailed studies of the organisations and trends that spanned the period from the 1920s to 1960s. With some notable exceptions, we are largely bereft of detailed studies of the non-state republican and unionist organisations in the intervening period (please note, throughout the text, I have tried to consistently use 'Unionist' to specifically designate actions by the Unionist Party's northern government and elsewhere 'unionist' where it is other members of that same political community). Similarly, historians have yet to capture a real sense of who participated in the violence of 1920-22 in Belfast on the unionist side, the depth of official knowledge and direction and what legacy that carried across into post-1922 politics. Arguably this gap in our knowledge compromises the idea that we fully appreciate the background to the intensification of violence in the late 1960s.

We are better served with histories of the republican side up to the early 1920s, in recent excellent contributions from the likes of Jim McDermott (*Northern Divisions*) and Kieron Glennon (*From Pogrom to Civil War*) and an increasing availability of archival materials that permit exploration of the individual republicans involved, their motivations and interactions. And it should be noted that neither were the I.R.A. the only players on the Irish nationalist side.

This book, essentially, provides a chronology of the activities of the Belfast I.R.A. from 1st November 1922 to the 22nd September 1969. That is, from when contact was broken between the I.R.A.'s Dublin-based G.H.Q. and what was then the 1st (Belfast) Brigade of the I.R.A.'s 3rd Northern Division (in 1922) and when the Belfast Battalion of the I.R.A. broke with G.H.Q. in Dublin in 1969.

Largely the evidence used to construct this chronology is contemporary news reporting and other official records, such as court reports. In this respect, it is very much a subaltern history, relying on the narrative generated through descriptions offered in court cases, officialdom's inferences of motive and blame and the partial view that provides. More significantly, though, it does secure a more robust chronological framework than the frailties of both oral history and the canonical studies of the I.R.A. over the relevant period, such as Bowyer Bell's *Secret Army* and Tim Pat Coogan's *The I.R.A.* (both essential reading as background). While indispensable both have minor chronological errors with regard to Belfast. More recently, Matt Treacy has shown the value of thematic treatment when writing about the period from 1956 to 1969 (in *The I.R.A., 1956-69*). To concentrate on developing an appropriately detailed timeline, I have largely avoided thematic exploration except where unavoidable.

Unfortunately, for most of this period, we lack a clear picture of who was involved on the Unionist side and who directed their activities. Almost immune from arrest or imprisonment, even subsequent academic histories have largely ignored the role of violence in unionist politics and so, to some extent, the history of the Belfast I.R.A. is stripped of some of it's significant context.

I've broken the history of the Belfast I.R.A. down into several phases for this book. The first follows immediately on from the intense violence of 1920-22 when the I.R.A. was paralysed by the vortex of a civil war in the south and coming to terms with its own traumatic experiences of the previous three years. The reburial of Joe McKelvey in 1924 then became a reference point for the re-organisation of the I.R.A. in the city.

The fragmentation of the republican position that had begun with the civil war continued with the de Valera split of 1926 which ushered in the next phase. This was a confusing era wherein Fianna Fáil and I.R.A. fortunes still appeared to be interdependent. Ironically, the natural partner for Fianna Fáil in the north, though, was the Nationalist Party, complicating the dynamics between the Belfast I.R.A. and G.H.Q. in Dublin. This appears to provide a more nuanced context, ultimately, to the Belfast I.R.A.'s reaction to the I.R.A. leadership returning to individuals like Sean Russell and Stephen Hayes who, to some extent, sought to at least not work against Fianna Fáil, if not actually work with them. Around Russell and Hayes the I.R.A. hemorrhaged senior personnel.

The southern Minister for Justice, Gerry Boland, in the 1940s referred to what happened over the period from 1938 to 1946 as the 'second civil war'. In 1941 the Belfast I.R.A. firstly ousted the remnants of Russell's leadership, in his deputy Hayes, and then relocated G.H.Q. to Belfast. All the while, Boland and de Valera, sought to crush the I.R.A. for good in the south and assist the Unionists to do the same in the north. The outworking of this saw the eclipse of an I.R.A. G.H.Q. to provide overall strategic direction but failed to eradicate local republican structures and, more significantly, sentiment for the organisation as enough survived for the I.R.A. to rebuild in the late 1940s. By that time Fianna Fáil too had succumbed to electoral defeat for its handling of the I.R.A. (at least in part).

The formal declaration of a twenty-six county republic provided the impetus for the I.R.A. to finally focus on a northern campaign. Paradoxically, after lobbying for a militant anti-partition push for decades the Belfast I.R.A. was to take a subordinate role. However, Belfast was mainly to supply internees to Crumlin Road jail. As with the end of the 1940s, the Belfast I.R.A. had to be rebuilt from scratch after the 1956-62 campaign. Given the directions the I.R.A. took from 1969 onwards, much energy has been expended on narrating a particular view of what transpired over the period from about 1962-69. The events that led up to the split appear less dramatic in hindsight than later histories have required them to be.

ACKNOWLEGDEMENTS
This book had started as background research for a biography of Jimmy Steele (which I do intend to publish in the future) before becoming a necessary pre-requisite. Thanks are due to all those who assisted in the research, answering queries, and helping and encouraging in various ways including Claire Breen, Fearghal Caughey, Tim Pat Coogan, Danny Donnelly, Martin Flynn, Anthony Fox, Kieron Glennon, Brian Hanley, Kathleen Hayes, Roddy Hegarty, Roy Johnston, Brian Keane, Ciaran MacAirt, Dónal McAnallen, Mary McConville, Jim McDermot, Tim McGarry, Máire McGinley, Billy McKee, Chris McLoughlin, Sean McNally, Danny Morrison, Niall Murphy, National Library of Ireland, Féilim Ó hAdhmaill, Stan Ó Cairbre, Gerry O'Hare, Niall Ó Murchú, Geraldine O'Neill (who read the whole book in draft), John O'Neill, Tómas Ó Néill, Eamonn Phoenix, P.R.O.N.I., Republican History Museum in Conway Mill (particularly Susan and Johnny), Ciaran Steele, Liam Steele, Seamus Steele, Siobhan Steele and Danny Turley. Apologies if I've overlooked anyone.

i ndíl gcuimhne Niall Largey, 1972-2004

"A SUSPENSION OF OFFENSIVE OPERATIONS": 1922-26

harassed by the enemy and in need of rest

In November 1922 the Belfast I.R.A. was in chaos. By July that year, Ireland had been on a war footing for almost ten years. The importation of German rifles by unionists in 1912 had signaled their intent to violently oppose Home Rule and the outbreak of war between Europe's imperial powers in 1914 merely delayed the outbreak of conflict in Ireland rather than prevented it.

For republicans the short-lived Irish Republic in 1916 became a touchstone. Susequently, republican political aspirations were usually given as the 'restoration of the republic declared in 1916'. Commemorations for those executed after the 1916 republic was suppressed also joined the tributes for the United Irishmen at Bodenstown (and, in Belfast in the 1920s, on Cavehill) as integral to the annual republican calendar.

When a separate Irish parliament (Dáil Éireann) was formed, based on the 1918 election results, the military forces organised to defend it (the Irish Republican Army, the woman's revolutionary organisation Cumann na mBan and the youth organisation Fianna Éireann) inevitably clashed with the R.I.C., the British Army and the temporary special constabularies created to bolster the R.I.C. (and to carry out reprisals and other counter-insurgency actions). The latter were the Special Reserve (who became known as the Black and Tans), the Auxiliary Division (the 'Auxies') and the Ulster Special Constabulary (U.S.C.).[1] As the latter incorporated various unionist paramilitary groups intent on violently resisting Home Rule, the reprisals carried out by the Special Reserve and Auxiliary Division paled in comparison with the killings carried out in Belfast.

A proposal to temporarily install parliaments in Dublin and Belfast led to an arbitrary partitioning of Ireland from May 1921. This nominally applied the logic that it included counties with unionist majorities, but in reality incorporated the likes of Fermanagh and Tyrone which had nationalist majorities. A Boundary Commission was to review partition and it was generally assumed it's report would end the partition experiment.

In Belfast, violence didn't end with the truce of July 1921 and continued until conflict broke out between republican and Free State forces in the south in June 1922. Unionists intended the combined experience of extreme violence and an aggressive internment policy to drive the Catholic professional and business classes to move away and to attack opposition to partition.[2] Up to June 1922, around 25% of the 2,000 or so fatalities since 1919 had occurred in Belfast where republican forces had lost over 30 members, while the R.I.C., Special Constables, British Army and paramilitary groups had lost just over 40. Michael MacConaill, the Belfast Brigade's Medical Officer, described this period as the 'Battle of Belfast'. Over 80% of casualties in Belfast had been civilians compared to less than 20% elsewhere in Ireland. That experience of intense violence very much shaped the attitudes of the Belfast I.R.A. into the 1920s and much later.

As an I.R.A. had evolved between 1916 and the formation of Dáil Éireann in 1919, the existing battalion of Irish Volunteer companies in Belfast had simply become A and B Company of the I.R.A.'s Belfast Battalion, with 'C' and 'D' companies added in early 1919.[3] These units didn't have strict geographic catchment areas. The Belfast Battalion was re-structured in September 1920, when the companies were divided into a 1st Battalion (centred on the Falls and sometimes referred to as the 'West' Battalion) and 2nd Battalion (stretching from Ardoyne to Ballymacarrett). From April 1917 the Belfast Battalion reported to the Belfast, Antrim and East Down Brigade. By March 1921, officers and experienced volunteers had been used to staff four companies in each of the two battalions, which now formed the 1st (Belfast) Brigade of the 3rd Northern Division. The 1st Battalion was quickly expanded to six companies: 'A' centred roughly on Leeson Street, 'B' on Cullingtree Road and the Pound, 'C' on Carrickhill and Smithfield, 'D' on Clonard, 'E' on the upper Falls, while 'F' was an engineering company. The 2nd Battalion companies were 'A' in Ardoyne and the Bone, 'B' in Ballymacarrett, 'C' in the Market and 'D' in North Queen Street/York Street. By April 1921, the loosely independent Fianna Éireann and Cumann na mBan structures had been aligned onto the I.R.A.'s divisional command structure.

Local conditions dictated that differing divisional areas of the I.R.A. had to adapt their tactics accordingly. This included some holding territory while others went on the offensive with rural and urban guerilla operations. The Belfast Brigade faced conditions unlike that faced by any other command in having to carry out urban guerilla raids and attacks alongside mounting an almost continual defence of some districts against intensive communal attacks by heavily armed unionists.

In August 1921, after the truce, three additional battalions were added to the Belfast Brigade. The 2nd Battalion and 3rd Battalions seem to have covered the city centre, north Belfast and Ballymacarrett. Pat Thornbury, O/C of the 4th Battalion, states that it covered the Whiterock, Hannahstown and Randalstown (O/C or 'Officer Commanding' was the designation the I.R.A. typical gave to the leader of a unit). Many of those who joined the 3rd and 4th Battalions supposedly enlisted after the truce (July 11th 1921) and were later derided as 'Trucileers' by pre-July 1921 veterans. The 1st Battalion's engineering company ('F') also became the 5th (Engineering) Battalion. It is a measure of the chaos of 1922 that it is difficult to reconstruct the organisation of the Belfast Brigade with any huge degree of certainty.

The conventional view is that Belfast I.R.A. officers largely took the pro-treaty side although this was largely down to Eoin O'Duffy insisting that if they supported pro-treaty G.H.Q. it would provide them with more arms than the anti-treaty Executive (as it was G.H.Q. never made good on the offer). Those that agreed to support the treaty mostly relocated to I.R.A. G.H.Q. in Dublin while awaiting instructions and the Belfast I.R.A. effectively acquired two, parallel, command structures. One was pro-treaty and mostly made up of the existing staff officers but now Dublin-based and reporting to I.R.A. G.H.Q.. The other was anti-treaty, in Belfast, and reporting to the I.R.A. Executive. According to *An tÓglách*, those supporting the treaty ousted Joe McKelvey as Divisional O/C by April 1922.[4] His replacement was Seamus Woods, who had enlisted in the new (pro-treaty) Free State Army as a Colonel on 1st February. But as far as McKelvey and the (anti-treaty) Republicans were concerned, Pat Thornbury had succeeded McKelvey as Divisional O/C. This confusion perpetuated itself into the attempt to concentrate on a northern campaign in May, which basically became isolated upsurges in a couple of locations, including Belfast. By June, both Roger McCorley (pro-treaty) and Willie Ward (anti-treaty) seemed to consider themselves as Belfast Brigade O/C.

Meantime the Cumann na mBan staff had remained anti-treaty, while eleven of the fourteen Fianna staff officers had gone pro-treaty.

The intended shape of the northern offensive in May isn't really clear. It began with attacks on the Special Constabulary, police barracks and R.I.C., alongside targeted arson attacks against businesses, all with the intention of demonstrating the inability of the Unionists to control Belfast. Nationalist districts were subjected to intense assaults by unionists, the R.I.C. and Specials to pin down the I.R.A. into defensive actions. May 1922 was the most violent month in Belfast over the period from 1920 to 1922.

One long term impact of the May 1922 offensive was that the Unionist Home Affairs Minister Richard Dawson Bates issued regulations on 22nd May outlawing membership of the I.R.A., I.R.B., Irish Volunteers, Fianna Éireann and Cumann na mBan, as well as possession of any documents related to those organisations. Less than a year previously the I.R.A. had operated a public office in Belfast city centre.

Pro-treaty and anti-treaty sentiment in Belfast had even extended to clashes over control of arms dumps with occasional, if fleeting, physical and verbal confrontations. In one episode, the competing divisional intelligence officers, Dan Turley (anti-treaty) and David McGuinness (pro-treaty), vied to secure the services of Pat Stapleton, a productive I.R.A. plant in military headquarters in Belfast.[5] The May 1922 offensive, as a combined effort, staved off any real threat of outright conflict within the I.R.A. in Belfast. But the lack of a clear plan or strategy meant the northern campaign was already a failure when violence broke out in Dublin in June between pro-treaty and anti-treaty forces. By August 1922 both sides agreed to halt the I.R.A. offensive in the north-east.

At the end of the summer, a proportion of the Belfast Brigade officers and volunteers were sent to the Curragh where they were to rest and train in anticipation of renewing the campaign in the north. It was also agreed that they would not be asked to participate in operations in the south. The first groups to go were "...officers and men who were harassed by the enemy and in need of rest." According to Joe Murray, by September 1922 the scale of departures for the south had depleted the Belfast I.R.A..[6]

Pat Thornbury, divisional O/C in July 1922, his vice O/C James O'Donnell, quartermaster Hugh Corvin and director of intelligence, Dan Turley, continued to form the leadership of the Belfast I.R.A. into the mid-1920s and later.[7] All but O'Donnell were to end up imprisoned (Corvin in September 1922, Thornbury in October 1922, Turley in January 1923) but returned to active service once released. Thornbury, though, was served with a notice excluding him from the six counties (his brothers remained active in Belfast). Thornbury had been succeeded as O/C by O'Donnell in October 1922 (by then the Division had been reorganised as a Brigade). O'Donnell remained as Brigade O/C until Corvin was released in December 1924.[8]

I.R.A. G.H.Q. regarded Seamus Woods as Divisional O/C and Tom Fitzpatrick as Brigade O/C in the summer of 1922 (the anti-treaty forces recognised Willie Ward as Brigade O/C). In reality, though, both sets of staff officers were struggling with the attitude of the (pro-treaty) Dublin G.H.Q. towards the north.[9] Amidst the growing confrontations in the south between pro-treaty and anti-treaty forces and tensions in Belfast at the end of August 1922, it was agreed by both sides that I.R.A. offensive operations would formally cease in the north.

Kieron Glennon, in *From Pogrom to Civil War*, shows how a complex matrix of motivations led Belfast volunteers to take the pro-treaty or anti-treaty side. Loyalty (particularly to Michael Collins), politics and events influenced individual choices, alongside the prospect of a regular pay packet or relief from the intense violence in Belfast. At the end of September, with 3rd Northern Division men in camps in the south and Collins now dead, former Belfast I.R.A. officers in the Free State Army wrote to the Chief of Staff, Richard Mulcahy, at G.H.Q. asking what the plans were for the north. Their letter went unanswered.

All the while, violence still continued in Belfast, even though the intensity and scale of casualties had dropped significantly. For instance, over the weekend of 30th September and 1st October, a bomb was thrown at the corner of Stratheden Street and Lepper Street and shots were fired from Cupar Street into Lucknow Street, wounding two.[10] Shots were also fired into Stanhope Street, and from vacant ground in Bray Street into Herbert Street, wounding Henry McAuley.[11]

That violence formed the immediate backdrop to the Free State officers (who had written to Mulcahy) meeting Belfast I.R.A. representatives on 4th October. They outlined the only current proposal from Mulcahy: to recognise the Unionist government. The Belfast I.R.A. officers dismissed the idea and walked out. Another meeting in the Falls Road Boys Hall two days later went even worse. The pro-treaty officers present included Denis McCullough, President of the Supreme Council of the I.R.B. at the time of the Easter Rising, a Belfast Sinn Féin councillor and Mulcahy's brother-in-law. The Free State officers were slammed by those in Belfast for taking comfortable paid positions while the city was still under pressure (McCullough now had a shop in Dublin, where he lived). It was an accusation that stubbornly followed many of them around for the rest of their lives. Within a week of the meetings Pat Thornbury, the Belfast Brigade O/C, was arrested and interned.

By October, there was also discontent in the Curragh. Since it was recognised that continuing the northern campaign was futile, and following instructions from Dublin, pro-treaty officers in Belfast placed some arms in dumps, destroyed files and some left for the south. According to Tom Fitzpatrick, those who couldn't return home were transferred to Dundalk (where one hundred and thirty-four are listed in the November 1922 census as part of the 5th Northern Division) or to the 3rd Northern Division Reserve in the Curragh (seventy-one were listed in the November census). A total of three hundred and sixty-six Belfast men were later recorded as having been supplied with pensions information by 1926.[12]

Joe Murray records that, as 3rd Battalion O/C, he supervised the dumping of arms on 31st October 1922. That last weekend in October saw a bomb thrown into Vulcan Street and a huge arms find by the R.U.C. in Dunmore Street including thirty seven rifles, bayonets, thirty Mills bombs, four eighteen pound shells, revolvers, pistols, parts of a Thompson machine gun and six thousand rounds of rifle ammunition (was this what Free State officers meant by 'ensuring the removal to safety' of arms?). Through into November, bombing and shooting incidents continued, albeit at a decreasing intensity. The violence in Belfast was dying down, but never formally stopped.

By then, the Belfast I.R.A. was effectively on its own.

---

[1] The U.S.C. had four sections: A, B, C and C1. The A, C and C1 sections were discontinued, with only the B Constables (generally known as 'B Specials') retained.

[2] Kleinrichert, D. 2001 *Republican Internment and the Prison Ship Argenta 1922* deals with how the business and professional classes were targeted by internment. Official unionist policy was to 'encourage' Catholics to move out of the north.

[3] This was the 1st Battalion of the Belfast, Antrim and East Down Brigade, under the command of Sean O'Neill in 1919-20 (Military Archives, SP12109). In his pension documents, Sean Cusack seems to indicate that this was known as the 1st West Belfast Battalion, although he dates this from 1916 onwards (it may be that the name was used later when the 2nd Battalion was formed), see Military Archives, SP308. Liam Gaynor suggests the organisation into four companies began as early as 1916 (BMH/WS0183).

[4] *An tÓglách*, 22nd April, 1922.

[5] See Military Archives, MSPC/RO/402 which refers to the Executive Forces and names Ward, while BMH/WS0395 names Fitzpatrick. Similarly, see witness statement from David McGuinness (BMH/WS0417) naming the relevant pro-treaty staff. Woods had actually joined the Free State forces and was attached to its intelligence staff from February 1922 (see Military Archives, SP11139). Fitzpatrick's pension file indicates he spent 1922 trying to recruit to the Free State army in Belfast as well as 'ensuring the

removal to safety' of Belfast I.R.A. arms dumps so they could not be used in the civil war (he doesn't explain what this means), only formally joining the Free State army in September 1922 (Military Archives, SP13219). Oddly, some Brigade documents also list Sean O'Neill as Brigade O/C in 1922 (eg see Military Archives, MSPC/RO/402).

[6] See BMH/WS0412.

[7] This is based on the divisional staff as retrospectively recorded by the Brigade Committees in the 1930s.

[8] O'Donnell is listed on the nomination papers for Paddy Nash, who had been vice O/C to Ward for the 1924 election. O'Donnell may have been acting as O/C by then (see *Belfast Newsletter*, 20th October, 1924).

[9] See Kieran Glennon's *From Pogrom to Civil War* (2013) for a good synopsis of the background.

[10] Hugh Stevenson (age 7) and Joe McNally (age 17).

[11] As reported in the press (where dates are given in the text, the details are taken from contemporary newspaper reports – some of these are cited where there is additional detail provided).

[12] See Military Archives, WM/MSP/10. This figure wouldn't include those Belfast men still serving with the Free State army in 1926. The list does identify those from Belfast who were officially enlisted in the Free State army.

suspending operations

When the formal link to G.H.Q. was severed in November 1922, prospects for the Belfast I.R.A. were bleak. Volunteers continued to drift down both to join and to fight the Free State army. The 3rd Northern Division Reserve in the Curragh (dismissively called the 'special refugee unit' by Ernest Blythe) was disbanded in mid-November and some joined the 17th Battalion of the Free State army.[1]

A significant number of Belfast I.R.A. volunteers were held in prison camps (north and south) and the prison ship Argenta.[2] The number imprisoned kept increasing as new internments continued to exceed releases until June 1923.[3] Embroiled in a civil war in the south, the Belfast I.R.A. was left on a fragile defensive footing with no immediate prospects.

While the city itself remained relatively quiet towards the end of 1922, events elsewhere were to have a deep emotional resonance among Belfast republicans. On December 8th, 1922, the Free State government executed the former 3rd Northern Division commander Joe McKelvey along with Rory O'Connor, Liam Mellows and Dick Barrett in a reprisal for the shooting of a pro-treaty T.D., Sean Hales. All four had been in Mountjoy at the time of Hales death and had no involvement in the killing. The executions merely served to heighten the bitterness of the clashes between the Free State forces and the I.R.A..

In mid-December, perhaps to assuage criticism for executing McKelvey, the job of taking control of the Viceregal Lodge in Dublin on behalf of the Free State army was given to former volunteers from the 3rd Northern Division. That same month, though, there were still arms finds and occasional shootings in Belfast, such as an attempt to kill a publican on the New Lodge Road on 13th December. Clearly a lot of weapons were still in circulation in Belfast and there were almost daily reports of armed robberies across the city.

The I.R.A. sought swift revenge for McKelvey's execution. Barely a month later a landmine blew out the front of the shop and house owned by Denis McCullough in Dawson Street in Dublin, injuring three people and badly damaging premises on either side.[4] McCullough (a former Belfast O/C) had recently been nominated to the Free State's Senate. In early October 1922 he had been directly criticised in Belfast for his role in promoting the treaty. He had also personally tried to persuade McKelvey, as commandant, to get the 3rd Northern Division to support the treaty.

There is no record of direct Belfast involvement in the bombing although Belfast-based engineering units had been manufacturing explosives for the I.R.A. in the south. More pointedly maybe, the I.R.A.'s Dublin-based Director of Intelligence at the time was Mick Carolan from Belfast, who went back a long way with McCullough.[5]

From February 1923 it was apparent that the Free State forces were winning in the civil war. It's hardly coincidental that at the end of that month and into early March, now sensing defeat and hoping to avoid future prosecution, some people gave away arms dumps to the R.U.C. in Belfast. This included one in the Falls Road A.O.H. hall, two in the Cullingtree Road district, and others in Stranmillis, Cinnamond Street and Library Street.[6] Over the same period in March and into early April, a number of Belfast volunteers were captured by Free State forces, in Roscommon, Sligo, Longford and Tipperary.

In Belfast, Jack McNally reckons there were only around eighty active members left that summer and contact with Dublin was almost non-existent. Company meetings happened about once a month but the continuous arrests meant that there were constant changes in company officers and staffs. Although the city was largely calm, violence could still break out randomly. On 9th May, a soccer match in the Bog Meadows between teams from Ballymacarrett and Sandy Row led to an exchange of gun fire and three arrests. The Belfast Brigade had been reduced to having what McNally describes as "...practically no means of responding to any emergency." For that reason, McNally was tasked by the Brigade O/C, James O'Donnell, with putting an active service unit of around seven volunteers together, drawn from units across the city.[7]

In the civil war, the I.R.A. called for a "...suspension of offensive operations" on 30th May, with an order to units to dump arms by 23rd May.[8] The influence of the civil war on Unionist security policy was immediately visible as June became the first month in which prisoner releases in the north exceeded new internments. A substantial batch of raw materials for making explosives was intercepted the same month, with the Free State and Unionists having begun to jointly operate border posts and customs from 1st April 1923.[9] Of more immediate concern to the Unionist government was the return of Free State soldiers to their homes in Belfast. Barely ten percent of the two thousand northerners who served with the Free State army ever returned to live permanently in the north. But the Unionists feared they would provide a pool of trained and experienced soldiers that the I.R.A. might seek to recruit or reinstate.

While the R.U.C. regularly arrested and harassed men they believed were home on leave from the Free State army, it became much more frequent from mid-March 1923. From then until early May, Free State soldiers Hugh Donnelly, Joseph McKeating, Joseph McPeake, Hugh O'Neill, John O'Hagan and William Somerfield were all arrested on various pretexts. The latter two were involved in a clash that followed a search of O'Hagan's house. Outside the house, an I.R.A. volunteer, John Leathem, was also arrested as shots were fired at the B Specials involved.[10] Clearly, casual incidents in Belfast still had the potential to rapidly escalate in intensity.

In June, following the suspension of operations in the south, the I.R.A. prisoners on the Argenta and in Larne Camp re-organised along pro/anti-treaty lines with Pat Thornbury

as O/C and Paddy Nash, Dan McCann, James McGouran and Richard Ryan all representing the Belfast prisoners in different sections of the Argenta. Hugh Corvin became O/C in the Larne Camp. Both reported, via the Belfast Brigade's Intelligence Officer, Eamonn Murphy, to G.H.Q. in Dublin.[11]
Without a short term plan, the I.R.A. focus was mainly on the prisons and securing the release of internees and sentenced prisoners. Politically, it was hoped the Boundary Commission would make two separate governments in Belfast and Dublin unworkable. This would at least reduce the main issue to the question of Ireland's degree of independence from Britain rather than partition.
So, over the summer of 1923, discontent, protests and hunger-strikes become frequent on the Argenta, in Larne Camp, Derry Gaol, Belfast Prison and elsewhere. Hugh Corvin, who had contracted TB, was moved to the notoriously cold and damp Derry Gaol for taking a lead role in these. Many prisoners were moved around making visits difficult for their families. The large group of Belfast prisoners also got a reputation for not mixing well with other prisoners which occasionally caused tensions.[12]
That year's Twelfth of July demonstrations passed off relatively peacefully, although Daniel O'Neill from Carrickhill, was arrested on the Whiterock Road with a loaded revolver.[13] At the end of July, the R.U.C. raided an I.R.A. headquarters in Smithfield, at Toners Bar in Winetavern Street.[14] In it they found a dump of eight revolvers and ammunition. Patrick Loughran, who had been in the Curragh camp the previous summer, was arrested and charged with possession of the dump (he received an eighteen month sentence in November).[15]
The involvement of Leathem alongside two Free State troops in the same incident and then Loughran's arrest probably strengthened the Unionists' fear that battle-hardened I.R.A. volunteers were now returning after the Civil War. The atmosphere in the city again grew tense. Another street confrontation in early August saw shots fired by the R.U.C. in Lancaster Street and arrests made. The R.U.C. intensified raids on Catholic districts and further arms finds were made in the Short Strand and in Stanhope Street.[16]
Then, on 4th September, unionists shot a Catholic publican, John Shevlin, outside his pub on the corner of the Oldpark Road and Byron Street. Shevlin had just taken the pub over from the same James Toner who had owned the Winetavern Street bar. When he was shot he fell in front of a tram and died within minutes.[17] Even though the R.U.C. knew he was killed by unionists, they continued to raid for I.R.A. weapons, while putting up a £1,000 reward for information.
Within a few days of Shevlin's death, a raid on Kashmir Road had netted an I.R.A. volunteer, John Cooper, with a revolver and ammunition. As they were in the back yard he was acquitted, but the Unionists interned him anyway. Later the same day John Craig and another revolver were captured.[18] On 11th September, another small I.R.A. arms dump with a revolver and ammunition was found to the rear of a shop on the New Lodge Road.[19] The next day a pedestrian reported finding four bombs in a unionist district. Close to where John Shevlin was killed, a bomb was thrown by unionists at the end of October, seriously wounding one man.

The return of Free State soldiers and others meant that the poor treatment of northern I.R.A. volunteers by the Free State army was also becoming common knowledge in Belfast. After the summer of 1923 the Unionists were even happy to let Free State army recruits entice militant young northerners over the border, knowing it was more likely to lead to them emigrating or being held in a prison camp than a career in the Free State army (never mind returning, better trained, to the north).[20] By early 1924, Richard Mulcahy, the Free State's Minister for Defence, was even complaining that the Unionists were allowing their side of the border to be used as a sanctuary by the I.R.A..[21]

Meanwhile, republicans agitated to get prisoners released. At the end of October and until the middle of November 1923, internees on the Argenta and the other prisons were on hunger strike and many of the leaders were taken off and removed to onshore prisons. From November 1923 to July 1924, most months began to see increasing numbers of internees being released. From July a core group of around 140 internees were kept until November that year.

Although it was less frequent, finds of arms by the R.U.C. continued in early 1924. Old dumps of I.R.A. weapons were found in Andersonstown in February and Osman Street in April.[22] At the end of March, James McKeon lost two fingers when he handled a box containing detonators on a windowsill in a Protestant district on the Shore Road (the exact circumstances are unclear). The same week grenades were left out to be found on the roof of a business in Henry Street. People were clearly get rid of arms dumps rather than risk arrest. Shevlin's death and the Oldpark bombing in October had already shown that the threat from unionists was still real.

In August 1924, the Belfast Brigade reported its strength as two hundred and forty men.[23] Its strength in July 1922 was at least four hundred and thirty-two. More than two hundred from Belfast were in the Free State army in November 1922 (not all had been in the I.R.A.) and there were also losses due to internment.[24] But many of those still at liberty in Belfast now only nominally remained members of the I.R.A., given that Jack McNally (as quoted earlier) reckoned only eighty of those volunteers were still active in mid-1923. Despite the lack of observable I.R.A. activity, targeted R.U.C. raids continued. Early in the morning of 19th September, the R.U.C. and B Specials put a cordon around the Short Strand and carried out searches from 2 am until 9 am. At 9 am, the R.U.C. uncovered six Mills bombs, detonators, a Verey pistol, two rifles and one hundred rounds of ammunition. The press reported that the R.U.C. believed that a number of people had managed to escape their cordon. In reality, just hours before the raid, John Walsh had managed to get a taxi, driven by Patrick Woods, to move arms from the Short Strand to Currie Street off Cullingtree Road. There, about 10.30 pm, the arms were taken through number 18 Currie Street and hidden in a shed at the rear. The organised nature of the raid made it seem clear that the R.U.C. were acting on a tip off.[25]

This was even more apparent when the R.U.C. immediately began another targeted raid in Currie Street, starting with a 'dance hall', known locally as the 'Currie Institute'. They then raided houses in Currie Street itself. There they uncovered the large dump in a shed in the entry behind 18 Currie Street. The R.U.C. found twenty-four service rifles, a Thompson, eight Mills bombs, detonators, 'cheddar' (explosives), thousands of rounds of ammunition and literature on weapons.[26] Dan O'Kane, of 18 Currie Street, was arrested along with his stepson John McAstocker. An R.U.C. Sergeant later testified in court that O'Kane and his wife had been in Ballymacarrett on the night the arms were moved.[27] The R.U.C. also detained eleven men found in the hall in Currie Street including John Leathem. John McAstocker also appears to have been in the hall.[28] One of those arrested, David Walsh, had been captured in the same hall in July 1922 when the R.U.C. had swooped on thirty volunteers from C Company, 1st Battalion.[29]

In court, O'Kane and McAstocker's defence pointed out that there was public access to the building where the arms were found and so it could not be shown that they could have had any knowledge that the arms dump was there. It was clear from the R.U.C. evidence that they had a tip-off that an arms dump was being moved to Currie Street (in the Cullingtree Road area) from the Short Strand.

In October 1924, the Belfast I.R.A. put forward two prisoners to contest the 29th October election to the Imperial parliament in Westminster. Paddy Nash, former vice O/C, 1st (Belfast) Brigade, was selected to stand in West Belfast. Hugh Corvin was chosen as the candidate for North Belfast. The Sinn Féin President, de Valera went on an election tour north of the border as political divisions saw competing nationalist and republican candidates in the elections.

Republican influence in Fermanagh and Tyrone was still sufficiently strong to prompt calls for a Nationalist Party to be formally created as an alternative to Sinn Féin, implying it might then recognise the authority of northern government.[30] Then, with the media debating his role in the election, de Valera was arrested in Newry and got served an exclusion order. He was arrested again in Derry on 2nd November and received a one month sentence in Crumlin Road. From 1924 until well into the 1930s, the Unionists regularly applied exclusion orders under the Special Powers Act to individuals canvassing for republican candidates in elections, like Mary McSwiney, Constance Markiewicz, Hanna Sheehy-Skeffington and de Valera.[31]

While imprisoned, de Valera apparently remained aloof from the other republican prisoners (not exactly endearing himself to the Belfast I.R.A.), and was released on 28th November.[32] With its President in jail in Belfast, the election was held. Sinn Féin staged only its second Árd Fhéis since 1921 on 4th November. More significantly, for the Belfast I.R.A., though, Joe McKelvey's remains had been released for reburial on 29th October.

---

[1] See Lynch, R. 2006, *The Northern I.R.A. and the Early Years of Partition, 1920-22*, p314.
[2] At its peak, the prison ship *Argenta* and Larne Workhouse prison camp alone contained around 540 prisoners, out of a total of around 900 men who were interned. It has been estimated, though, that only roughly 10% of those interned were active in the I.R.A. (see Kleinrichert 2001). At least two hundred were interned after the break with Dublin in November 1922.
[3] Kleinrichert 2001, p300.
[4] *Ulster Herald*, 6th January, 1923.

[5] MacEoin, U. 1997, *The I.R.A. in the Twilight Years, 1923-48*, p78.

[6] See *Irish News* and *Irish Times* in March 1923 for the various finds.

[7] McNally, J. 1989, *Morally Good, Politically Bad*, p20.

[8] MacEoin 1997.

[9] Frank McGeough was later given a nine month sentence for this in November 1923.

[10] Leathem was in E Company, 1st Battalion (Military Archives, MSPC/RO/403), see also *Irish Times* 31st May 1923. Incident happened on night of Tuesday 29th May and is reported in *Irish Times*, 31st May. O'Hagan was originally from Grove Street but is not listed in the (incomplete) return for D Company, 2nd Battalion (see Military Archives, MSPC/RO/404). Leathem's brother Thomas was arrested for firing the shots in August.

[11] Kleinrichert 2001, p129.

[12] Kleinrichert 2001, pp296-7.

[13] O'Neill was a member of Fianna Éireann.

[14] Several I.R.A. volunteers gave this address in the Free State army census of November 1922. See Military Archives, HA/5/151G.

[15] He was a member of C Company, 1st Battalion, see Military Archives, MSPC/RO/403.

[16] See press, eg *Irish News*, for 6th August, 13th August and 29th August 1923.

[17] See *Irish Independent, Irish News*, 13th September 1923 and press reports from the preceding week.

[18] See his twin Joe's medal file: Military Archives, MD39003.

[19] The shop belonged to the aunt of two I.R.A. volunteers, Bill and Jimmy Steele. The latter had been arrested and detained for a few weeks in August.

[20] Robert Lynch's PhD thesis, *The Northern I.R.A. and the Early Years of Partition, 1920-22*. https://dspace.stir.ac.uk/bitstream/1893/1517/3/robert%20john %20lynch-24072009.pdf.txt

[21] MacEoin 1997, p95.

[22] The R.U.C. received information on the locations of dumps, including Osman Street, in October 1923 but couldn't locate it (see P.R.O.N.I., HA/5/424).

[23] Hanley, B. 2002 *The I.R.A. 1926-36*, p11.

[24] Military Archives, MSPC/RO/609 for establishment strengths in July 1922 (as retrospectively estimated in the 1930s). These figures underestimate some units and ignore others.

[25] September 1925 below and *Sunday Independent*, 6th October 1924.

[26] *Irish News*, 10th September and 22nd September 1924.

[27] *Irish Independent*, 4th October 1924.

[28] Some clearly had I.R.A. connections and so this could well have been an I.R.A. meeting. In 1922, Bernard Mervyn had been a 1st Lieutenant in C Company, 1st Battalion, John Leathem was a volunteer in E Company, 1st Battalion, John McKay is

also probably the I.R.A. volunteer of the same name in F Company, 1st Battalion (see Military Archives, MSPC/RO/403).

[29] *Belfast Newsletter*, 31st August 1922. The eleven arrested in 1924 were Michael Mervyn, James Leonard, John McKay, John Leatham, Bernard Mervyn, Joe Barnes, William McAuley, Patrick Kelly, David Walsh, Thomas Morris and John McRory.

[30] *Irish Times*, 20th October 1924.

[31] P.R.O.N.I., HA/4/2/29.

[32] MacEoin 1997, p109.

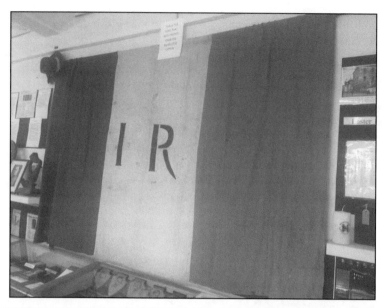

Top: The flag, emblazoned with I.R. (Irish Republic) used on Joe McKelvey's coffin during the reburial in Belfast in 1924 (now in the Irish Republican History Museum). Bottom: Joe McKelvey GAA club, 1925-26 with some names suggested (after Quinn 1999).

Joe McKelvey's funeral

To understand the significance of Joe McKelvey's funeral in Belfast, you have to go back to 1915 and the burial of veteran republican O'Donovan Rossa. That had provided a rallying point for the I.R.B. to mobilise support for the declaration of a republic, with Pearse giving a famous graveside oration. In Belfast, the O'Donovan Rossa G.A.A. club was formed and named in his honour, drawing its membership from the I.R.A.. The Belfast I.R.A. was to come to see Joe McKelvey's funeral as its own particular O'Donovan Rossa moment.

In the Westminster election both Corvin and Nash did badly. The same day, the Free State had announced that McKelvey's was among a group of remains from 'official' executions by pro-treaty forces in 1922-23 that were being released for burial.[1] His mother, Rose McKelvey, was allowed into Mountjoy Prison for the removal. A Cumann na mBan delegation, Count Plunkett and Joe Clarke were also present and she had been permitted to be accompanied by a family member or friend. She brought Maud Gonne McBride but the authorities refused to allow her access and Sarah Mellows went with her to receive her son's remains. Cumann na mBan brought tricolours emblazoned with I.R. (for Irish Republic) which were draped on the coffins as they were brought in a procession to Hardwicke Street Hall in Dublin where they briefly lay in state.[2]

From there McKelvey's coffin was brought in a procession to Amiens Street (now Connolly) Station accompanied by Rose and Sean McBride.[3] At Amiens Street the remains were formally handed over to a guard of honour (dressed in trench coats and soft black hats) that had been dispatched from Belfast to meet it.

At Drogheda, Dunleer and Dundalk the train was held up as crowds came to place wreaths and a tricolour on the coffin in the mortuary car. By the time McKelvey's body arrived in Belfast, a large crowd had gathered at the station with the Craobh Ruadh Pipe Band. Brigade and Battalion officers from Belfast had also assembled at the station. The R.U.C. were also present in force to try and intercept the train.

At 2.30 pm the train arrived at the Great Northern Railway Station. While the train slowed to a halt at the platform, a large force of armed R.U.C. men stepped forward and surrounded and searched the mortuary car as soon as the train stopped. Determined to prevent any public display of republican sentiment, they insisted that they remove the tricolour from McKelvey's coffin and, so, refused to allow it to even leave the train with the flag in place. Sean McBride, son of Maud Gonne and Major John McBride (the executed 1916 leader who had attended St Malachy's College in Belfast), was himself a senior I.R.A. figure and, at the time, involved in re-organising the I.R.A.. He unsuccessfully challenged R.U.C. District Inspector Stevens over having to remove the flag.

With the flag removed, the R.U.C. permitted the coffin to leave the station. A funeral procession then formed up behind the Craobh Ruadh Pipe Band in Glengall Street and the coffin was again covered with a tricolour. The hearse was followed by volunteers from the I.R.A., Fianna Éireann, Cumann na mBan, members of Sinn Féin, the clergy and the public. The cortege moved along Great Victoria Street, College Square East, King Street and Mill Street, then on into St Mary's in Chapel Lane. As if in mitigation for the R.U.C. permitting this display, the R.U.C. Inspector General apologetically described it as the 'shortest route' in his report to the Minister of Home Affairs.[4]

At St Mary's, the coffin was carried in by the bearer party and placed before the high altar where it lay in state, with the bearer party forming a guard of honour. Afterwards the public came to pay their respects while Fianna Éireann provided a guard of honour.

The next morning a crowd began to gather outside St Mary's for the funeral which was to take place at 1.30 pm. A guard of honour was again stationed around the coffin as soon as the church was opened in the morning. Some of those who had arrived to pay their respects carried photographs and pictures of McKelvey. McKelvey's coffin was once again draped with the 'IR' emblazoned tricolour.

After requiem mass the coffin, still covered in the tricolour, was carried by a bearer party of young men out to the awaiting Craobh Ruadh pipe band which was to accompany it along the route to Milltown cemetery. By now a large crowd had assembled outside St Mary's in the narrow confines of Chapel Lane and the top of Bank Street. A large detachment of R.U.C. men was also present and Stevens again attempted to halt the procession and remove the tricolour from McKelvey's coffin.

The R.U.C. used batons and waved their guns to force a way through to the coffin and bearer party. Within the tight space of Chapel Lane, by now crowded with mourners and R.U.C. men, an already emotional atmosphere almost reached boiling point. The funeral procession itself was halted at the doors of St Mary's as the bearer party and mourners attempted to physically prevent the tricolour from being seized by Stevens. The bearer party managed to pin down the tricolour onto the corners of the coffin and to move it backwards into the church. The flag still shows repairs that were made where it was torn during the struggle to prevent it being seized by the R.U.C..

The R.U.C. later described this incident as 'protests of a trivial nature'. For a few minutes it appeared that the funeral was going to descend into chaos. The Belfast O/C, James O'Donnell, with the bearer party inside St Marys, ordered that they remove the tricolour to avoid any further dispute.[5] An agreement was reached out in Chapel Lane that Fr Murray could take possession of the tricolour and deposit it in the church.

However, the reason why O'Donnell backed down soon became apparent. The funeral organisers had already anticipated that the R.U.C. would intervene and prevent the procession displaying a tricolour on McKelvey's coffin. But as it formed up in Chapel Lane, led by the hearse bearing the coffin and the Craobh Ruadh Pipe Band, a number of girls then joined the cortege around the hearse, carrying wreaths and other emblems in green, white and orange. The funeral proceeded from St Mary's, along Chapel Lane to Castle Street and from there along Divis Street to the Falls and then to Milltown Cemetery. Newspaper reports state that the whole route was lined with crowds. At Milltown, the R.U.C. had two Lancia armoured cars drawn up outside the gates. Inside the cemetery, a large R.U.C. detachment armed with carbines were also on duty. At the graveside, the tricolour was once again placed on the coffin whilst the burial service took place.[6] By this stage, the R.U.C. kept their distance and didn't try to remove the flag. The ceremony passed off without incident as the R.U.C. appear to have been awaiting an attempt to hold a military funeral including a colour party and a volley of shots over the grave, neither of which materialised.

When the funeral party reached the Harbinson plot, McKelvey's remains were interred there. Sean Lemass delivered a short oration to those present: "We are gathered here to pay a solemn tribute to one who was a true soldier of Ireland. General McKelvey was a man who died for his principles, and he thought it was the noblest and truest thing a man could do. When he walked across the yard of Mountjoy Prison and stood before the firing squad, he did so confident in the thought that the people he left behind would carry on where he had left off. He was being buried among his friends and foes, not as a traitor to a foreign country, but as a hero and a true Irishman. It is up to all of us to carry on until our efforts are crowned with success, then, and not till then will we have a free undivided and prosperous Gaelic Ireland. "[7]

The mourners then sang Faith of Our Fathers and, in defiance of the R.U.C. presence, The Soldiers' Song.

McKelvey's burial marked a symbolic end to the War of Independence and Civil War in Belfast, coming just before the release of internees and intentional moves to give the I.R.A. in the city new impetus. Sean McBride, effectively acting as a nationwide organiser, strengthened operational command between Belfast and G.H.Q. and the I.R.A.'s Army Council in Dublin. Notably this also coincided with a growing expectation that the boundary commission would be a flop. All of this was happening as news came out that Nash and Corvin had both done poorly in the election. This was taken to signal the utter apathy of nationalists and republicans towards electoral politics in the northern state.

Almost every republican source that refers to McKelvey's funeral cites it as the key event in the re-organisation of the I.R.A. in the city after the Civil War. Mirroring the founding of a G.A.A. club to honour O'Donovan Rossa in 1916, the I.R.A. staff formed a Joe McKelvey G.A.A. club. By the late 1920s and early 1930s it was one of the most prominent G.A.A. clubs in Antrim. The club was neither low key nor subtle. It sponsored overtly political motions at G.A.A. conventions and played in black jerseys with a tricolour on the front (the O'Donovan Rossa club had played in white jerseys with a tricolour on the front).

Within a couple of months of McKelvey's funeral, the former vice O/C of the Belfast Brigade, Paddy Nash died. Nash was first imprisoned for trying to buy a rifle from a British soldier but was released in time to go to Coalisland and take part in the mobilisation for the Easter Rising in 1916. He was arrested the following week and interned in Frongoch. On his release he was again active in the I.R.A. and interned in Ballykinlar. Released from internment, he was a leading figure in the 'Loney' area and the area of the Falls Road, right up to the signing of the Treaty in 1921. He was later interned (at various times) in Crumlin Road, Derry Gaol, Larne Camp and the Argenta prison ship.[8] Leading protests and hunger-strikes had impacted his health, which was so badly damaged that he was released from internment. He died less than a month later, on the 31st January 1925. His brother George was to be a leading figure in the Belfast I.R.A. into the 1930s.

More practically, Joe McKelvey's funeral also marked the formal restoration of communications with I.R.A. G.H.Q. in Dublin. The Belfast I.R.A. now began a process of review and re-organisation. Its recorded strength in 1924 was two hundred and forty. It was apparent that the divisional structure that had been put in place in 1920 now needed to be replaced. Not that I.R.A. strategy was particularly clear. At this time, Frank Aiken was Chief of Staff, while de Valera was still head of Sinn Féin. It only recognised the authority of the Dáil Eireann elected in 1921 whose power, it believed, was only legitimately exercised by the 'Second Dáil' organisation (Comhairle na dTeachtaí). Cumann na mBan members also swore continued allegiance to the Second Dáil. It wasn't until an I.R.A. convention in Dalkey on the 15th November 1925, that the I.R.A. severed the formal connection with the Second Dáil organisation.

Liam Mulholland recalls that a G.H.Q. organiser had advised the Belfast I.R.A. that there would be a period of training and organisation before resuming a campaign. He also reckoned they could access about two hundred rifles although many of those involved in storing them in dumps had left the city. The I.R.A. had to go around identifying houses that had contained dumps and ask the current occupants if they could try and recover the contents.[9]

By now the former divisional staff, Pat Thornbury, Hugh Corvin and Dan Turley had all been released from imprisonment. Corvin took over as O/C of the Belfast I.R.A. and Jim Johnston took over as Adjutant. All were simultaneously trying to rebuild lives and careers, Thornbury eventually as a teacher (in Westmeath), Corvin as an accountant, Turley ultimately as an insurance salesman. The Belfast I.R.A. wasn't in a position to support full-time staff, with no resources or secure supply of weapons. With a brigade and two battalions, each with a number of companies, it was also top heavy with staff officers. On paper that would be roughly thirty-five to forty posts (depending on whether there were separate divisional and brigade staffs). Given Jack McNally's estimate of around eighty active volunteers, almost one in two held a staff post (roughly one in six based on the official figure of two hundred and forty volunteers). This was the Belfast I.R.A. that needed re-organisation and a strategic direction from a republican movement that, in 1925, still had Eamonn de Valera as its head.

---

[1] The exact number of executions by the Free State government has never been clearly established, since it should include both 'official' executions and summary executions

in the field, including surrendered men killed out of hand without any pretence to formal proceedings.

[2] Account of the removal is given in *Southern Star*, 1ˢᵗ November 1924.

[3] This section is largely based on that given by Jimmy Steele in *Anrrim's Patriot Dead* with details added from *The Irish News* and an account by Leo Wilson in Munck, R. and Rolston, B. 1987 *Belfast in the 1930s: An Oral History.*

[4] P.R.O.N.I., HA/5/1383 (S.524).

[5] I am assuming that James O'Donnell was still the O/C in late 1924 (he was also included on Paddy Nash's nomination papers for the 1924 election).

[6] The tricolour placed on McKelvey's coffin can still be seen today in the Irish Republican History Museum in Conway Mill, Belfast.

[7] Contemporary police documents (P.R.O.N.I., S.524) say the speaker was Sean McBride who was present. But Jimmy Steele (who was present) identifies the speaker as Sean Lemass (in *Antrim's Patriot Dead*). Lemass was also named as the speaker in the *Derry Journal* account of McKelvey's funeral (31ˢᵗ October, 1924).

[8] Colloquially the Belfast Prison is invariable known as Crumlin Road, or simply 'the Crum'. Armagh's Jail (or Gaol) was also known as Armagh Prison while Derry's was often just called Derry Gaol.

[9] See Munck and Rolston, 1987, p166.

WAITING FOR DE VALERA, 1926-37

internment

In 1925, the Belfast I.R.A. headquarters was a wooden building called the McKelvey Hut (sometimes, more grandly, 'McKelvey Hall') in Rockmount Street. The I.R.A. continued to use the Willowbank huts on the Falls Road as well. Security was so lax that both of these addresses were public knowledge. The Joe McKelvey G.A.A. club also used the hall as its base. Since the likes of *The Irish News* published team line-ups when reporting on G.A.A. games, the R.U.C. simply had to pick up a copy to get a list of active I.R.A. members. Certainly the Belfast I.R.A. was not overly security conscious in the 1920s.

The future for the I.R.A. was to remain unclear while everyone waited for the Boundary Commission to end partition. I.R.A. membership was limited, both by a general refusal to accept anyone who hadn't fought in 1920-22 and a dismissive attitude towards younger recruits. Bob Bradshaw, having joined Fianna Éireann in 1925, went to the McKelvey Hut to ask Tony Lavery, the local company O/C, if he could join the I.R.A., only to be refused.[1] Bradshaw was only fourteen years of age. Lavery told him: "Come back when you are out of short pants." Lavery himself was barely twenty years of age but, crucially, had fought in 1920-22.

Throughout 1925, I.R.A. operations in Belfast were mainly confined to recovering and securing existing arms dumps. Not all were worth retrieving. In June of 1925, a party of R.U.C. and ordnance experts descended on Raglan Street to remove a mine. It may have been discovered during an attempt to recover an earlier dump and was deemed too dangerous to move. Certainly the authorities believed it was a leftover from 1920-22 rather than that the I.R.A. was still manufacturing them in Belfast.

At the end of July, Mick Carolan, still the I.R.A.'s Director of Intelligence, got a year in prison after a Free State raid on his headquarters in Adelaide Road in Dublin. His replacement was his assistant, Frank Kerlin, another northerner. Carolan was then sprung from Mountjoy by George Gilmore, in a plan hatched by Kerlin. Eighteen others, including Jim Killeen and Sean Russell also escaped.[2] But for much of the next ten years

there was an increasing gap in Belfast representation at the most senior levels of the I.R.A..
In Belfast, other arms discoveries by the authorities led to arrests. In July, John Walsh of Chemical Street in Ballymacarrett, was arrested and charged with possessing the explosives, arms and ammunition captured by the R.U.C. in Currie Street the previous year. Evidence was given against him by Patrick Woods.[3] Woods had been involved in moving the arms and may even have provided the R.U.C. with the information used to pinpoint the location in the initial raids. In September, Walsh was given eighteen months. Two weeks later Joe McGurk, also living in Chemical Street, was charged with possessing illegal documents and I.R.A. membership. McGurk refused to recognise the court and was sentenced to three months. The documents read in court ominously noted that an unnamed person had been found guilty by the Belfast Brigade and sentenced to death.[4]
The Unionist government wasn't only targeting republicans, though. That autumn the Minister for Home Affairs banned a proposed unemployment march, while the Labour Party's Samuel Patterson got six months for delivering a 'seditious' speech. Locally and nationally, harmonising relationships between the organised left and the I.R.A. was to be a recurring theme throughout the next five decades, with varying degrees of success. During 1925, I.R.A. G.H.Q. in Dublin was even exploring a deal with the Soviet Union to secure financial support.
By that autumn, the Belfast I.R.A. had decided on a response to the loss of the Currie Street and Short Strand arms dumps and John Walsh's arrest. On the evening of 19th November, Patrick Woods was walking down Seaforde Street in Ballymacarrett when he was approached by a single gunman who shot him three times, including twice in the heart. After being shot, he was brought into a shop where he died before he could be given medical assistance.[5]
After Woods' death on the Thursday evening, the R.U.C. carried out a series of raids starting at 1am on the Saturday night. Little was found in the raids although John Connolly, from Ballymacarrett, was charged with possession of seditious documents and sentenced to a month in prison.[6]
Only one man was specifically detained for questioning about the shooting of Patrick Woods but the R.U.C. used the opportunity to seize a total of fifty men across Belfast including former internees and ex-Free State soldiers.[7] Those arrested included the Belfast O/C, Hugh Corvin and many of his staff and senior I.R.A. figures, including Dan Turley and Davy Matthews. An ulterior motive to the scale of the Unionist response became rapidly evident. From 21st November, press reports were making it clear that the Boundary Commission was a failure. This was officially announced on 4th December. The significance of this moment for the northern I.R.A. probably can't be underestimated. Hope that the Boundary Commission would render partition unworkable had meant the issue of partition was, to some extent, parked in the treaty debates and even civil war. The reality that the Boundary Commission wouldn't end partition came too late for a unified political response from the now bitterly fractured pre-treaty republican movement.

Given that the press reported that only one of those arrested was a suspect in Woods' death, it seems clear that a significant motivation in the mass arrests and subsequent internment of twenty-two men until January 1926 was to limit any potential I.R.A. response to the demise of the Boundary Commission. But in Belfast any belief in the Boundary Commission had long evaporated and the streets remained quiet.

---

[1] See MacEoin 1997, p424 and Quinn 1999, *A Rebel Voice*, p16.

[2] On 27th November, 1925. See MacEoin 1997, p123.

[3] *Irish Independent,* 10th September 1925.

[4] See *Irish News* and *Irish Independent,* 23rd September 1925.

[5] See press on 20th and 22nd November, eg *Irish News* and *Irish Independent.* See also the inquest report in *Irish Independent,* 4th March 1926 where the I.R.A. is specifically blamed.

[6] See *Irish News,* 24th November and 5th December 1925.

[7] See *Irish Independent* 10th September and 23rd November 1925. Many appear to have been held until January 1926 (see list published by Kleinrichert 2001, p299: Frank Burns, Charles Connolly, Hugh Corvin, Patrick Cullen, Alex Johnston, John Keenan, Thomas Kellett, John Martin, Davy Matthews, Willie McCurry, John McDermot, James McGouran, Charles McKee, P.J. McKenna, Patrick McWilliams, Arthur O'Donnell, Samuel O'Neill, Patrick Quinn, Peter Quinn, Peter Trainor, Dan Turley and John Wallace).

Top left: Hugh Corvin (*Irish Press*, 1970); top right: Dan Turley (Danny Turley); bottom left: Bridie Dolan (*An Phoblacht*, 22nd February 1975); bottom right: Jimmy Steele.

Ulster No I Area

It seems odd in retrospect but initially no-one had really taken partition seriously as there had originally been a general assumption that the Boundary Commission would remove the border entirely. Not least, the various political groupings that were emerging from the I.R.A. and Sinn Féin which hadn't a strategic response prepared.

The Belfast I.R.A., though, continued to gather intelligence, source rifles, ammunition and grenades, secure dumps, recruit, train with rifles and build organisational structures. The shooting of Patrick Woods aside, the focus appears to have been on restoring some form of operational readiness to defend districts in the event that there was further violence. Alongside the internments, the Unionists continued to pressure republicans.

At the end of November, Joe Rogers from Hawthorn Street, was caught with ammunition in a search.[1] In January Jimmy Steele, was arrested over 110 copies of *An Phoblacht* that had been destined for Cumann na mBan but were intercepted by the Post Office (it had been banned under the Special Powers Act from 11th January 1926).[2] The Unionists struggled to make a charge stick in either case as neither had the items in their actual possession (in the end Steele was imprisoned for a banned edition of *An Phoblacht* found at his home).

While Hugh Corvin had been interned his Adjutant, Jim Johnston, had presumably acted as Brigade O/C. But he was suddenly arrested at his Tyrone Street home in mid-February. The R.U.C. found him in possession of letters sent to the Belfast Brigade O/C, a letter from I.R.A. Chief of Staff, Frank Aiken, and documents about the re-organisation of the I.R.A. in Belfast. Johnston refused to recognise the jurisdiction of the court and got six months hard labour. A few days later an I.R.A. arms dump, containing a rifle, bullets and a bomb, was found beneath a manhole in Donard Street.

Johnston's documents showed that a sum of £4,000 had been set aside for reconstruction of the I.R.A. in the north by the White Cross with a monthly allowance of £8 for the Belfast O/C with responsibility for the Ulster No 1 (Divisional) area of Antrim and Belfast City.[3] Belfast was now a Battalion, rather than a Brigade, with two companies, one centred on the Falls, and one covering the city centre, north Belfast and Ballymacarrett.[4] Overall command was managed by creating a 'Battalion Council' with a staff including representatives for each I.R.A. section across the city. The Belfast leadership reported directly to G.H.Q. in Dublin through a Communications Officer.[5] In 1925, Tony Lavery and George Nash were the company O/Cs. Jack McNally's active service unit seems to have been disbanded as part of this reorganisation. The recorded strength of the Belfast I.R.A. in 1926 was two hundred and forty-two, largely the same as in 1924. The Tyrone Street raid had shown that the I.R.A. was recruiting again by December 1925 but new members must have just replaced resignations.[6]

At the Sinn Féin Árd Fhéis in March, de Valera proposed that, on removal of the oath of allegiance, attendance at the assemblies in Dublin (and, notably, Belfast) be downgraded to a 'policy' issue rather than a 'principle' (basically the line he had pushed in the Treaty debates with his 'Document No 2'). An un-named delegate from Belfast's Joe McKelvey Cumann tersely stated "…That the present time is not opportune for the discussion [on recognising either parliament], and that it be deferred until the oath has actually been abolished…".[7] When the Boundary Commissions report was officially accepted in April, the now inevitable split followed and de Valera founded Fianna Fáil on 16th May.

This was not, however, a clean break with de Valera. The I.R.A. was to continue working with his political movement for some time and struggled to develop a strategy that was not, to some degree, sensitive to the political fortunes of Fianna Fáil. While Fianna Fáil grappled with accessing power through the Free State parliament, with all that might promise to deliver, the I.R.A. had to continually re-calibrate its behaviours to avoid damaging the prospects of Fianna Fáil. However, relations between I.R.A. G.H.Q. and Fianna Fáil were caustically observed by abstentionist Sinn Féin, Comhairle na dTeachtaí and the Belfast I.R.A..[8]

Notably there was considerable Sinn Féin influence among senior Belfast I.R.A. staff like Dan Turley, Davy Matthews and Jack McNally. It was to be increasingly obvious, though, that the Nationalists who swiftly entered the northern parliament had greater synergies with Fianna Fáil. This added a further complication to the web of relationships, not only between the I.R.A., Fianna Fáil and Sinn Féin, but also the I.R.A. structures in the north and the Dublin-based centre of the I.R.A.. From the perspective of the Belfast I.R.A., its relationship with a Dublin-centric G.H.Q. and leadership of the I.R.A. was to be a perpetual source of tensions.

---

[1] The officer involved, William Heffernan, was part of the political unit of the R.U.C. suggesting Rogers was a republican. In court Heffernan said they were also looking for an automatic pistol.

[2] *Belfast Gazette,* 8th January 1926.

[3] This appears to be the date at which Belfast was re-designated a 'Battalion', although the terms 'Brigade' and 'Battalion' were almost always used interchangeably.

[4] Fianna Éireann and Cumann na mBan had largely the same structure labelling the two units as West and East.

[5] Munck and Rolston 1987, p189.

[6] Hanley, B. 2010, *The I.R.A. – A Documentary History*, p12.

[7] *Irish Independent*, 10th March 1926.

[8] Comhairle na dTeachtaí was made up of T.D.s elected to the Second Dáil who didn't recognise the authority of subsequent assemblies.

the de Valera split

The immediate impact of the de Valera split on the Battalion was the loss of its O/C, Hugh Corvin. When Corvin resigned in April 1926, officially citing business reasons, G.H.Q. sent an organiser to Belfast, called Wilson, who notified Dublin that Dan Turley was taking over as O/C.[1] G.H.Q. seemed to think Turley was difficult to deal with and he didn't last long in charge in Belfast with Davy Matthews taking over the post of O/C, while Turley served (at various times) as his Adjutant or Intelligence Officer.

The de Valera split did prompt further consolidation of Cumann na mBan, the I.R.A., Fianna and Sinn Féin. G.H.Q. had Wilson get the Belfast branches to collaborate on a Wolfe Tone commemoration in June on Cavehill but Wilson feared that a certain amount of lethargy had taken hold in Belfast.[2]

Perhaps to counter this, there were now further organisational changes made. District-based companies were formally re-established, beginning with Ballymacarrett. Eventually (by the early 1930s) there would be seven companies, labelled A to G.[3] In the short term, there was to be a decline in I.R.A. strength between 1926 and 1930, from two hundred and forty-two to one hundred and seventy-seven. To some degree this must reflect some resignations over the split with de Valera.[4]

A letter sent to G.H.Q. by the Battalion lists the weaponry available to Ulster No 1 Area at this time. It included a Thompson, one hundred and eighteen revolvers, sixty rifles, twenty-four parabellum pistols, forty grenades, twelve boxes of detonators, over five thousand rounds of rifle, revolver and Thompson ammunition, with a further two hundred thousand rounds apparently accessible.[5] But from the start of 1924 the R.U.C. had recovered at least a Thompson, a pistol, thirty rifles, twenty-three Mills bombs, detonators, a landmine and several thousands of rounds of ammunition. Notably rifles were harder to conceal from the R.U.C. than pistols. Given the number of recent and later arms finds, the G.H.Q. list appears to be on the low side. But it does reflect an emphasis on weapons useful for defensive street fighting. The utility of rifles in defending urban areas meant that sourcing rifles was a recurring obsession of the Battalion.

While avoiding parliamentary politics, some in the I.R.A. were promoting a greater role in social justice campaigns, like Peadar O'Donnell and Sean McCool. At least one robbery of a rent-collector in Belfast may have been by republicans (see below).[6] A more widespread campaign saw I.R.A. units sporadically attacking pro-British films and newspapers. But political considerations in the south kept a brake on any significant

I.R.A. activity in Belfast. The assassination of Kevin O'Higgins in Dublin on 10th July had been followed by the Public Safety Act and moves against both the I.R.A. and Sinn Féin. To counter abstentionist Sinn Féin in the south an oath now had to be taken to stand for election meaning republicans would refuse to field candidates.

Despite the O'Higgins assassination, the inactivity of (and lack of significant threat from) the I.R.A. in 1926 and 1927 is shown by the fact that only a dozen republican prisoners were left in Free State jails by end of the year. In the north, Patrick Thornbury was imprisoned for ignoring an order banning him from Belfast (Thornbury got six months for stating that, as an I.R.A. volunteer, he was ignoring the order).

De Valera finally took the Free State parliament's oath of allegiance on 11th August and Fianna Fáil entered the Dáil. Having lost a large number of members (and access to financial support from the U.S.A) to Fianna Fáil, the oath now saw the collapse of Sinn Féin as a political power in the two Free State elections of 1927. The I.R.A., though, hadn't remained completely neutral as *An Phoblacht* had carried a half page advert for Fianna Fáil prior to the September election. At its annual Árd Fhéis, though, Sinn Féin still reaffirmed support for the I.R.A. and Cumann na mBan.

In the north, proportional representation was abolished for elections on 22nd October, furthering unionism's gerrymandering of the electoral system. Following the founding of Fianna Fáil, and its ending of abstentionism, a non-abstentionist National League (usually known as the Nationalist Party) was formed in the north in 1928.

Another noticeable outcome of the Fianna Fáil split was a dramatic upsurge in the volume of arms finds both in the Free State and the north. At the start of December 1927, the R.U.C. began a search in the Whiterock area. In a disused house on the Whiterock Road, they found ninety hand grenades, a Thompson submachine gun, a range finder, seven automatic pistols and revolvers, 2lb cordite, twenty-three Verey lights, eighty-four detonators, seventeen thousand rounds of rifle ammunition, twenty-thousand rounds of revolver ammunition, a thousand rounds of Morris tube ammunition and 'warflour' explosives.[7] The *Belfast Newsletter* reported that the search took place because "Some time ago, information came into the hands of the authorities…".[8] Regardless of that R.U.C. statement, the I.R.A. would have immediately began compiling a list of those who knew about the dump to investigate any potential treachery. The R.U.C. arrested Michael O'Dwyer and charged him with possession of the dump. A jury later decided that the R.U.C. had provided no evidence that he knew the dump was present and found him not guilty in January 1928.

Ironically, even given the availability of the Civil Authorities (Special Powers) Act and a suitably accommodating justice system, the R.U.C. could be incredibly inept at prosecutions. Non-recognition of the courts (which, technically, was required by I.R.A. Standing Orders) facilitated a swift guilty verdict while requiring no effort from the prosecution. Where republicans allowed themselves to be defended the R.U.C. were regularly caught off guard as juries and even the prosecutors threw out ill-prepared cases. I.R.A. G.H.Q. could, and clearly did, provide waivers on recognising the court to allow individuals to escape conviction.

To put that December 1927 Whiterock arms find in context, in August 1924 the Quartermaster General, Andy Cooney, had reported on the arms available to the I.R.A.[9] The return included one hundred and seventy-three thousand rounds of ammunition and two hundred and fifty-six Mills bombs. Even though Cooney's return appears to be incomplete, ninety hand grenades and thirty-eight thousand rounds of ammunition were a substantial loss, being equivalent to a quarter of all ammunition captured in the Free State between 1923 and 1931 and nearly 10% of all grenades captured over the same period.[10]

Given the reported I.R.A. weapon stocks in Belfast, this brought discoveries since the start of 1924 to two Thompsons, eight pistols, thirty rifles, one hundred and thirteen Mills bombs, over one hundred detonators, more than forty thousand rounds of ammunition and explosives. This amounts to 50% of the reported stock of rifles, in excess of the reported ammunition, three times as many grenades and one more Thompson than the Battalion supposedly had in its possession.

Another dump was found by workmen in Belvoir Hall Public Elementary School in Dee Street on 23rd December. Under a floor that was being repaired they found seven rifles and ten grenades. But given the location this seems unlikely to be an I.R.A. arms dump. In 1928 the Unionists decided to ban Easter Rising commemorations from Milltown Cemetery (for the third year in a row).[11] The I.R.A. planned to post up notices on Easter Sunday morning anyway. Jimmy Steele and another I.R.A. volunteer were observed putting up posters in North Queen Street and arrested.[12] At Milltown itself, the R.U.C. arrested eight men who refused to remove Easter Lilies while trying to stage a commemoration, including James Connolly, Jack Gaffney and Arthur Thornbury. Despite now holding ten prisoners, the R.U.C. struggled to find a charge that would stick for any of them. Eventually they decided to release the two arrested in North Queen Street as they believed it was '…doubtful if any charges would succeed.' The other eight were then released on 16th April.

Another big R.U.C. success came on 12th June 1928. At 6 a.m, twelve R.U.C. men broke down the door of George Nash's house at 52 Gibson Street. They found a copy of *An Phoblacht*, a pocket-book containing codes and other documents. Bricked up in a hide alongside the chimney, they uncovered an arms dump, including twenty-three service rifles and some drill books. Nash contested the trial and the R.U.C. couldn't prove he knew of the arms. Instead he was given three years for the documents in his possession. In the context of the reported weapons available to the Battalion and R.U.C. seizures since 1924, the Gibson Street arms dump appears to have contained at least a substantial portion of the remaining rifles theoretically available to the I.R.A. in the city.

The reality for Nash of being in prison in Belfast in the 1920s and early 1930s is described in John McGuffin's book *Internment*. He relates how an old republican (probably Nash himself), who was first jailed in 1929 for political offences, recalled that: "In the first week we lay on a board and mattress. For food we got gruel, rotten potatoes and porridge. We got out of our cells only for one hour a day, and not at all on Saturday. We tried everything, but it wasn't until the Treason Felony men came in, in 1936, that things improved." At any given date in 1928-29 there were generally only between ten and twenty republicans in prison in total, north and south.

During 1928 the annuities campaign continued, as Peadar O'Donnell chaired meetings in Dublin, with related activity in Clare and Galway.[13] From 1926 the I.R.A. had also been publicly targeting money-lenders and those accused of robbing the rich to feed the poor.[14] This began in Dublin and spread to Limerick. In July 1928, Cecil Lyons, a twenty-two year old rent collector, was shot and wounded by a gunman in Boomer Street in Belfast. Lyons was carrying £38 8s 2d in rent money. Peter Carleton was subsequently arrested, tried and found guilty of the robbery and shooting (a medical condition prevented him being jailed). Active in Fianna Éireann in 1920-22, Carleton was subsequently interned and later got involved with Saor Éire.[15] His relationship with the I.R.A. by 1928 is unclear, though. His co-accused, John Martin, appears to be the I.R.A. volunteer who was interned in 1925-26.[16]

During the year the Unionists continued to curtail political opposition. First, a proposed Wolfe Tone commemoration on Cavehill was banned. Then, in July, Lord Craigavon announced the abolition of proportional representation in all elections (the formal date of abolition was 22nd October 1928). Ironically, by then, the I.R.A. had been edging into politics via Comhairle na Poblachta.

Comhairle na Poblachta was convened in Dublin in late 1928 and called for all volunteers to give it active support. It was described as an '...agreement and co-operation on the basis of co-equality between the civil and military arms of the Republic' including the I.R.A., Fianna Éireann, Cumann na mBan, Sinn Féin and Comhairle na dTeachtaí. It was backed by Maud Gonne, Count Plunkett, Mary MacSwiney, Peadar O'Donnell, Frank Ryan, Margaret Buckley, Brian O'Higgins and J.J. O'Kelly. O'Kelly was chair and, to emphasise its left-wing credentials, Mick Price was secretary.

A November 1928 editorial in *An Phoblacht* had stressed the '...need to secure popular backing for the physical force movement...'. A draft Constitution of the Republic of Ireland was prepared by Mary McSwiney and presented in January to a public sitting of the Second Dáil organisation (Comhairle na dTeachtaí), made up of the T.D.s elected to the Second Dáil who still refused to recognise the authority of the Free State government. While the draft pushed for liberty, equality and fraternity, it wasn't left wing enough for some at I.R.A. G.H.Q. and O'Donnell refused to print it in *An Phoblacht*. To further complicate matters, at an I.R.A. Convention in Dublin in late February O'Donnell proposed the formation of Saor Éire as an I.R.A. political vehicle, although delegates opted instead to support Comhairle na Poblachta.[17]

The year ended on a further sour note for the Battalion as an R.U.C. raid in the Falls uncovered yet another substantial dump. After surrounding the area and beginning a house to house search, the R.U.C. located the dump hidden in various pieces of furniture in 17 Linden Street. The dump included fifteen service rifles, five Martin-Henry rifles, a Thompson gun, a shot gun, eleven pistols, over 700 rounds of ammunition and 300 Morris tube rounds, thirty-one grenades and other assorted items. There were no immediate arrests. The Battalion was now investigating the loss of three major dumps instead of one.

[1] For more on this see Mahon, T. and Gillogly, J. 2008 *Decoding the I.R.A.*.

[2] Mahon and Gillogly 2008, p309.

[3] See the documents produced in court for Tony Lavery's trial in 1936 (see later in this book).

[4] Hanley 2002, p12-14. In comparison, numbers in 1932 (Ulster No 1) were 564, and, Belfast in 1934 was 460.

[5] The letter was later captured and referred to in court in Dublin. It was also read by the Minister of Home Affairs in a Stormont debate on 15th May 1928.

[6] The Peter Carleton involved noted in court that he had a brother living in the Whiterock. The Carleton close to Peadar O'Donnell also had a brother Paul in Britton's Drive although he doesn't mention this incident in his account in Uinseann MacEoin's 1980 book *Survivors*.

[7] A Morris tube was an attachment for a gun barrel designed to permit practice firing in a confined space. Finding of Morris tubes and suitable ammunition tended to indicate that covert weapons training was taking place.

[8] *Belfast Newsletter*, 12th December 1927.

[9] MTUCDA P69/179, 126-9; also Hanley 2002, p28. Cooney took over as Chief of Staff from Frank Aiken for a year and was then succeeded by Moss Twomey.

[10] Hanley 2002, Appendix 2.

[11] Donohoe, L. 1998 'Regulating Northern Ireland: The Special Powers acts, 1922-1972', *The Historical Journal*, Vol. 41, No. 4, p1089-1120.

[12] See internal memos from Department of Home Affairs describing this incident P.R.O.N.I., H.828.2959.

[13] MacEoin 1997, p147-8.

[14] MacEoin 1997, p138.

[15] Carleton was also a member of the revived (but short-lived) Irish Citizen's Army in Belfast.

[16] It is unclear, but this may be the same John (Sean) Martin who died in an accidental explosion in 1940 which may indicate that this may have been an I.R.A. operation.

[17] MacEoin 1997, p157ff.

the Fianna Éireann project

As mentioned earlier, by 1929 I.R.A. strength in Belfast had declined to one hundred and seventy-seven.[1] In 1928, Tony Lavery and Jimmy Steele had been appointed by Davy Matthews to work with Fianna Éireann, a project that would see I.R.A. numbers triple over the next three years. Lavery looked after the 'West' Battalion, Steele looked after the 'East'. The timing of the Fianna re-organisation suggests a deliberate strategy to increase I.R.A. numbers over the next few years (this would coincide with the next general election in the south in 1932).[2]

In comparison, the R.U.C. in Belfast officially numbered between 998 and 1,273.[3] The ratio of R.U.C. to I.R.A. volunteers in 1929 was in the order of 5.6-7.2 to 1. The throughput from Fianna Éireann to the I.R.A. was to reduce the ratio to below 2 to 1 by 1932. B Specials and British soldiers would increase the ratio again but it was likely that both would only be deployed during high tensions or violent conflict which would also see an influx into the I.R.A.. Psychologically the size of the Battalion in the 1930s, relative to the Belfast R.U.C., was surely a significant factor in the belief that they were capable of withstanding a pogrom like that of 1920-22 or, otherwise, confronting the R.U.C..

Training and parades were now held in groups of up to seventy or eighty individuals. However this made for lax security as individuals had knowledge of a significant number of names of other members. Large gatherings could also attract attention and provide the R.U.C. with an opportunity to swoop on a large body of the I.R.A., Fianna or Cumann na mBan and make arrests. Some discoveries made by the R.U.C. like Whiterock Road, Linden Street or George Nash's house couldn't just be by chance and came either from close observation or informers. Investigation of the loss of those dumps by the Belfast I.R.A. led the Intelligence Officer, Dan Turley, to believe an informer had given them away. A comparison of those who had knowledge of each dump would have identified potential suspects which included Turley himself. Another suspect was Jack McNally, then the Battalion Adjutant. Seemingly held responsible for the loss of the dumps, McNally was suspended from active duty.[4] For the next few years the R.U.C. made no major finds of arms dumps in Belfast.

However, Turley's own suspicions that McNally wasn't actually the informer were raised further when he was pulled in and held for questioning by the R.U.C..[5] The ongoing investigation into the dumps seems to have created friction between Turley and Joe McGurk.[6] With the added pressure from the R.U.C. Turley resigned his post in the I.R.A.. The I.R.A.'s social agitation actions over the annuities and landlord campaign in the south, as well as lobbying by Peadar O'Donnell and others, had drawn elements of the I.R.A. closer to organisations like the Irish Labour Defence League and the Friends of Soviet Russia. All this was during the global economic crisis that followed the Wall Street crash.[7] Prominent members of I.R.A. G.H.Q. in Dublin, like O'Donnell, Mick Price, Frank Ryan and George Gilmore, continued to explore possible political projects (other than Sinn Féin).

Through 1930 and into 1931, the I.R.A. kept a relatively low profile both in Belfast and across Ireland generally. Notably, the discovery of arms and other arrests were almost non-existent in 1930 and most of 1931. This was in spite of the I.R.A.'s poor security precautions although the R.U.C. may have substantially captured its available stock of rifles, while revolvers were easier to conceal.

At the same time, despite the relative absence of I.R.A. activity, known republicans were subject to frequent arrests and raids by the R.U.C.. The Unionists continued to utilise the provisions of the Special Powers Act which were now treated as the norm rather than temporary provisions only to be used in extraordinary circumstances. As well as being used to detain individuals, confiscate materials and create a series of questionable offences, the Special Powers Act was continually used to ban meetings of political opponents of the Unionists. This mainly targeted the I.R.A., but also was used against left wing groups and trade unions. Films, records and books could be banned, as well as newspapers. Memorials and commemorative monuments, too, could be banned and removed (such as happened in Carrickmore in 1931).

Art Thornbury gives an example of how republicans were subject to the attentions of the R.U.C. during this time. He was constantly followed, had his house raided at all of hours of the day or night, was regularly taken in for questioning and stopped and searched on the street.[8] He reckoned this had been the case for much of 1930, 1931 and 1932. So while the I.R.A. was very much in the background, it was still being actively pursued by the R.U.C. There is no reason to believe Thornbury's experience wasn't typical of I.R.A. volunteers in Belfast. This happened alongside gerrymandering and other elements of the Unionists' ongoing 'cold pogrom' against Catholics.

In 1930 the Battalion faced its usual conundrum on how to commemorate the Easter Rising. That April, while defying a ban on a commemoration in Milltown, there was a violent clash between the R.U.C. and I.R.A. at the gates of the cemetery. But it was possible to defy the ban by holding a prayer service as a religious ceremony couldn't be restricted. So republicans knelt and said prayers at Milltown to beat the ban. This time an altercation with the R.U.C. followed the service, for which Art Thornbury, Tommy O'Malley, Michael McBriarty and Hugh Matthews (brother of the Belfast O/C) all got three months.[9]

For good measure the Unionists again proscribed any Easter Rising commemoration at Milltown in 1931. To enforce the ban, the R.U.C. posted a large force in the cemetery and the surrounding fields. They did let women in and out of the cemetery but only allowed men to enter on specific business.[10] Despite the ban and R.U.C. presence, Emmet Sweeney tried to give a political speech and got six months in prison for his efforts.

Over that Easter, the I.R.A. held an Army Convention in Glendalough in County Wicklow where it now adopted the Saor Éire proposal for widespread nationalisation. That year, the Free State government had tried to institute a last minute ban on the traditional gathering at Wolfe Tone's grave in Bodenstown but ten thousand still managed to get through. Some later speculated that Bodenstown that year was a test mobilisation of the I.R.A.. Uinseann MacEoin dismisses this claim and notes that, at the time in 1931, the I.R.A. had "…no focus; no real notion of its role; should it stage a coup d'état; should it be purely agitationary; a machine for boycott; engage only social issues; be subsumed into a political party."[11]

Mainly the I.R.A. was paralysed by the realisation that its agenda may be achieved through the elevation of Fianna Fáil to government by the next Free State election. Sinn Féin was even distancing itself from the I.R.A. over its loose connections to Fianna Fáil (which was undoubtedly awkward for the likes of Belfast O/C Davy Matthews who was a Sinn Féin member). The assumption was that Fianna Fáil would deliver on restoring the 1916 Republic once in government (rather than de Valera's Document No 2). The I.R.A. appeared to have lost its purpose.[12] To the likes of Frank Ryan, George Gilmore, Mick Price and Peadar O'Donnell this justified re-engineering the I.R.A. into a left-wing political movement. However, unlike elsewhere, in Belfast the I.R.A. also had to consider the likelihood that it would be called upon to fulfil a defensive role as it had done in 1920-22.

Ominously too, for much of 1931, *An Phoblacht* began to warn of an impending pogrom in the north. Rifles had been proven to be effective in the street battles of 1920-22 in Belfast and warning of a pogrom may have prompted concern among ther Battalion staff at the loss of the bulk of their stocks.[13]

After the summer, political tensions also began to rise with the first major incident involving the new generation of Fianna Éireann. In September, the R.U.C. surprised a Fianna party who were drilling at Breda, arresting Bernard and Patrick Rooney, but letting the remaining eleven go home. Both were detained for a period of time. Earlier that month a raid on Pat McGrath's home in Ardilea Street had netted the R.U.C. copies of *An Phoblacht* and a revolver.

---

[1] Hanley 2002, p13.

[2] Watt, J. 1981 *Na Fianna Eireann, Case Study of Political Youth Organisation.* PhD submitted to University of Glasgow. Watt suggests a more general renewal in republicanism was responsible, while highlighting the more distinctive nature of the Belfast Fianna Éireann where progression to the I.R.A. was almost automatic.

[3] See, eg, statement from Dawson Bates in *Belfast Newsletter,* 23rd March 1927.

4 McNally glosses over this in his own memoir (1989, p24) where he states he was "…taken out of active duties" although Moss Twomey (then Chief of Staff) notes McNally had been originally accused of leaking the dumps (MacEoin 1997, p845).

5 MacEoin 1997, p179.

6 The friction is implied in a letter Turley wrote on 5th May 1933.

7 Hanley 2002, p13.

8 *Irish Independent,* 9th July 1932.

9 See press, eg *Irish News, Irish Independent,* for 30th April 1930.

10 *Irish Times,* 6th April 1931.

11 MacEoin 1997, p196.

12 Document No 2 was a variation on the Treaty as signed in 1922 with the oath constructed by a different formula.

13 Claiming a pogrom may be imminent may have been a ploy for the Battalion to secure fresh stocks of rifles. At the same time, the threat of a pogrom may have been responsible for subsequent Battalion policy.

rifle raids

At the end of September 1931, the I.R.A.'s Saor Éire project was formally inaugurated although Peadar O'Donnell continued to use non-I.R.A. members in Belfast. According to Peter Carleton, O'Donnell started a Belfast section of Saor Éire with Carleton, his brother Paul, an ex-B Special called Robert McVicker and a former Stormont M.P., William McMullen.[1] O'Donnell was clearly attempting to cultivate a Belfast power base outside the I.R.A. command structures in the city. Intentional or not, friction increased between the Battalion staff and left republicans at I.R.A.'s G.H.Q. in Dublin. By December 1931, the Battalion was founding Wolfe Tone Republican Clubs, apparently as an alternative to Saor Éire.

In October, the Free State government banned a series of organisations including the I.R.A., Cumman na mBan, Fianna Éireann, the Women Prisoners Defence League, a number of left wing groups and now added Saor Éire. Not to be outdone, the Unionists also banned Saor Éire.

According to Jack Brady, Charlie McGlade and Barney Boswell, 1930s Battalion volunteers usually had left-wing sympathies and worked closely with the local Belfast socialists (like McVicker and McMullen in Saor Éire). However they made a distinction between left wing politics and support for 'communism' which was viewed as simply the implementation of Soviet Union foreign policy.[2] In Belfast, the Soviet-aligned communists had re-organised in January 1930 as the Worker's Revolutionary Party (branches were known as Revolutionary Worker's Groups or R.W.G.). The Belfast O/C, Davy Matthews, was close to some of the trade unions whom the R.W.G. viewed as direct competition.[3] Matthews also appears to have saw echoes in R.W.G. and Saor Éire strategy. A Battalion staff officer, Art Thornbury, first persuaded Dan Turley to attend a Saor Éire meeting and then to return to full duties in the I.R.A. and, under pressure from Davy Matthews and Joe McGurk, he rejoined the Battalion staff. Turley took the same view of Saor Éire as Matthews and began to actively lobby against it.

He later wrote that while "…never being much of a Catholic I considered it my duty to do all in my power to smash it up and thank God I succeeded." In May 1931 a Papal Encyclical, *Quadragesimo Anno* had stated that "No one can be at one and the same time a good Catholic and a true Socialist…". That type of reasoning clearly had an impact on some but it should be noted that active I.R.A. volunteers repeatedly disregarded excommunication and refusal of Catholic sacraments and continued their involvement.[4]

On a whole they may have been no more or less religious than the society they came from but, unlike most, did repeatedly exhibit greater defiance to the Catholic Church.

Overall the Battalion was distinctly unenthusiastic about Saor Éire, anyway. Volunteers were more interested in training and raising money to purchase weapons than debating the Saor Éire constitution or other similar socio-economic issues. And not that the I.R.A. was focused purely on action - I.R.A. volunteers typically took a course of lectures on Irish history and guerrilla warfare and had to pass an entrance examination (this process took a year if the volunteer hadn't been in Fianna Éireann).

At this time the unemployment rate in Belfast was rapidly doubling. It rose from 14% in 1929 to 28% in 1931. Some 39% of jobs had been lost in the construction industry by 1932, where many republicans had been employed.[5] Competition for employment raised the threat of Catholic workers being forced out so Unionist supporters could take their jobs.

Increasing unemployment also diminished the capacity of the Battalion to purchase weapons, usually stolen military and police arms. On top of the threat of another pogrom and the loss of dumps, there were also continuous rumours that if Fianna Fáil took power, de Valera would seek to restore the republic declared in 1916 and the I.R.A. campaign in the north would restart. Harry White relates how the Battalion was put on alert in February 1932 after Fianna Fáil was elected to power. In March Chief of Staff Moss Twomey and George Gilmore, representing the I.R.A. had met with de Valera in Dublin but it was clear that he expected the I.R.A. to simply follow Fianna Fáil policy and he had no strategy to tackle partition.[6] However, the elevation of Fianna Fáil to power had already raised expectations.

The Battalion had deliberately increased in size to coincide with this election but more volunteers and no money put further pressure on weapons stocks. So it now needed to source more rifles. On 17th March, the Battalion raided the home of Charles Newell, a retired sergeant-major and former gamekeeper to various prominent unionists, looking for rifles. Arthur Thornbury and James Connolly were immediately arrested. Thornbury was a star footballer and hurler with the McKelveys G.A.A. club, the Antrim county teams and Ulster provincial teams (while in prison he was even proposed for the position of secretary of the Ulster Council, but lost out in a ballot).

It wasn't just Belfast that was restless. At the next I.R.A. General Army Convention, in April, the Down and Tyrone Battalions called for a Northern command within the six counties to deal with issues arising from partition.[7] Meanwhile Belfast moved that "…the Army retain its arms until its aims are achieved. That the I.R.A. sever its connections with Saor Éire as its political arm. That if the Army requires a political arm, an effort be made to re-organise and build up Sinn Féin as the political arm of the Republic." The criticism of Saor Éire and promotion of Sinn Féin sounds like Davy Matthews.

Afterwards, many left republicans at G.H.Q. tried to publicly pressure Belfast over Saor Éire despite the fact that O'Donnell had set it up outside the Battalion structures. Mick Price claimed "Conservative minds… will allow no discussion of this plan for social reconstruction in Ireland." Whether Price meant the Battalion or not, George Gilmore clearly did, as he slammed "..certain people who are suggesting that we are 'sullying the flag' by introducing 'bread and butter politics' and that we should keep our movement on a higher and more spiritual plane…".[8] Presumably 'sullying the flag' and 'bread and butter politics' and the aspiration to '…keep the movement on a higher and more spiritual plane…' were phrases used at the Army Convention. The prose sounds very much like Matthews. As Harry White was later to describe him, "…when he gave talks on Irish history … he could make you cry."[9]

Matthews told the I.R.A.'s Chief of Staff, Moss Twomey, that Belfast was of the "…firm opinion that the army has deviated from the path of nationalism and has taken the road of materialism through Saor Éire."[10] Twomey got the attacks against Belfast in *An Phoblacht* toned down.

Within a couple of weeks, *An Phoblacht* was more constructive: "There are progressive forces in North-East Ulster, and economic conditions, growing rapidly worse, are forcing a new consideration of 1) the value of the close British connection, 2) the whole economic and social system, as revealed in the appalling conditions of industry and trade and consequently employment. Those who are really Nationalist should take up this question immediately."[11] According to Bob Bradshaw, the Battalion wasn't rejecting left wing politics, though, it was growing concerned that another pogrom may be imminent.[12] To complicate matters, G.H.Q. then heard that a visit to Armagh by Moss Twomey had come to the R.U.C.'s attention. The finger of suspicion seemingly pointed to Belfast. Given some of the hostility between Belfast and G.H.Q., it probably couldn't have come at a worse time as it was also feared that Thornbury and Connolly had been given away to the R.U.C..[13] At their trial, both refused to recognise the court while Charles Newell and his son James gave evidence against them. According to Bob Bradshaw, Joe McGurk, the Battalion Adjutant, wanted reprisal action taken against the Newells for testifying.[14] There was also a campaign to protest Thornbury and Connolly's innocence. Slogans were painted on walls around the Falls Road saying Thornbury and Connolly were '… in jail on a trumped up charge'.

The I.R.A. posted handbills calling for their release. The Unionists had learnt their lesson. It prosecuted the printers Joseph and Thomas Cahill as well as Dan Turley, Tommy O'Malley and Willie McCurry for ordering the handbills.[15] Turley got three months and O'Malley and McCurry a month each. On the 9th July, Thornbury and Connolly received sentences of eighteen months.

---

[1] MacEoin, U. 1980 *Survivors*, p308. Carleton erroneously dates this to 1930.

[2] See Munck and Rolston, 1987, p169-174, where Barney Boswell, Charlie McGlade, Jack Brady and Jack McNally discuss these issues. Bob Bradshaw is even more forthright in a series of article published in *The Irish Times* in March 1969 where he described the I.R.A. at the time as being far to the left. The Wolfe Tone Republican Clubs in Belfast first get mentioned in December 1931. It's early activity appears to be in connection with commemorations such as for Dick Barrett, Joe McKelvey, Liam Mellows and Rory

O'Connor (*Anglo-Celt*, 19th December 1931) or the 1916 Rising (*Ulster Herald*, 2nd April 1932).

[3] Munck and Rolston 1987, p21.

[4] The comments were made in a letter from Turley to his wife in May 1933. The Papal Encyclical was issued in May 1931.

[5] Munck and Rolston 1987, p18-19.

[6] MacEoin 1997, p846.

[7] N.L.I. MS 44,069/7.

[8] See Munck and Rolston 1987, p174 citing *An Phoblacht* 2nd April 1932 and 30th April 1932.

[9] MacEoin, U. 1985 *Harry*, p41.

[10] See MTCUDA P69/52 (190) quoted in Hanley 2002, p146.

[11] *An Phoblacht*, 21st May 1932.

[12] Bradshaw contributed a number of articles to *The Irish Times* in March 1969 on Belfast in the 1930s where he insisted the Belfast I.R.A. was very much left wing at this time.

[13] Hanley 2002, p47.

[14] MacEoin 1997, p422 and p435.

[15] The father and uncle of future leading I.R.A. figure Joe Cahill.

we have sometimes exchanged shots

During that year the I.R.A. issued an address to the Orange Order, written by Peadar
O'Donnell, trying to appeal directly to northern Protestants (and again bypassing the
Battalion). This is the text as published in *An Phoblacht* on 16th July 1932:

Fellow Countrymen and Women,
It is a long call from the ranks of the Irish Republican Army to the marching throngs that hold the 12th
July Celebrations in North East Ulster. Across the space we have sometimes exchanged shots, or missiles
or hard words, but never forgetting that on occasions our ancestors have stood shoulder to shoulder. Some
day we will again exchange ideas and then the distance which now separates us will shorten. For we of
the Irish Republican Army believe that inevitably the small farmers and wage-earners in the Six County
area will make common cause with those of the rest of Ireland, for the common good of the mass of the
people in a Free United Irish Republic. Such a conviction is forming itself in an ever increasing number
of minds in North East Ulster.
The Irish Republican Army – within North East Ulster as well as in the rest of Ireland – believe that
the mass of the Working-Farmers and Wage-earners must organise behind revolutionary leadership if
they are to rescue themselves from a system within they the few prosper and the many are impoverished.
It is our opinion, a conviction driven in on our mind by the facts of life around us, that capitalism and
imperialism constitute a system of exploitation and injustice within which the mass of the people can know
no freedom.
The burdens of to-day's bad times are falling with increasing weight on Working Farmers, who must
surrender an increasing part of their produce to meet rents, taxes, bank interest, etc, while their incomes
diminish The unemployed workers are being torn at with economies in social services – adding daily to
the destitute. The wage earners are finding their conditions of employment and standard of living steadily
worsening.
We can see no permanent solution of these evils except by the transfer of power over production, distribution
and exchange to the mass of the people. The power to produce what the many require exists; the
Organisation and its distribution presents no insoluble difficulty. But the vested interests of a privileged
minority are across the road and progress is impossible, unless we are prepared to clear away these
obstacles. These interests that deny their rights to the many are those on which the Empire rests. Touch
or threaten these privileged interests and the whole force of the Empire is invoked for their protection.
Thus it is that we see and say that the freedom of the mass – of the Irish People is impossible without

breaking the connection with Imperial Britain and with all the Imperial system connotes. Do you see any other road to freedom for yourselves and your families?

You must realise that the chief industries on which the former alleged prosperity of North East Ulster rested are gone beyond hope of being revived; that the same thing has occurred in Great Britain; that everywhere the pinch grows tighter on those who are unemployed as a result of this breakdown in the whole structure of capitalism. Can the British people help you while their own workers and industries are struggling desperately to exist and are not succeeding in these days? Where do you see any hope?

Working-farmers and Wage-earners of North East Ulster. You surely must see that your future is bound up with the mass of the people in the remainder of Ireland. To preserve yourselves from extinction, you and they must combine and go forward to the attainment of A Free Irish Nation within which life and living will be organised and controlled by you to serve your needs and thus end the present economic and social injustices for ever.

The industrial capacity, and training of you industrial workers, of North East Ulster ensure you a leading influence and place in the economy and life of a Free Irish Nation.

EXPLOITATION OF RELIGIOU.S. PREJUDICES

To prejudice you it is emphasized that we of the Irish republican Army and the mass of Republicans are mainly Catholic, and that your religious beliefs would not be respected in a free Ireland! It is quite true we are mainly Catholics, but in Southern Ireland the same political and economical interests and voices that tell you we are Catholics, tell the Catholic population of the South that we are Anti-God fanatics, and yearning for an opportunity to make war on the religion to which the majority of us belong!

The fact is we are quite unaware of religious distinctions within our Movement. We guarantee you, you will guarantee us, and we will both guarantee all full freedom of conscience and religious worship in the Ireland we are to set free. This is the simple truth, and just now when Imperial interests are attempting to conceal themselves behind the mad fury of religious strife you and we should combine to make certain that no such escape should be provided them.

In the process of exploitation of the wage-earners and small producers, do you not realise how little religion matters to the exploiters? Orangemen and Catholic, Catholic women and yours toil side by side in the factory and mill, all equally victims Those who thus exploit mercilessly your labour and energies, would outside set you at one anothers throats, because it is to their advantage to divide you and lead you into conflict by arousing religious issues and inflaming passions.

Do yon not find yourselves queued shoulder to shoulder outside the Unemployed Exchanges waiting for the 'Dole', that crumb which the exploiters throw to the exploited of different religions? In these vital matters jour religion or your membership of the Orange Older counts for little, nor does Catholicism to the unemployed and starving Catholics in Southern Ireland. The fact is that the religious feelings of the masses of both Orangemen and Catholics are played on and exploited by the Imperialists and Capitalists the more surely to enslave them.

THE VICTORY OF THE BOYNE!

You celebrate the victory of the Boyne. This battle was a victory for the alliance of the then Pope; and William of Orange; strange alliance for you to celebrate; strange victory for Catholics to resist! History has been muddled to hide the occasions when your forefathers and ours made common cause, and passions are stirred to manufacture antagonisms. If William of Orange and His Holiness could achieve an alliance, there is hope that "NO SURRENDER" may come up from a throng which also roars "UP THE REPUBLIC".

Your stock were the founders and inspiration, the North East Ulster the cradle, of the modern Revolutionary Movement for National Independence and Economic Freedom. Your illustrious ancestors and co-religionists, the United Irishmen, by their gallant struggle in 1798 set aflame the ideals of Republicanism which never since have been extinguished. We ask that you should join us to achieve their ideals — National Freedom and religious toleration.

It was John Mitchel, a Newry man of your stock, who addressed these words to your forefathers: "In fact religious hatred has been kept alive in Ireland longer than anywhere else in Christendom. Just for the simple reason that Irish landlords and British statesmen found their own account in it, and so soon as Irish landlordism and British domination are finally rooted out of the country it will be heard of no longer in Ireland any more than it is in France or Belgium, now."

Fraternally, Your Fellowcountrymen,

The Army Council, On Behalf of the Irish Republican Army

Correspondence between Matthews and Moss Twomey makes it clear that the Battalion delivered it door to door in districts like Sandy Row, despite a feeling that O'Donnell lacked a real understanding of the sectarian dynamic behind the likes of the 1920-22 pogrom.[1] Outdoor Relief workers intended to protest just after the Twelfth but G.H.Q. warned Matthews to avoid Battalion involvement in any violence as it might diminish the address' impact.

Under the guise of McKelveys G.A.A. club, Matthews had been organising training camps at Harp Hill near Carnlough and in Louth at Gyles Quay. After trouble was threatened in Ardoyne, though, Matthews mobilised sixty volunteers to defend the district. When there was a suggestion of threats to the Falls Road, two sections were recalled from training camps to come back to Belfast.[2] Once mobilised, potential flashpoints were cleared of people by the I.R.A. to prevent any violence.

One outcome of a 1932 R.U.C. raid on the Carnlough camp was a decision to only hold training camps south of the border at Gyles Quay, halfway between Dundalk and Greenore. That camp was quietly tolerated by the authorities, even when there were outbreaks of violence between the Blueshirts and the local I.R.A. in Dundalk in 1934.[3] The Battalion staff and Fianna also used nearby Omeath for training.

---

[1] *An Phoblacht,* 16th July 1932.

[2] MTUCDA P69/158 (228-33), these sections had returned from Gyles Quay in Louth.

[3] McNally 1989, p30.

the Outdoor Relief Riots

On Sunday 17th July, a thousand people gathered at the Custom House to hear speeches on the provision of Outdoor Relief in Belfast given, among others, by an ex-I.R.A. volunteer, Tommy Geehan, now of the R.W.G.. Outdoor Relief was felt to be a punitive and humiliating form of assistance for the employed. Even setting aside the dreadful humiliations applicants were put through, the basic rate in Belfast was twelve shillings, less than half of what was given elsewhere. The R.W.G. had organised Outdoor Relief workers committees and were preparing them for a strike.[1]

The next Tuesday morning at 4 am, the R.U.C. stormed into the Harp Hill camp. In the wooden hut, Farrell John Leddy from Rockdale Street in Belfast was arrested. He was a 22 year old doctor and son of a former R.I.C. man (his brother Charlie was on the Belfast I.R.A. staff). A bugle and a book with notes about the use of arms was found on a table in the hut. The twenty-five young men found at the camp had their details taken then were released on probation back in Belfast.[2] At the start of August the wooden hut at Harp Hill was burnt down.

Three days later, a rifle and ammunition were found in a derelict house in Bradford Square just off Tomb Street, close to Belfast city centre. It was found by chance, by some children who played in the house and saw the ammunition. There were no arrests but the location suggests this might well have been an I.R.A. arms dump.

Since O'Donnell's address to the Orange Order had fallen on deaf ears, *An Phoblacht*'s writers decided the blame lay with the Battalion. An article called 'Belfast Bigotry' stated that "…we have those who speak of Tone and emulating all Irishmen, 'Catholic, Protestant and Dissenter' in the country's interest. The intention is good. And they make it honestly. But it is not acted upon. Belfast Republicans, on the whole, are possessed of a bigotry that is all the more dangerous to the cause they have at heart since they themselves are unconscious of its existence."[3]

Since he doesn't cite examples, the form of this bigotry isn't detailed by O'Donnell. His issues with the Battalion staff really seem to revolve around its failure to provide himself, Price, Gilmore etc with a powerbase to challenge for leadership of the I.R.A.. Oddly, O'Donnell seems to have expended considerably more effort on developing the left in Belfast outside of I.R.A. channels than working with the Battalion staff.

The end result was that relations between some of the Belfast I.R.A. staff and some of those on the Dublin G.H.Q. staff were now seriously strained. Further marches by

Outdoor Relief workers in Belfast brought out crowds of ten thousand (on 18th August) and twenty thousand (on 31st August).[4] All the while Stormont was on a recess (it wasn't to sit at all from June to September, only sitting to adjourn for all of October and November on 30th September).

Dan Turley's release from Crumlin Road in September after four months included a céili to welcome him home.[5] Turley had decided to remain active in the I.R.A.. He later wrote that, despite his misgivings about the left-wing political emphasis, he "..went in body and soul to do everything to stop the information that was breaking out somewhere." He believed that, before his arrest, he was "…close on it and the person, or persons, responsible for it were getting afraid..".[6] Turley returned to the Belfast I.R.A. staff again. According to Peter Carleton, later that September he was asked to deliver a letter to Davy Matthews at Pearse Hall and found Turley there with Joe McGurk, the Belfast Adjutant. The letter was from George Gilmore who had been openly critical of the resistance of Matthews and others to Saor Éire. Although Matthews was out at a Painter's Union meeting, Turley wanted McGurk to open the letter but Carleton objected. Matthews then appeared and read it. He told Carleton, "This is Communist philosophy, Peter. And there is as much difference between Republicanism and Communism as there is between day and night."[7] After riots took place in Liverpool at the end of September, Peadar O'Donnell told Matthews that something similar might happen in Belfast but Matthews dismissed his concerns.[8] The Liverpool riots took place in the days leading up to the hunger march in Britain, promoted by the Communist Party of Great Britain through the National Unemployed Workers movement.

In early October, the second week of the hunger march in Britain, the National Unemployed Workers in Belfast organised an Outdoor Relief strike. The chair of the strike committee was Tommy Geehan.

The Battalion was reluctant to get directly involved, despite (according to Bob Bradshaw) being "…fairly far to the left..". As a company officer, he was told by the Battalion Adjutant (Joe McGurk) that the staff feared that open participation by the I.R.A. would "…immediately be known, as it was not a stone-throwing organisation, and returning the fire of the 'B' Special's with Mausers and Lugers, which constituted a large part of its armament, would amount to a proclamation of intent. This would have split the strikers along the old lines of sectarian demarcation. When left to themselves they might have forged a new unity…".[9]

Tommy Geehan was also a former I.R.A. volunteer. He had shot dead the unionist M.P. William Twaddell in an unsanctioned operation on 22nd May 1922 and then served in the Free State army until 1923. Both Davy Matthews and Dan Turley had been treated as suspects in Twaddell's death and were imprisoned while Geehan fought in the pro-treaty forces. How far those kind of personal histories coloured attitudes towards some of the Belfast left in 1932 isn't clear.

When the Outdoor Relief strike began on Monday 3rd October, many I.R.A. volunteers got involved as individuals and with the committees in their local areas. An estimated sixty thousand marched on the first day of the strike. There were marches each day and on the Wednesday (5th October), there were violent confrontations as the R.U.C. baton charged protestors on the Lisburn Road and some of the crowd damaged and looted shops. At around the same time, a couple of miles across the city, the R.U.C. baton charged a crowd outside St Mary's Hall (the strike headquarters).

Calm then returned until the evening of the next Monday when the R.U.C. broke up a meeting in Cromac Street. A major march planned for the next day was then banned by Dawson Bates under the Special Powers Act. On the Tuesday, the R.U.C. violently enforced the ban, attacking the marchers coming from East Belfast before they even left their assembly point. Resistance to the R.U.C. breaking up the marches was much more intense on the Shankill and Falls. In Catholic districts, though, the R.U.C. (and B Specials who had been called up) very quickly resorted to using their guns. A Protestant flower seller, Samuel Baxter, was shot dead in Albert Street and John Geegan, a Catholic from Smithfield, was badly wounded. A curfew was put in place from 11 pm to 5 am that temporarily calmed the violence but the next day it began again. While no-one was killed on Wednesday, John Geegan died from his wounds.

As paving stones had been pulled up and barricades built, the R.U.C. dragged people from their beds to remove the barricades, including James Collins one of the Board of Guardians who oversaw the Outdoor Relief scheme. Collins was a leading member of the Nationalist Party which had reluctantly supported the strike.

There were rumours of I.R.A. weapons being lifted from dumps and used to resist the R.U.C. on both the Falls and Shankill.[10] That Wednesday, the Unionists tried to split the strikers, with Craigavon announcing work in the shipyards and saying the strikers' intent was 'obtaining a republic'. Divide and conquer worked as the strike petered out, finally ending on 17th October after an offer of increases in the rates by the Board of Guardians. The curfew was then lifted and Belfast returned to its own form of normality.

In his memoir *Harry*, Harry White recalls Jimmy Ward firing an old Martini rifle from on top of a bin on Raglan Street (and falling off with each recoil). He also states that others like Albert Price, Tony Lavery, John Rainey, Liam Mulholland and Bob Bradshaw were also prominently involved in street-fighting. White says that the Outdoor Relief riots were "…the first political baptism of fire for a lot of us, and it was the frustration that arose from that, that consolidated the I.R.A.". He pointedly states though that "I do not say that it drove us into it because we were in it already."[11] The new generation brought through Fianna Éireann and into the I.R.A. were getting their first experience of street-fighting. The unionist press were also eager to assign the I.R.A. a leading role in the Outdoor Relief strike, as were some in G.H.Q. in Dublin. Ironically the officers on the Belfast I.R.A. staff, who had been the subject of so much overt criticism from G.H.Q., were now wary of a sectarian pogrom following in the wake of the strike.[12]

In Britain, the hunger marches were to culminate in a large rally at Hyde Park which was broken up by the police and led to clashes in the centre of London. As the role of the police and the suppression of public protest in the hunger marches later came under critical scrutiny, the British National Council for Civil Liberties was established in 1934. It quickly began to focus on the actions of the Unionists and R.U.C. at the time.

Arrests of republicans began to increase significantly after the Outdoor Relief riots. In November 1932, immediately after a robbery a few miles from Belfast, Mick O'Kane,

Dominic Adams and Bob Sloan were arrested on the Springfield Road by the R.U.C. O'Kane had a revolver in his possession and some incriminating 'documents'. Three men with no connections to the I.R.A. were charged with the robbery before the end of the month.[13] When the Prince of Wales came to open the Unionist parliament at Stormont, Davy Matthews attended a protest but it was with Sinn Féin in Dublin.[14]

In December, there was a confrontation between the R.U.C. and I.R.A. in Finaghy when the R.U.C. found seventy men drilling.[15] The R.U.C. arrested Dan Turley's son Sean and Chris McLoughlin, both of whom were jailed (Turley for twelve months, McLoughlin for eight). Finaghy, like the Upper Springfield Road, Black Mountain and Cavehill were locations volunteers would go to with a few rounds to experience firing live ammunition. On Black Mountain they would also get the opportunity to train using explosives.

Over the winter of 1932 and 1933, Harry Diamond, a Board of Guardian member, organised a meeting of republicans and some other nationalist politicians, including the likes of Joe Devlin, to review tactics.[16] Devlin intimated that he wouldn't stand for election again. Davy Matthews and Dan Turley were both present at the meeting. According to Diamond, Devlin criticised I.R.A. tactics and strategy saying that "I don't believe in people dying because they're angry." Matthews and Turley both argued that the political path followed by Devlin and others was pointless as it had never succeeded. There appears to have been no significant outcome to the meeting.

---

[1] Munck and Rolston 1987, p23-34. Munck and Rolston collected a series of oral histories on the context of the Outdoor Relief strike and riots from various perspectives. Recently Seán Mitchell (2017) has published a detailed account using additional archival material.

[2] The twenty-five were William Barrett, Bob Bradshaw, Walter Brennan, Hugh Brennan, Brian Burns, James Crawford, James Devlin, Daniel Ferran, Michael Fitzsimmons, John Maguire, Patrick Martin, Peter McGowan, Thomas McGrogan, John McMullan, Martin McParland, Hugh O'Hagan, Michael O'Kane, Tommy O'Malley, Joe Pimley, Edward Reilly, Jim Shannon, Bob Sloan and James Stewart (see *Belfast Newsletter,* 20th July 1932).

[3] *An Phoblacht,* 20th August 1932.

[4] Munck and Rolston 1987, p22.

[5] MacEoin 1997, p223.

[6] *Irish Press,* 21st September 1945.

[7] MacEoin 1980, p308.

[8] Munck and Rolston 1987, p175.

[9] Bradshaw included this in article in *The Irish Times,* 3rd March 1969.

[10] *An Phoblacht,* 29th October 1932.

[11] MacEoin 1985, p36-7.

[12] Hanley 2002, p150.

[13] *Irish Times,* 8th and 28th November 1932

[14] MacEoin 1997, p227.

[15] Press reports for 21st December 1932.

[16] Diamond's account is given in Munck and Rolston, 1987, p188. There was a Wolfe Tone Republican Club which used Pearse Hall in King Street (effectively the Battalion's headquarters). It features in various charges related to 'seditious' documents over the period from December 1931 to November 1933 and then again in the summer of 1936. Dan Turley implies that he was involved in setting up the Wolfe Tone Republican Clubs and that they were specifically intended as an alternative to Saor Éire (see P.R.O.N.I., Belf/1/1/2/139/5). The Clubs appear to have been formed a year before the I.R.A. permitted volunteers to participate in electoral activity (in November 1932) and may have been intended to oversee commemorations of the likes of the 1916 Rising. The I.R.A. Convention decision of November 1932 is likely what prompted the meetings with Devlin and Diamond but it may all have been part of a more general politicisation process that included the Wolfe Tone Republican Clubs and just never fully got under way.

the 1933 rail strike

January 1933 saw de Valera call a snap election with the I.R.A. leadership now leaning in two directions (neither towards Sinn Féin). The I.R.A. Army Convention in November 1932 had finally authorised members to work and canvas during elections. Frank Ryan, George Gilmore, Mick Price and Peadar O'Donnell felt a new left-leaning party was needed. But Moss Twomey, Sean McBride and Sean Russell blocked it and endorsed working with Fianna Fáil. They also instructed that *An Phoblacht* be less a mouthpiece for the left in future, and that Frank Ryan's editorials be 'looked at.'[1]

Ironically, the Belfast I.R.A. now felt it should have been formally involved in the Outdoor Relief strike and decided to work more closely with the trade unions. When a request came from the dockers union to bomb new grain mills at the docks, the Belfast I.R.A. agreed to help only for the Irish Transport and General Workers Union to veto it from Dublin.[2] Oddly, the support for the Outdoor Relief strike did not translate to the Belfast Corporation elections as left-wing candidates fared particularly badly (this, in part, was equally a reminder that property qualifications meant not everyone had a vote while others had many more than one).

In late 1932, the rail unions got increasingly militant over pay cuts being imposed on their members and proposed a major strike from 31st January 1933. One night, a few days into the strike, two Protestant railway union men arrived at Davy Matthews house and asked for I.R.A. assistance to prevent blacklegs running lorries and trains to break the strike. Matthews pointed out that would mean blowing up the railway lines. The union men said that was what they hoped the I.R.A. would do.[3] The Battalion was then mobilised and prepared to carry out sabotage against the railway companies.

This marked a sudden shift in tactics by the Battalion. Judging by the material lost in dumps and references to training, Battalion volunteers had been trained in defensive measures but were now going to shift to adopting urban guerrilla tactics like sabotage and gun attacks. Once it made that tactical shift, it would be difficult to simply return into the shadows.

From early February, the I.R.A. began mounting operations in support of the strike, including holding the bus up along the Dublin-Belfast route. On the 13th February, Bob Bradshaw and May Laverty (of Cumann na mBan) blew up a culvert at Dunmurry using gelignite and a battery-operated detonator. On the 19th February, strike-breaking drivers were hauled off buses on the Dublin-Dundalk route. By the 26th February, the I.R.A. was throwing Mill bombs into empty buses in Dundalk and in the York Road and Great Victoria Street termini in Belfast. Damage was minimal but the risk of injury or worse was increasing. A live bomb was found near the Adelaide depot on the morning of Tuesday 28th February.

The same day, Matthews summoned Bob Bradshaw. Matthews sent him to the Great Northern's lorry exit (at the corner of Durham Street and Grosvenor Road). There he was to fire warning shots at strike-breaking lorry drivers, supported by Joe Pimley and others. The drivers were being guarded by about twenty-five R.U.C. men. Matthews instructed Bradshaw that he was to fire at the cab but not injure the driver. According to Bradshaw, Pimley's brother Isaac used to describe Matthews as having a heart of gold but a head of ivory.[4]

When Bradshaw opened fire on the lorries, Pimley discovered that the ammunition in his pistol was defective and couldn't provide covering fire. Bradshaw's firing position was now given away so he and Pimley ran into Stanley Street as the R.U.C. opened fire on them.[5] Turning into Cullingtree Street then Fox Row, they were joined by one of the lookouts, Jack Crosskerry.[6] They cut through an entry half way down Fox Row and came out on Durham Street where they crossed the road to a short lane way at the back of Christchurch. Here they ran into R.U.C. Constable John Ryan in Durham Street. Ryan and another R.U.C. Constable, Lally, had been in Albert Street and heard shots from the Grosvenor Road. Ryan headed for Durham Street. Lally started down Stanley Street only for the R.U.C. to open fire on him from the Grosvenor Road. He saw two men running from Stanley Street into Cullingtree Road so he headed back to Albert Street to catch up with Ryan. Ryan, meanwhile, had encountered Bradshaw, Crosskerry and Pimley in Durham Street. When Lally then entered Durham Street he saw Ryan and three men rather than two.

Ryan pointed his gun at Pimley and Bradshaw and shouted "What are you fellows up to?" and they replied "It is alright." Crosskerry separated from the other two at this point. Ryan shouted to Lally "Watch, watch!" and Lally looked around to see where Crosskerry had gone. Seeing Ryan and Lally distracted, Bradshaw drew his own gun and fired at Ryan and Lally as he and Pimley ran up Durham Street and down College Square North.[7] Lally emptied his revolver at the escaping I.R.A. men. Ryan fired three shots but was hit in the face and chest by Bradshaw and died within minutes. Ryan was the first R.U.C. constable killed by the I.R.A. since 1922.

Bradshaw, Pimley and Crosskerry all fled to Dublin (despite R.U.C. reports, none were wounded in the incident). The strikers, who were mostly Protestant, were not put off by the fatality and the strike continued. Meanwhile the R.U.C. tore the Grosvenor Road apart searching for the I.R.A. unit involved. The Unionists even offered a reward of £1,000 for information.

Outside Belfast, there was interference with railway lines between Omagh, Donemana and Strabane leading to a derailment that injured thirteen people and caused £30,000 worth of damage on lines, stock and cargo being transported. There was also an attempt to blow up the line near Coleraine.

While the R.U.C. carried out widespread searches there were limited arrests but, on the Thursday, they hauled in Billy McAllister and Tommy O'Malley and put them up on a charge of possession of a revolver. At the end of March, over two days, five revolvers and three grenades were also found beside Queens Bridge on the banks of the River Lagan.

I.R.A. actions in support of the strike continued for a few more weeks, with further shots being fired at strike-breakers and attempts to bomb the rail line. The railway unions finally agreed to go back to work (and take a 7½% pay cut) at the end of April. The Irish Catholic bishops had now become vocal critics of 'communism' and the left-wing policies of the I.R.A. and there was a quite public debate in the press on the issue. And clearly not everyone in the I.R.A. agreed with supporting the strike (see Dan Turley's letter quoted elsewhere here).[8]

---

[1] MacEoin 1997, p231.

[2] Jack Brady and Liam Mulholland, quoted in Munck and Rolston 1987, p177.

[3] According to Bob Bradshaw in MacEoin 1997, p424.

[4] MacEoin 1997, p425.

[5] *Irish Independent,* 2nd March 1933. The version here largely relies on this account, Bradshaw's, the *Belfast Newsletter,* 1st March 1933 and another in the *Evening Herald,* 10th April 1933.

[6] Bradshaw (in MacEoin 1997, p426) identifies Crosskerry as the third man in Durham Street.

[7] Another eye-witness statement was reported in *Irish Examiner,* 3rd March 1933.

[8] *Irish Press,* 21st September 1945.

Top: Republican election rally, 1933 (*Irish Press,* 28th November 1933).
Bottom: R.U.C. guard the gates of Milltown cemetery as republican 1916 commemoration kneels on the road outside (*Irish Independent*, 3rd April 1934).

Dan Turley and Davy Matthews

Dan Turley now intended to resign from the I.R.A. for good. He had been unable to expose the informer he suspected to be inside the Battalion. He also disagreed with I.R.A. strategy and the relationship between himself and Belfast O/C Davy Matthews was strained. Turley appears to have been acting as Finance Officer for the Battalion but Matthews instead had Cassie O'Hara (of Cumann na mBan) look after the Battalion's money.[1] Davy Matthews ordered Turley to attend a meeting on the 5th April at which Matthews informed Turley that he was under arrest. Turley assumed it was over the Battalion finances. He left with a member of I.R.A. G.H.Q. in a motor car and was only then told what he was charged with. An R.U.C. C.I.D. Sergeant, Heffernan, had told a bailiff called Frank Moyna that Turley was an informer. Moyna passed it on through I.R.A. channels, hence Turley's arrest.[2] Moyna had dealt with Heffernan before, having given evidence to support firearms charges (not involving the I.R.A.) brought by Heffernan in 1927. Moyna had also pursued various other people through the courts including a man called George Gibson in 1930 for fraud.

The car took Turley away from Belfast. A Belfast staff officer who was also in the car told Turley the Belfast staff were as bewildered as he was. Turley was sure he'd be exonerated by a court-martial. Held for a week without anything happening, he then was questioned by a G.H.Q. staff officer and badly beaten.[3] He was told to admit he had given away the Whiterock Road, Linden Street and Gibson Street arms dumps for £20, £10 and £10. He refused but eventually agreed to confess at a court-martial.

In the morning Turley was given a statement to sign which now also included that he had given away Thornbury and Connolly in 1932. He refused and was again beaten for an hour and a half until he signed a statement. The G.H.Q. officer who prosecuted Turley at the court-martial was Mick Price, who had been involved with O'Donnell and Gilmore in the long running feud with Turley and other Battalion staff since the 1920s. The court-martial found him guilty (solely on the basis of Heffernan's information which Turley insisted even Heffernan would refute if they asked him) and sentenced him to death.[4] Sean Russell, a member of the I.R.A.'s Army Council, got involved and the sentence was commuted to exile, first in Canada (which Turley refused) then Glasgow. Russell accompanied him to Glasgow to confirm he had complied. By May, Turley had already requested permission to return to Belfast and was awaiting a response from I.R.A. G.H.Q. in Dublin.

Despite the usual ban on Easter Rising commemorations the I.R.A. made a public call for recruits for which Joe McGurk was arrested and got three months.[5] As Turley was now held responsible for the loss of the dumps a few years previously, Jack McNally was brought back into active service by Davy Matthews at Easter 1933, presumably to offset any issues raised by Turley's exile and McGurk's arrest.[6] Like Matthews and Turley, McNally was in Sinn Féin.

Paradoxically, the I.R.A. was both legal and high profile in the south. In June a Battalion contingent went to Bodenstown for the annual Wolfe Tone commemoration. Ominously, Fianna Fáil held their own, separate, Bodenstown commemoration that year. The press reports on the I.R.A. commemoration list the G.H.Q., Army Executive and Battalion leaders present, giving a who's-who of the 1930s I.R.A.: Moss Twomey, Domhnall O'Donnchada, Sean Russell, Sean McBride, Mick Price, Jim Killeen, George Gilmore, Mick Fitzpatrick, Frank Ryan, Peadar O'Donnell, Andy Cooney, Peadar Kearney, John Joe Sheehy, Paddy Fleming, Liam Leddy, Tom Barry, Paddy McLogan, Stephen Hayes, Con Lehane and George Plunkett. Davy Matthews and Jimmy Steele are listed for Belfast. The main speaker, Twomey, was introduced as Chief of Staff of the Irish Republican Army.[7]

The obvious contradiction in the publicity was that the I.R.A. was engaged in urban guerilla actions in Belfast. The I.R.A. was still struggling with strategy though, with Twomey and Sean McBride reduced to considering stunts like seizing the Lia Fáil (the 'Stone of Scone' used as a Coronation Stone at Westminster) and bringing it back to Ireland, via Belfast.[8] Whether the Battalion was every formally asked to consider the scheme isn't clear.

The left, whilst also fractious, was slightly better organised. That same month the Revolutionary Workers Groups reformed as the Communist Party of Ireland.

Famously at the Twelfth of July demonstrations that summer, Lord Brookeborough (the future Unionist Prime Minister) urged employers not to employ Catholics saying "I have not one about my place…".

Security was a major concern of the Battalion in September 1933. The increasing numbers of volunteers, and continuing economic depression, brought its own security risks. More volunteers heightened the probability of recruiting someone who was susceptible to pressure to inform to the R.U.C., either due to financial or psychological pressure. That summer, one man was found chained to a tree in the grounds of St Matthews on the Newtonards Road on which it was written: "Silence is Golden, others beware." This punishment, the public shaming of individuals, was to be occasionally used by the I.R.A., as was tarring and feathering (literally pouring tar over a victim then covering them in feathers).[9] But there were clearly still security leaks from somewhere within the Battalion. On the 17th September, the R.U.C. raided Tony Lavery's house in Balkan Street at 2.15am and detained him. Lavery had been acting as Matthew's Adjutant after Dan Turley's court-martial.

A few days later, the I.R.A. attempted to shoot Charles and James Newell (who had testified against Thornbury and Connolly) as they walked along Talbot Street after leaving work.[10] Miraculously, both Newells had bullets pass through their clothing yet were unharmed. The two of them were armed and attempted to give chase but their attackers escaped. Joe McGurk, who had called for a reprisal against the Newells in 1932, had taken over as the Belfast Adjutant again after Lavery's arrest. He obviously wanted it carried out before Thornbury and Connolly's imminent release.

The Battalion staff also weren't prepared to let Dan Turley's case go. George Gibson, the former employee Frank Moyna had prosecuted for fraud in 1930, was picked up and questioned by the I.R.A., seemingly for posing as an I.R.A. intelligence officer. Gibson was taken to a hall in King Street for questioning and was asked specifically about Moyna and what he knew of Moyna's work and presumably, his relationship with Heffernan.

At the end of that month, Gibson was found handcuffed and gagged in a field off the Falls Road. The R.U.C. put a guard on Gibson's Roumania Street home and Tom Hunter and Gerard Moyna (Frank's son) were arrested based on testimony from Gibson and then brought to court.[11] Gibson's story was that, walking through Willowbank to meet Joe McGurk, he was stopped by two men who knocked him down. He was then surrounded by twenty men, beaten, then handcuffed and his legs bound. Gibson claimed he managed to roll away and raise the alarm. Hunter and Moyna were charged and a warrant was put out for McGurk who refused to recognise the court and was imprisoned for contempt.[12]

On top of the imprisonment of both Lavery (who had been sentenced to three months) and McGurk, rumours began to circulate that Turley had returned to Belfast at the end of September. Two masked men arrived at his family home in Dunmore Street and searched it, finding nothing. Presumably the Turley rumour was connected to Gibson's interrogation by the I.R.A. and Turley's own requests to return home. At the end of September, the press were also beginning to sense a change of atmosphere and hardening of attitudes among unionists, wryly noting that an election to the northern parliament was imminent.[13]

Apparently, after George Gibson's interrogation, Turley did actually return to Belfast during October 1933. As he later lived openly in his family home, his return was presumably sanctioned by the Battalion following its own investigations of Gibson and Moyna and his information sources.

In early October the Communist Party proposed to commemorate the anniversary of the previous year's Outdoor Relief strike (later that month the Unionists reverted to the pitifully low rates that prompted the strike). On 7th October, Joe McGurk was brought back in to court and given an opportunity to purge his contempt and agree to be bound over. McGurk refused on the grounds that he was an I.R.A. volunteer. Like Lavery, he was given three months.

The next evening, R.U.C. Constables Charles Anderson and John Fahy had just come on guard duty outside Gibson's house when three masked men approached them and told them to put their hands up. Anderson drew his revolver and at least one of the gunmen opened fire, hitting Anderson in the wrist. He staggered out into the road where a second bullet hit him in the stomach. Fahy threw himself on the ground, then fired off a few wild shots from his revolver. The gunmen escaped back down Servia Street. The next day a revolver, with two chambers empty, was found inside the railings of Dunville Park, five hundred metres away. One eyewitness reported that the three men involved were followed by four youths, suggesting this was an organised I.R.A. operation.[14] During the night Anderson died from his wounds in hospital.

It is not clear now what the intent was in Roumania Street, although it has echoes of a wild Davy Matthews 'plan'. The next day, Gibson fled the house (presumably recalling the fate of Patrick Woods less than ten years previously). The R.U.C. flooded the district with Lancia cars and carried out a series of raids over the next couple of days, mainly between 4 am and 5 am in the mornings. They arrested suspected I.R.A. volunteers in Belfast, including most of the Battalion staff.

After the arrests Jack McNally took over as Adjutant. He brought back two other veterans, Jim Johnstone and Sean Carmichael, to form a temporary staff.[15] More were arrested in follow-up raids. On Friday 13th alone, thirty-three were detained across Belfast. By the Friday evening the R.U.C. had served detention orders on forty-nine men who had been moved into Crumlin Road Prison. At one stage sixty men were detained. Arthur Thornbury and James Connolly were released the day after Anderson was killed. They had been served with orders excluding them from the north apart from the town of Limavady.[16] Both had ignored the order and were re-arrested early Thursday morning when the R.U.C. found them at home. Each received a further month in prison.

During the waves of arrests that followed Anderson's death, the proposed commemoration of the Outdoor Relief strikes on 11th October was banned by the Unionists. The secretaries general of the Communist Party of Great Britain and the Communist Party of Ireland were both then served exclusion orders in mid-October.

A few days later, on the night of 14th October a well-known Catholic publican, Dan O'Boyle, was shot in Brougham Street while waiting for a tram. One hour later, a Catholic man, John Gillespie, was badly beaten by a crowd at the corner of Nelson Street. Afterwards a mob came through Vere Street attacking the houses of Catholic residents. They were chased off before the R.U.C. arrived. O'Boyle died in hospital the next afternoon. On the Monday night, further shots were fired in Michael Street and there was trouble in the Old Lodge Road. The raids and arrests of republicans continued. There was no R.U.C. response to unionist violence. Although most of the staff were being held by the R.U.C., the patched up staff temporarily re-organised the Battalion companies into smaller units. This would mean that individual volunteers would know less names and places.[17]

Then, on 26th October, Major John McCormick, an Ulster Protestant League supporter and Unionist M.P. was shot and wounded in Barnetts Road after a struggle. He later claimed that he had been warned five days previously that his life was under threat. Some of the press reporting noted that it had been widely rumoured that McCormick would not be reselected as the Unionist candidate for the upcoming election. The revolver used in the attack on him was an unusual calibre, .320, but the attack was dismissed as an attempted bag snatch.[18] Despite this, the R.U.C. carried out further raids on republicans. The next day Arthur Thornbury's brother Gene's house was searched as part of the investigation. The R.U.C. found a notebook recording the movements of the Newells in the days before they were attacked in September and Gene was detained for further questioning.

The widespread arrests of republicans prompted a crowd of six hundred to gather in Smithfield in support of the detainees on the Sunday, 5th November. Speakers included Harry Diamond and Brendan Kielty (on behalf of the I.R.A.). Kielty was also a regular county delegate for McKelveys G.A.A. club.[19] The meeting was baton charged by the R.U.C. and Diamond and Kielty were arrested and charged with breach of the peace. Both got a months imprisonment as did Eileen Morrissey from Divis Street.

Eventually twenty of the republican detainees were sentenced to three months in prison for 'refusing to answer questions' (a Special Powers Act offence).[20] Charlie Leddy and Isaac Pimley were kept in detention without charges. Separately, Hugh Matthews (brother of Davy) and John Dunn were each fined £10 for possession of I.R.A. documents, while Seán Murray, secretary of the Communist Party of Ireland, was sentenced to one month's imprisonment. A few days later, on the 11th November, Gene Thornbury was charged with shooting the Newells.

While all those arrested in late October were being detained in prison, the election to the northern parliament took place. It had been decided that republican candidates would stand. Various names were suggested including Arthur Thornbury, James Connolly, Joe McGurk, George Nash and Frank Devlin. Having got a tip-off, thirty R.U.C. officers swooped on McKelvey Hall at 10 pm on 15th November to raid the selection convention. But the convention was held elsewhere and selected Thornbury. Instead the R.U.C. arrested fifteen 14-19 year olds who were present, charging them with drilling (eight of whom received two months in prison).[21] The authorities refused visits to Thornbury so he couldn't sign nomination papers. His brother Pat, the former 3rd Northern Division O/C stood instead, in Belfast Central.

Sean McCool also stood in Foyle, Paddy McLogan for South Armagh and Tom McGrath for South Down, while de Valera stood for the Nationalist Party in South Down. Despite having said at the conference with republicans back in 1932 that he would not stand again, Joe Devlin stood for election in Central Belfast.

During the campaign there were the usual clashes. The authorities also arrested Davy Matthews who was acting as republican Director of Elections.[22] Jack McNally took over as acting Belfast O/C. In the last week of the election campaign, Gene Thornbury was brought to court (on the 23rd November). He allowed himself to be defended claiming he had left the I.R.A. nine months previously. His alibi managed to stand up to scrutiny and he was found not guilty.

A couple of days after the not guilty verdict, a big election rally was held on 26th November in Belfast which was attended by about twelve thousand people. It was to be the largest republican rally in the city for more than thirty years. On the eve of the election the Communist Party issued a statement urging people to vote for the Republican candidates (much to the irritation of Tommy Geehan who wanted them to back him). While only Paddy McLogan was elected in the end, the Belfast rally coincided with Thornbury pushing Joe Devlin very close and Harry Midgeley, a Labour candidate, taking a seat off the unionists in the Dock Ward.

As well as a taste of political campaigning, the Battalion also began to produce its own publication, *An Síol*, during the election. At first it was put together by Jack McNally and Michael Traynor, later Charlie Leddy took over as editor as it became more regular.[23] Typically it included political statements, news items, republican poetry, G.A.A. notes and Irish language articles.

On 30th November, the day of the election, Davy Matthews was sentenced to three months while Charlie Leddy and Isaac Pimley got two months.[24] Tommy Cormican was bailed on an undertaking to leave the I.R.A.. Matthews, a 1920-22 veteran, first imprisoned in 1924 and a lifelong dedicated I.R.A. and Sinn Féin activist, then signed an undertaking to cease his I.R.A. membership and get an early release before Christmas.[25] He was joined in signing out by George Nash, another long-term activist.

On 15th January 1934, McKelvey Hall was raided yet again by the R.U.C.. Gerald O'Toole from Spinner Street was questioned along with four others.[26] O'Toole refused to answer on the grounds that he was a member of the I.R.A.. He got three months with hard labour for his admission.

---

[1] In an (undated) letter Turley wrote to his wife (P.R.O.N.I., Belf/1/1/2/139/5).

[2] In a letter he wrote a few months later, Turley said "I believe I was closing on the source, that the person or persons responsible for it were getting afraid, and that the only way was to get me out of the way, by possibly dropping some hint from the C.I.D." (P.R.O.N.I., Belf/1/1/2/139/5).

[3] The staff officer was one of Tom Barry's Cork Battaltion.

[4] I assume it is Heffernan from references elsewhere. In a letter Turley suggests the dumps were given away to 'Fergy' but his real name isn't clear.

[5] Bob Bradshaw has McGurk as the Belfast Intelligence Officer (see MacEoin 1997, p423) other sources have him as the Adjutant – he may have temporarily filled both roles after Turley's court-martial.

[6] McNally (1989, p24) records his return as Easter 1933.

[7] Twomey's speech is quoted in, eg, *The Kildare Observer* 24th June 1933.

[8] MacEoin 1997, p846.

[9] Harry White discusses tarring and feathering in *Harry*. This appears to be first instance of it being used by the I.R.A. in Belfast since May 1922.

[10] A third man appears to have acted as a lookout.

[11] See *Belfast Newsletter*, 1927, 21st March 1930, 23rd November 1933.

[12] This story appears in fragments in newspaper reporting in late September and early October 1933.

[13] For instance, see *Sunday Independent,* 1st October 1933.

[14] None of the contemporary accounts identify any of those involved. The only possible hint of involvement is that Gerard O'Toole left Belfast for Dublin at this time (as had Bradshaw, Pimley and Crosskerry had after the shooting of John Ryan earlier that year).

The account here is mainly based on the *Irish Press* and *Irish News* of 9th/10th October 1933.

[15] McNally's timeline in *Morally Good, Politically Bad* for 1933 is unclear as he merges events in February and November. He also states he was made Adjutant but it isn't clear who acted as O/C while Matthews was detained in November (I assume, as he states that he re-organised the companies in November, McNally was then O/C).

[16] Under the same regulation that confined republicans to Limavady, communists were internally exiled to Clogher.

[17] McNally 1989, p24. The Belfast I.R.A. undertook a similar process in the 1970s moving to what was known as a cell structure.

[18] The .320 calibre is recorded in *Irish Press* 27th October, 1933. The same report suggests McCormick was about to be de-selected for his seat. It may be coincidental, but on 28th December 1934, Liam Watson of Fianna Éireann was caught and charged with possession of a .320 revolver and ammunition.

[19] He later went to Spain with O'Duffy's Bandera – on his return he had to face an I.R.A. board of inquiry before he could be accepted back by the Battalion.

[20] The names are reported in the press, eg *Irish Press* on 8th November 1933: Dominic Adams, Paddy Adams, Philip Campbell, William Connolly, Jack Gaffney, John Hall, Jimmy Hasty, Bobby Hicks, Hugh Keenan, Patrick Largey, William McAllister, Michael McBriarty, Willie John McCurry, Peter McGowan, Robert McKnight, George Nash, Mick O'Kane, Tommy O'Malley, Frank Pimley and Jimmy Steele. Charles Leddy and Isaac Pimley were kept in detention without any charges.

[21] Rory Campbell, Frankie Doherty, Tom Graham, Vincent Kelly, Patrick Lavery, Patrick McCann, Francis McGoldrick and John McKenna.

[22] It is not explicitly stated anywhere, but Jack McNally seems to have deputised as O/C in Matthews absence.

[23] McNally 1989.

[24] Irish Press 1st December 1933.

[25] *Northern Whig* 23rd December 1933; Hanley 2002, p156; *An Phoblacht* 3rd February 1934.

[26] Bob Bradshaw places O'Toole in Dublin in late 1933, so he may have been involved in the Anderson (or possibly McCormick) shooting.

Republican Congress

The reaction to Davy Matthews signing the undertaking to cease his membership of the I.R.A. was swift. G.H.Q. in Dublin decided that he should also be held responsible for Nash signing out. In January 1934 Matthews was charged and a court-martial held. He was dismissed from the I.R.A. with ignominy with the result published in *An Phoblacht* in February 1934. Tony Lavery, who had been Belfast Adjutant until his imprisonment in September, had since been released and now took over as O/C. Jimmy Steele took on the role of Adjutant. Many of the current I.R.A. volunteers had come through the ranks of Fianna Éireann under Lavery and Steele.

In early March, with one eye on the election campaign of the previous November, the Unionists brought in a Representation of the People Bill to unseat any abstentionists who got elected. Joe Devlin also died, which meant a by-election in Belfast Central.

An I.R.A. Army Convention in Stephen's Green on 17th March rejected a radical socialist motion which was put forward by Frank Ryan, George Gilmore and Peadar O'Donnell. To the I.R.A. the national issue still had primacy over social and economic matters. Many of those supporting the defeated motion then left to found Republican Congress.

The Battalion staff summoned the membership and told them about Republican Congress and its aims. They then asked each volunteer whether they wanted to stay. Some, like Liam Tumilson and James Pimley joined Republican Congress. Congress also reformed the Irish Citizen's Army to provide protection to its political activities. Having been collectively at the receiving end of so much criticism from Gilmore and O'Donnell, the Battalion stayed loyal to the Army Convention decision.

That Easter Unionists again banned the 1916 commemorations at Milltown cemetery (and elsewhere in the north).[1] Some two hundred R.U.C. men were even stationed around Milltown on Easter Sunday to prevent a ceremony taking place. By 2.15 pm a crowd of around five hundred had gathered outside. Shortly afterwards, Jimmy Steele led a group in parade formation up along the Falls Road to the gates where a decade of the rosary was said.

A week later, the Battalion mounted a raid on the Ballybraid Spinning Mill near Ballymena, which was used by the local B Specials. Seventeen rifles were captured along with a thousand rounds of ammunition, three thousand rounds of revolver ammunition, a large number of revolvers and other equipment.[2] These were taken away in a waiting car which was seen driving towards Toome.[3] The arms were then brought to Belfast and dispersed into dumps by transporting them around the city on a horse and cart. The R.U.C. carried out some raids and picked up various individuals for questioning but to no avail.

By the time of the Belfast Central by-election in early June, the political landscape had shifted further. De Valera's government had sought to buy support from former I.R.A. volunteers via the Military Pensions Acts. This coincided with the formation of the abstentionist Anti-Partition League (A.P.L.).[4] Hugh Corvin and other former I.R.A. volunteers were prominent in promoting the A.P.L. in Belfast which was distinct from the non-absentionist, and now Fianna Fáil-aligned, Nationalist Party. The A.P.L. was, basically, a proto-type for Sean McBride's later Clann na Poblachta project of the 1940s. In the Belfast Central by-election Harry Diamond stood as an A.P.L. candidate but lost to the Nationalist Party's T.J. Campbell.

The annual Bodenstown commemoration in 1934 saw its biggest crowd yet. Some thirty thousand attended, including the Battalion and a group from the Shankill in the James Connolly Workers Republican Clubs formed by Peadar O'Donnell. They were involved in an infamous dispute with the Bodenstown stewards over a restriction on banners being carried into the inner field. While O'Donnell and George Gilmore seemingly hadn't advised the Republican Clubs of the restrictions, they had a lengthy statement ready for de Valera's *Irish Press* the same afternoon which, in retrospect, gives the whole episode a contrived look. By now O'Donnell's people in Belfast, like Carleton, were no longer involved with the I.R.A. But Republican Congress and the Irish Citizen's Army both faded rapidly from the Belfast scene.[5]

By August the depth of sectarian divisions in Belfast was once again obvious. Clashes followed Orange marches in North Queen Street and Upper Library Street where a man was stabbed by a marcher. Then unionists fired shots into a crowd at the junction of North Thomas Street and Garmoyle Street, wounding an R.U.C. sergeant.[6] In mid-September, an Orange procession ended with an invasion of New Dock Street and Marine Street. Forty houses belonging to Catholics were wrecked and masonry thrown through a window, injuring a disabled man, Andy McCombe, who died from his injuries. The focus of the trouble was mainly North Queen Street.

Revisions to the unemployment assistance schemes kept economic issues high on the agenda. Another proposed commemoration of the Outdoor Relief Strike in early October was again banned by the Unionists.[7] With Republican Congress having split at the end of September, Roddy Connolly and Peadar O'Donnell bickered, while Mick Price first called for the Irish Citizen Army to disband then joined the Irish Labour Party.[8] While the left squabbled, sectarian violence still continued in Belfast as a bomb was thrown at four Catholics in the Old Lodge Road in October.

---

[1] See contemporary newspaper reports (eg *Irish News* and *Irish Press*).

[2] Initial reports on the 9th April 1934 were later revised to claim it was 5,000 rounds of rifle ammunition and 1,000 rounds of revolver ammunition (eg in press reports on 10th

April). The later R.U.C. reports also state it was 7 service rifles, 10 'old' U.V.F. rifles, a shotgun, a Webley revolver and two smaller revolvers.

3 *Irish Press,* 17th May 1934.

4 The name 'Anti-Partition League' had previously been used in Fermanagh and Tyrone in 1916 and again in 1921-22.

5 See Murtagh Morgan and Peter Carleton in Munck and Rolston 1987, p178-179. Congress did have some local successes in achieving rent reductions, but only in the Falls.

6 See contemporary press accounts for August 1934 (none of the accounts of events appear to be contested).

7 There is a discussion of the events of the autumn 1934 in Munck and Rolston 1987, p45-46.

8 A newssheet printed by *Arm Luchta Oibre na hÉireann* for G.H.Q. Dublin on 27th November 1934 claims only one Belfast Volunteer from the four Belfast companies has sided with Peadar O'Donnell in the emerging split in the Irish Citizens Army. (N.L.I., ILB04p5).

personal liberty

Violent clashes between the I.R.A. and R.U.C. now slowly increased in frequency. On the 22nd December, three men entered Samuel Leddy's house on Thomas Street (off York Street) and shot him in the arm in front of his family.[1] Since Leddy was an army reservist it appears the R.U.C. decided to treat it as a political action. The Belfast Adjutant, Jimmy Steele, and two of the other senior I.R.A. figures in the north of city, Chris McLoughlin and Liam Mulholland, were hauled in and served with detention orders. On the 26th December Liam Watson was arrested on the Falls Road after being searched and found in possession of a .320 revolver and ammunition, Fianna badges and the usual 'documents'.[2]

As *Habeus Corpus* was suspended Steele, McLoughlin and Mulholland were kept incommunicado. Seamus McKearney and Brian Burns were also detained in early January. They were reportedly beaten on the ribs and threatened with being shot by the R.U.C.. Steele's own treatment was bad enough that he had to be examined by Dr. McNabb on Donegall Street on his release.[3] Only on 14th January did the authorities even admit the men were being detained.[4]

Sectarian violence continued as well. On 25th February a man rolled a bomb along North Queen Street towards a nine year old girl standing near Hardinge Street. The bomb exploded although she wasn't injured and the man ran off up Spamount Street. The I.R.A.'s Easter commemorations were, of course, banned by Minister for Home Affairs Dawson Bates who said, "No person who is disposed to obey the law in Northern Ireland, and keep the peace need fear any interference with his personal liberty."[5]

The Battalion also faced other challenges. On 12th April, a group had met in Dublin to form a 'Pre-Truce' I.R.A. Association for Belfast, attended by Sean McEntee (the Fianna Fáil T.D. and Free State Minister of Finance), Joe Connolly (now a Fianna Fáil Senator and Minister for Lands) and Denis McCullough. While, nominally, this was part of the out-working of a military pensions review, it also served as a financial inducement to buy support for de Valera. McEntee also made it clear that Fianna Fáil's ambition was to be seen as the authoritative voice of northern republicans and nationalists.[6] It was also hoped that the new volunteer reserve for the Free State army (known as 'Aiken's Reserve') would siphon off young republican-minded individuals away from the I.R.A..[7] Notably, *An Síol*, the news-sheet first issued at the time of the November 1933 election, began to appear in numbered issues at Easter in April 1935. An edition, numbered and dated as Volume No. 1, 20th April 1935, is probably the earliest surviving issue.[8] The paper ran to five double-sided pages and was to be issued fortnightly, costing 2 pence. Now edited by Charles Leddy, it was put together by typing text onto waxed paper then duplicating it on a Gestetner. It also was subtitled 'The Voice of the Resurgent North' and 'Issued by the Republican Publicity Bureau' with an address at 58 King Street in Belfast.[9] In March 1935 the Gardaí had intercepted letters in Mick Price's office in Dublin from the Adjutant of the Belfast Battalion of the Irish Citizen's Army that indicated that the 'apathy' had taken hold and that they should push to hold a James Connolly commemoration at Easter.[10] The threat of competition may have encouraged the Belfast I.R.A. to regularise production of *An Síol*.

That Easter, a half hour long religious service was held outside the locked gates of Milltown cemetery where two hundred R.U.C. men were on duty. Through April and May, gunfire began to become a regular occurrence in York Street, the Docks, Antrim Road, Peter's Hill and North Queen Street. Employers also stood aside as Catholics began to be violently expelled from their workplaces whilst Unionist politicians sardonically complained at the R.U.C. being restrained from attacking Catholics. In June, a young Catholic girl, Annie Quinn, of Harding Street was shot on her way to Mass (a man accused of the shooting was from nearby Grove Street). On 17th June, shots were fired into North Queen Street. An attempt to ban orange processions by the Unionists was ignominiously over-ruled in public by the Orange Order.

During 1935 the R.U.C. made a number of arrests of republicans in Belfast where I.R.A., Fianna Éireann or Cumann na mBan documents or materials were reported from the court. This included Mick Traynor with Fianna documents in January and Paddy Cavanagh in March (in May he went on hunger strike for political status). John Clerkin, an I.R.A. organiser arrested in Armagh and I.R.A. volunteers arrested drilling in Ballymena also kept the organisation's name in the news. It's unclear how far the capture of documents contributed to R.U.C. intelligence gathering or whether it was heavily reliant on human intelligence via informers. As late as the 1938 the R.U.C.'s counter-insurgency strategy appeared to be relatively unsophisticated.

As the summer drew near and tensions heightened in June and July, more I.R.A. papers were found in John McKeever's house in Beechmount (ironically, McKeever had left the I.R.A. after a dispute the previous year and the papers were records of his departure). A raid on Patrick Lavery's house in Lincoln Street uncovered documents related to the Battalion's B Company including evidence of fundraising for arms and the activities of Fianna Éireann. These were all detailed in court in late June and reported in the press.[11] Lavery received two months in prison.

The 1935 commemoration at Bodenstown that June was to be the last of the mass gatherings for some time. Sean McBride gave the main speech followed by Paddy McLogan and Tom Malone, with Moss Twomey in the chair.[12] But the I.R.A. was now on a head-on collision course with both the Free State and the Unionists.

[1] *Irish News* and *Irish Times,* 24th December 1934.

[2] *Irish Press* and *Irish Times,* 28th December 1934. The same 'unusual' calibre was noted in the shooting of Major John McCormick.

[3] In statement given to Harry Diamond in 1946, read out by Diamond in Stormont.

[4] *Irish Press,* 14th January 1935.

[5] The order appears in the *Belfast Gazette,* no. 721, April 19th 1935.

[6] *Irish Times,* 20th April 1935.

[7] Anderson 2002, p28-29.

[8] P.R.O.N.I., HA/32/1/623.

[9] This was Pearse Hall.

[10] *Irish Independent,* 27th April 1935.

[11] *Belfast Newsletter,* 27th June 1935.

[12] MacEoin 1997, p340.

July, 1935

Despite the overt threat of further violent sectarian attacks, the I.R.A. had continued with its annual summer camp at Gyles Quay, just north of Dundalk. In 1932, the I.R.A. had to recall units from the camp to provide defensive cover in districts that were under threat. In 1935, the I.R.A.'s Army Executive recommended that the Belfast staff cancel the camp due to the potential for trouble in Belfast. In the end, the camp went ahead but an alert unit from Ballymacarrett under Jack Brady remained ready to contain any problems. Jimmy Steele, as Adjutant, would be the senior member of Battalion staff present, while the Training Officer Charlie Leddy was to be the O/C for the camp itself. The camp wasn't particularly discreet. There was little in the way of precautions, such as sentries. By the time the men had cycled the sixty miles from Belfast, an advance party had the tents erected and a meal cooking on the camp fire. In the mornings at a training camp participants usually formed up for parade and drill. The plan for Gyles Quay, over the course of the camp, was to deliver lectures on various military matters with opportunities to handle, maintain and fire weapons. This included firing live ammunition from rifles and revolvers, the chance to fire bursts from a Thompson gun and throw Mills bombs.

On the Friday at Gyles Quay the volunteers had carried out drills, attended lectures and sat knowledge tests. Rifle practice took place using a sand dune as a target. That evening was declared a free night and some cycled off to Dundalk to find a ceili, while others visited people they knew in the locality. Jack McNally remembers that they were advised to be careful in Carlingford, which was considered a Blueshirt stronghold, to the extent that their accents shouldn't be heard in the village.

Around the same time as the I.R.A. men were leaving the Gyles Quay camp for the evening, the Orangemen were marching home from the main demonstrations. There had been some shooting the previous night. Before the Orangemen reached York Street they clashed with residents in the Markets and Stewart Street and shots were fired. As the bands passed Lancaster Street on York Street a confrontation soon escalated into a major riot around Lancaster Street, Middle Patrick Street and Little Patrick Street. The RUC used cage cars and armoured cars that fired at the crowds.

Mrs. Kelly of Seaforde Street (in Ballymacarrett) and Sarah Trainor (from York Street) found Jack Brady and told him intense shooting had started in Lancaster Street. Brady immediately rounded up thirty men with guns (I.R.A. volunteers were already on duty and had been posted in pickets of six or seven men). They went straight across the city and set up headquarters in Trainor's Yard in Lancaster Street but there is little other information on how they were deployed although snipers positioned in the upper storeys of houses at the Great Georges Street/York Street junction and at the corner of Royal Avenue/Donegall Street tried to keep the crowds at bay. Bobby Hicks was also dispatched to Gyles Quay to warn the Belfast I.R.A. staff about what was happening. By the time the violence died down (around midnight), the hospitals reported seventeen people with gunshot wounds, twenty with other assorted wounds and two dead. Houses were burned out at several locations across the city.

While most of the Gyles Quay men were out for the evening, Bobby Hicks arrived and brought word on what was happening in Belfast. He reported that there had been a serious outbreak of violence and that it was mostly focussed on York Street. Jimmy Steele wanted to bring the North Queen Street men straight back to Belfast along with any other units that wanted to leave. Those present discussed the situation until around 2 am. Jack McNally pointed out that, since they had not yet word of casualties, the men might best go to bed and get up at 6 am, strike camp and head to Belfast. If they were stopped anywhere, they were to say they were a cycling club from the Markets on their way home. When the I.R.A. volunteers woke on Saturday morning they found large numbers of Gardaí, including the political unit, the Broy Harriers, walking up to 40 abreast in a wide sweep across the camp seizing men and weapons despite protests that both were needed immediately in Belfast.

When the men were brought up in court in Dundalk to receive their detention notices they refused to answer their names. Many, like Harry White and Bobby Hicks, gave false names and addresses (a favourite being Craig Street – a tiny street with one occupied house). When they were brought in front of the special court, Charlie Leddy made a statement from the dock: "We deny the right of this assembly to try us as we are subject only to the jurisdiction of the Republic. The camp at Ravensdale had been there in three previous years. It was significant that in this year, when the war dogs and agents of British Imperialism were let loose in Belfast, that the bloodhounds were let loose against soldiers of the North coming into the area for training."[1]

Meanwhile, Jack Brady's unit had remained in action around Lancaster Street for the rest of the Friday and Saturday. Barricades were erected to prevent attacks on individual streets. British soldiers were deployed and positioned at the barricades where the worst violence had occurred. On the Saturday Jimmy Steele managed to extract men from Gyles Quay and get back to Belfast. When he got there he told Brady: "You've done great work, but we'll take over from here." During Saturday, there was gunfire at Little Patrick Street around midday, in Vere Street around 5 pm and Nelson Street and Earl Street where unionists breached the R.U.C. cordon from 9 pm onwards. A house in Dock Street was also bombed. By 10 pm the military had been called out as a curfew was being imposed from 10 am to 6 pm.

The nature of the violence is recorded in various court cases that followed the riots. In one instance six men from around North Queen Street used buildings at either end of Washington Street as a firebase until they were disturbed and arrested by the R.U.C..[2] A story in Harry White's biography states that I.R.A. volunteers at the barricades used rifles to keep potential attackers at a distance.

By the Sunday night there were five dead, forty-two in hospital with gunshot wounds and thirty-one with other injuries. Most of the violence had been in York Street, although Sandy Row had also seen some trouble.[3] On the Monday, despite the barricades and a curfew being in place, violence and more shootings continued in Millfield, Brown Square, Percy Street and Queen Street.

By the 16th July, the violence spilled over the border as attacks and graffiti began appearing on Protestant-owned businesses in the south demanding they make public calls for the violence against Belfast Catholics to stop. While the attacks were largely unco-ordinated, the Blueshirts appear to have been active in a number of them (the I.R.A., though, was not involved). The same day, there was another fatality in Hudson Street as more gun battles and house-burnings took place despite heavy rain. The next day there was further trouble in North Street. By now the violence in Belfast was being reported as far away as Germany.[4] That Thursday a man injured on the previous Monday died as further violence took place in Conway Street. Then, the following weekend two more died as the trouble spread to Ballymacarrett and other districts around the city including Lisburn. The violence then began to peter out, but the injuries, arrests, home-burning and work-place evictions took a toll which didn't go away as quickly. Over 2,200 Catholics were forced from their homes and an unknown number from their jobs. As a result, the British National Council for Civil Liberties formally instigated an investigation into the Unionist government.

At the end of July all twelve arrested at Gyles Quay were sentenced to two years in Arbour Hill at the Military Tribunal sitting in Collins Barracks. Later, on their release, they found that their details had been passed on to the R.U.C.. Any remaining illusions the Battalion might have still held about de Valera and Fianna Fáil were being dispelled as quickly as any thought that sectarianism was on the wane.

The aftermath of the violence that summer saw many (including unionists) detained and jailed. In July Paddy Cavanagh received three months in jail for his six copies of *An Síol* (he had been arrested and fined for possession of banned newspapers the previous year as well but hadn't paid the fine).[5] By the 24th July, some one hundred charges had been brought over the violence and court proceedings continued into the autumn. Some of those arrested carrying revolvers and other weapons are likely to have been members of the Battalion although not many were subsequently listed by the R.U.C. as I.R.A. suspects or refused to recognise the court.

The I.R.A. also responded to the violence and arrests by carrying out its own punishments. Patrick Boyle and Pat McGrath were chained to the railings of St Pauls on 25th August, while Henry Healy was tarred and feathered on Donegall Street on 15th September.[6] When a unionist march accompanied by a band attacked the homes of Catholic residents in Greencastle, the subsequent clash ended with George Clyde being shot dead. The same day Bertie Magowan and Bertie Montgomery were clandestinely examining a revolver in the shipyards when Montgomery accidentally shot and killed Magowan. The next day there were a series of attacks against Catholic homes and business and in the evening John McTiernan was shot dead in his bar in Great Georges Street (this was 21st September).[7] Sophia McGahey, a Catholic married to a Protestant, was also shot at point blank range when she answered a knock on her door in Little Ship Street.[8]

As the violence died down, the I.R.A. decided to contest seats as abstentionists in the Westminster election held that November, fielding candidates in four constituencies. After the Outdoor Relief Strike it was clear that the I.R.A. feared others harnessing any political momentum and converting it into electoral successes that might be used to challenge the position of the republican movement. It was decided to field Charlie Leddy in West Belfast with Jimmy Steele to act as his director of elections. Leddy attracted considerable sympathy as he had been imprisoned by de Valera and Fianna Fáil at such a sensitive time. It also gave further exposure to the Arbour Hill prisoners who were involved in an ongoing prison protest including a hunger and thirst strike in October.

In October, the Catholic Bishop of Down and Connor, Daniel Mageean, was highly critical of the Unionist government and press for attempting to dismiss the violence over the summer as having a political rather than religious motivation. The Unionists had claimed that the conflict was between those who were loyal to the state and those who were disloyal. Bishop Mageean called on English Catholics to campaign for an independent inquiry into the violence in the hope that it would expose the nature of the Unionist government. The National Council for Civil Liberties then initiated an inquiry into the violence.

In the previous elections the gap between the unionist and Nationalist Party candidates had been considerable. Leddy standing meant that the nationalists, who had nominated de Valera to stand elsewhere in previous elections, did not field a candidate. As Leddy was in Arbour Hill after Gyles Quay, Jimmy Steele effectively deputised for him. During the campaign, the Chief of Staff, Moss Twomey came and spoke to a crowd of three thousand in Lurgan. A meeting on the eve of the election was held at the corner of North Howard Street and the Falls Road but came under gun attack and two people were wounded.

Leddy's sole opponent was the Unionist candidate, Captain Alexander Crawford-Browne (unionists had held the seat for over a decade). Crawford-Browne received 34,060 votes to Leddy's 20,313 and was carried out of Belfast City Hall on the shoulders of his supporters where he was cheered by the crowd.

After the result was declared, Jimmy Steele seconded a vote of thanks to the Returning Officer, the Belfast Under-Sheriff Robert Henderson, saying, "Despite all the intimidation, the people have voted well for Mr. Leddy. The support he secured is a lead to the rest of Ireland. Time will inevitably bring all classes to realise that their economic and spiritual necessities will best be secured in an undivided and free Ireland."[9] He also said that the election was a warning that the national spirit could not be simply swept aside.

After the result was declared, a bomb was thrown at houses occupied by Catholic residents in North Thomas Street and shots were fired in Little Ship Street.[10] As with almost all unionists bombings and shootings, the press did not report any follow-up searches or raids by the R.U.C..

---

[1] *Irish Independent,* 15th July 1935.

[2] The men, John Bailey, James McKinney, Gerard Gallagher, Robert Hamilton, Patrick Moylan and Francis McMullan were charged with 'rioting'.

[3] Accounts of the violence in Belfast are based on the reports in the *Irish News* and *Irish Times* from the 12th July 1935 through to the end of the month.

[4] *Irish Times,* 18th July 1935 reports that the riots had been refered to in *Nacht-Ausgabe* on 17th July.

[5] *An Síol,* 22nd February 1936.

[6] This appears to be the same Pat McGrath arrested with copies of *An Phoblacht* and a revolver in 1931 and again for armed robbery (of a pub) in November 1933 when he refused to recognise the court. He was arrested again for armed robbery with two other men in November 1935 and was eventually sentenced to three years and to be whipped. He was also found guilty of a robbery on 18th August 1935 which may have prompted the attack on him by the I.R.A. a week later. He is likely the ex-volunteer in prison that Tony Lavery later mentions.

[7] *Irish Press,* 17th October 1935.

[8] MacEoin 1997, p346-8.

[9] *Irish Press,* 16th November 1935.

[10] *Irish Times,* 16th November 1935.

Map of north Belfast showing limits of curfewed district in 1935 (marked in black line).

they'll have the whole crowd of us in jail

Clearly, the violence of the summer was taken as a warning that the Battalion needed more rifles. The value of rifles was demonstrated by the exchanges of fire in 1935 and during the Outdoor Relief riots. But historically rifles were the armament the Battalion was most lacking following the seizures ten years previously. Some more had no doubt been acquired on the black market. The raid at Ballybraid the previous year had probably given the Battalion an appetite for larger operations of that scale. At the end of 1935, a similar style raid was being proposed. On this occasion, the target would be the O.T.C. armoury at Campbell College in Belfast which was believed to hold between one hundred and fifty and two hundred service rifles.

The raid was initially proposed by I.R.A. G.H.Q. in Dublin. I.R.A. units were to empty the armoury into waiting vehicles then disperse them across the city. The raid itself involved three squads. Each would assemble at a gate lodge at 8.10 pm (only the rear gate lodge was not to be seized). Squad 1 was to commandeer a car and park up in the Old Holywood Road (roughly opposite Lodge 1). Squads 2 and 3 were to arrive on foot at Lodge 2 (at the junction of Hawthornden Road and Belmont Road) and Lodge 3 (on Hawthornden Road).[1]

A second car was to patrol the College perimeter from 8 pm. Once it observed Squad 1 in position, it would move down Belmont Road and signal to Squads 2 and 3 to proceed. Each lodge would be seized at 8.15 pm and the telephone lines cut. Two volunteers would remain on guard in each gate lodge while the others assembled at the armoury, remove the contents in the commandeered car and signal to the others to initiate a phased withdrawal.

On the night of the raid, when Squad 3 arrived at the Hawthornden Road at 8.15 pm, it immediately took over Lodge 3. As the squad leader left the gate lodge to join the rest of Squad 3 he met an R.U.C. Constable, Ian Hay, coming into the gate lodge. After an exchange of fire in the gate lodge, Hay was wounded and all three volunteers escaped although one had his gun shot from his hand by Hay. All of Squad 3 managed to leave the scene. Due to the late arrival of their weapons, Squad 2 didn't arrive at Lodge 2 until 8.35 pm where it awaited the I.R.A. patrol car to give the signal, sending three volunteers ahead to be ready to take Lodge 2. The three volunteers who had awaited the patrol car, headed down towards Lodge 3 only to encounter more R.U.C. heading towards the shootout with Squad 3 at Lodge 3. The R.U.C. gave chase, exchanging fire with Squad 2, and pursued all six of the squad back towards Belmont Road capturing Eddie McCartney. Squad 1 commandeered a car but the intended driver missed their rendezvous and they had to report to the Battalion O/C Tony Lavery and his Adjutant Jimmy Steele at 8.30 pm to advise them of the problem.[2] Deciding to call off the raid, Lavery and Steele took a tram to Campbell College. Meantime the I.R.A. patrol car withdrew from the scene as R.U.C. tenders began to arrive. Lavery and Steele arrived at 9.05 pm at Campbell College. Noting the R.U.C. presence at Lodge 3, they met one of Squad 2 who was disorientated by the shooting but informed them as to what had happened. McCartney had been the only I.R.A. volunteer arrested at the scene.

Meanwhile, the other members of the I.R.A. team, including Hugh Keenan, Sean McCaughey, Sean Hamill and Peter Fanning had got away. Keenan had the presence of mind to wait at a tram stop and was even searched by the R.U.C. as they combed the area immediately after the raid. R.U.C. searches and raids began straight away on the Friday night. On the Saturday morning, McCartney was charged. It was immediately clear from the R.U.C. evidence inflating the number of I.R.A. volunteers involved that they intended to perjure themselves to get further convictions.

That evening the R.U.C. carried out numerous raids including houses and premises on the Falls Road, and on the Saturday night, in several public houses. Among those arrested and then charged was Bernard Rooney, who was an I.R.A. company officer.[3]

The Sunday papers had been full of stories about the raid. By the Monday the Belfast staff and members of the raiding team were in hiding. That the R.U.C. had clearly inflated the number of I.R.A. volunteers involved was taken as a signal that the Unionists would use the raid as another pretext to detain a large number of men. And the I.R.A. was getting nervous about what had transpired on the night given that so many R.U.C. men happened to be in the vicinity.

Furthermore, the *Irish Press* was reporting that the arms had been moved from the college prior to the raid, causing serious anxiety among the I.R.A. on both sides of the border.[4] As the proposal to raid Campbell College had originally come from G.H.Q., this partly explained some of the nervousness about the report in Dublin. Tony Lavery then asked Joe Hanna, the Battalion Intelligence Officer, to check out the truth behind the statements that had been made just after the raid saying the arms had been moved from Campbell College in advance. Hanna advised Lavery that his sources confirmed that the arms had not been shifted.[5] More might become clear as the proceedings played out in court.

The Belfast staff also prepared a report on the raid which was then sent on to the I.R.A.'s Adjutant-General at G.H.Q. in Dublin, Jim Killeen. The Battalion staff quickly began its own analysis of the raid. It wasn't yet clear from the statements given by the R.U.C. in court whether the raid had failed through bad luck, or whether someone had tipped them off.

Those arrested would have to conform to the policy of non-recognition of the courts as set out in I.R.A. Standing Order 24. But according to Mick Traynor, the Battalion staff believed if they "…let them away with this, they'll have the whole crowd of us in jail."[6]

Permission to defend Rooney was unsuccessfully sought from G.H.Q. but Tony Lavery authorised Rooney's defence to see if proceedings would reveal if an informer had given the raid away. As remand hearings came and went, G.H.Q. became increasingly irate about Rooney being defended in court.

Meanwhile, Frankie Doherty, who had first been arrested and imprisoned as a 16 year old in 1933, died from tuberculosis which he was believed to have contracted while in prison. His death, even in the midst of the aftermath of the Campbell College raid, appeared to have a significant impact on some of the Battalion staff.[7] He is also commemorated in the song 'Belfast Graves' which became the anthem for Battalion events.[8] It is difficult to underestimate the significance of how popular ballads were used to communicate a political message. The words (and their message) were quickly committed to memory (particularly if the tune was catchy and the sentiment struck a chord). The medium was also extremely resistant to censorship, to the extent that attending an event at which such songs were song was probably the upper limit of many people's political activity.

On the 20th January, the I.R.A. Adjutant-General, Jim Killeen, wrote to Tony Lavery stating that the Army Council had ordered that legal aid to Rooney be withdrawn.[9] From this point on, the stakes were getting increasingly high as Lavery was now guilty of disobeying a direct order.

Nor did the Battalion maintain a low profile. On Sunday, 26th January, Patrick Carson of Foundry Street (in Ballymacarrett) was abducted, tarred and feathered, then left outside St Matthews Parochial Hall before mass (another brother, Hugh, was given the same treatment a couple of weeks later). The R.U.C. also made further raids based on evidence from Ian Hay who had been released from hospital. John Monaghan was arrested and charged, protesting that he didn't "…even know where Campbell College is…". Hugh Keenan was also charged. Another man named Magee was picked out from an identification line-up by Hay. He had been dragged in from the street to make up numbers and was promptly released by the R.U.C..

For good measure, on the 8th February the Unionists banned *An Síol*, which, judging by the surviving issues, was covering the Campbell College trials in some detail. The I.R.A. also remained active and visible. In the same week as the ban, Alexander McDonald was stopped on the New Lodge Road by Gerry O'Connor and a second I.R.A. volunteer. Other volunteers, including Arthur Corr, cleared the street while O'Connor held McDonald at gun point. McDonald was tied to a lamp-post, had tar poured over him and a placard placed around his neck. O'Connor and Corr were both arrested on McDonald's evidence.[10]

The day after the *An Síol* ban, an I.R.A. party drilling off the Glen Road was spotted by an R.U.C. Sergeant who tried to get close and observe them. An I.R.A. look-out confronted him and, in the ensuing struggle, fired off two shots but lost his revolver. As the look-out ran off the sergeant fired two shots after him but was knocked to the ground by the other I.R.A. volunteers who also made good their escape.

In mid-February, Ian Hay was cross-examined during a Campbell College remand hearing. To the question "Was there not a regular cordon of police around Campbell

College that night?" Hay replied: "I know nothing about that. I was given my instructions." When press speculation about the rifles being moved had raised suspicions that the raid had been given away, the assurances provided by Joe Hanna had allayed those fears somewhat.[11] But now the implication of Hay's answer was that the R.U.C. may have not been there by chance.

The Campbell College raid trial finally began at Belfast City Commission on the 20th February. Again, individual R.U.C. witnesses admitted that, rather than being there on regular police duties, a detachment of ten constables and a Head Constable had been specifically positioned there. The R.U.C. had not been there by chance. The Battalion now knew the raid had been given away.

At the end of the trial Rooney, Keenan and Monaghan were all acquitted and discharged (at least one genuinely was innocent). McCartney, though, was found guilty as charged and got ten years (the length of the sentence shocked people). The acquittals were a partial success for Lavery's strategy (and defiance of G.H.Q.). But the R.U.C. evidence, under examination, pointed to prior knowledge of the raid.

As the Army Council had specifically ordered Tony Lavery to withdraw legal aid to Rooney, G.H.Q. debated what it should do. Meanwhile, another of the I.R.A. unit involved at Campbell College, Peter Fanning, had been picked up in a raid on the Wolfe Tone club and charged with possession of a copy of the 1916 proclamation.[12] What was worse (for Belfast-Dublin relations), Gerard Deans was picked up in Belfast with a copy of the current I.R.A. cypher for sending communications in code.

The I.R.A. now also tried to kickstart another political project as Moss Twomey announced the formation of a new abstentionist party, Cumann Poblachta na hÉireann, on 9th March. The Ulster organiser was Battalion veteran Jack McNally. The Army Council also issued an order banning membership of Sinn Féin. On St Patrick's Day, de Valera's usual radio broadcast was briefly (and embarrassingly) interrupted by a voice that said "Hello, everybody. This is the I.R.A.".[13]

A week later, Sinn Féin's standing committee condemned the I.R.A. which, it said, had made itself a political organisation through its involvement in Cumann Poblachta na hÉireann. On the same day, the Cork I.R.A. shot and killed Vice-Admiral Henry Boyle Sommerville at Castletownsend in West Cork citing his role in recruiting locals to join the British armed forces. A few days later, Cumann Poblachta na hÉireann held its first official organising meeting.

In Belfast, there was continued friction between republicans and the R.U.C..[14] Constable John. Harrison of Glenravel Street Barracks, who had been active during the violence in 1935, claimed he was accosted by three youths when on his bicycle. One aimed a revolver at him, wounding him on the shoulder. This may have been one of the first actions of a group of maverick I.R.A. volunteers (called the 'Ginger Group' by Harry White). When Harrison later applied for compensation it was dismissed and implied he had faked the shooting.[15] On April 9th, another R.U.C. Constable signalled to a suspect car to stop on Balmoral Avenue and was shot twice in the chest then had his revolver stolen.[16] The culprits were never identified although the I.R.A. was blamed by the R.U.C. in press statements. They also carried out searches and raids on houses of republicans.

---

[1] The Adjutant's report was captured at Crown Entry and quoted by the press in May.

[2] The driver had gone off to meet his girlfriend and was late (as recounted to Sean Hamill's son Feidhlim).

[3] He seems to have been known as 'Art' Rooney (see *An Síol*, 22nd February 1936).

[4] Letter from Adjutant General to Belfast Battalion, dated 20th January and captured at Crown Entry later in 1936 cites the impact the *Irish Press* report had (see *Irish Independent,* 30th May 1936).

[5] *Irish Independent,* 30th May 1936 states that, in documents uncovered later, assurances had been given to the Belfast Battalion commander (Lavery) that the arms had not been moved. I assuming this came from Hanna as I/O.

[6] Munck and Rolston 1987, p183.

[7] Doherty's death is commemorated in the song *Belfast Graves* and quoted by Brendan Behan in *Borstal Boy* (1958): "When but a lad of sixteen years, a felon's cap he wore, God rest you, Frankie Doherty, Ireland's cross you proudly bore".

[8] It was performed at every event in Pearse Hall in King Street (according to Billy McKee).

[9] He used Lavery's formal rank - Commandant of No. 1 Division in the Ulster Area.

[10] See press coverage of O'Connor and Corr's trial, eg *Irish Press,* 24th July 1936. When they appeared in court Frank Duffy was arrested in the public gallery and charged with the same offence. McDonald claimed Duffy had followed him just before the attack but he wasn't present when it happened and the jury discharged him even though he had refused to recognise the court.

[11] As above, I assuming it was Hanna based on statements made by others afterwards.

[12] MacEoin 1997, p365. There were other arrests during raids on 1st March, with Leo Boyle, Frank McGrogan and Dickie Dunn all picked up and charged over possession of various 'documents'.

[13] MacEoin 1997, p366 (the *Irish Times* of 18th March 1936 neglects to mention this other than headlining an account of de Valera's 11 am broadcast as 'The Interrupted Address').

[14] MacEoin 1997, p367.

[15] He uses the term in *Harry.* It simply means a 'pressure group' but I am retaining here to keep a clear distinction between the activities of this group and official Belfast Battalion actions.

[16] See *Irish Press* and *Irish News* on April 10th and 11th 1936. A couple of days later, another stolen car was used in a robbery and shots were also fired.

Tony Lavery's court-martial

On the 18th April G.H.Q. finally wrote to the staff in Belfast ordering that Lavery be court-martialled on Saturday 25th April. The President of the court was to be Sean McCool, the other members included almost every senior I.R.A. commander in the north. The location of the court was kept secret until the last minute. Even though he was a courier, Jack McNally wasn't told the location until the Saturday morning. He and Charlie McGlade, who was also a courier, brought members to the Craobh Ruadh club (run by the former Belfast Adjutant Jim Johnston) on the top floor of No. 10 Crown Entry for the court-martial to take place. McNally was to leave before proceedings started, whilst McGlade remained to provide security.

Battalion staff present as witnesses included Jimmy Steele, Liam Mulholland and Mick Traynor. The number of senior I.R.A. commanders present was way above that necessary for the court-martial. In that regard this appears to have been doubling up as a northern I.R.A. command conference. Many of those present received the most recent issue of *An Síol* which said: "It is becoming more and more obvious that the North will become the cockpit of the coming struggle." The emphasis on a northern campaign in *An Síol* may reflect what was intended to be a wider agenda in Crown Entry.

Battalion officers met different members of the court from trains in Belfast and accompanied them to the Craobh Rua Club. John Fox was to meet Liam Rice but they managed to miss each other at the train. After leaving the station, Rice bumped into Joe Hanna in Castle Street. Rice reported that he had missed Fox to Hanna and had decided to head home. Hanna told him to go to the court instead.

Once at the Craobh Rua Club, Rice reported directly to Steele who told him to stay as part of the security team. Rice and Charlie McGlade acted as look-outs. Jack McNally had been a courier and was to leave before the court convened. He recounts that everyone had assembled by 3 pm, including Joe Hanna, who was not part of the court.[1] McCool was late arriving, but once he had, the court convened, Hanna left with McNally about to follow. Rice guarded the door, with one eye on the stairs and floors below. Since the Craobh Rua Club was on the top floor there was no escape route.[2]

Then sixteen R.U.C. men rushed up the stairs, pushing Rice and McGlade back into the Club. Only Joe Hanna managed to leave the building. Everyone else was arrested and various documents seized by the R.U.C..[3] Waiting cage cars took them to Chichester Street police station, then, by tea-time to Crumlin Road jail. They were now being detained under the Special Powers Act. It was clear to all present in Crown Entry that the R.U.C. knew exactly what they were doing.

On 21st May, a significant move was also made against the I.R.A. in Dublin. Moss Twomey was picked up leaving mass, whilst Con Lehane was arrested elsewhere and Maud Gonne's home at Roebuck House was raided in a search for Sean McBride. For the I.R.A., the immediate priority had been to re-organise as three members of the Executive (Killeen, Kelly and McNally) and most of the senior commanders from the north had been captured, never mind that the Belfast staff had been practically decapitated. Twomey and Lehane's arrests meant even more re-organisation as Sean McBride took over as Acting Chief of Staff in Twomey's absence. Sean McArdle took over as Belfast O/C with Liam McAllister as his Adjutant.

For several weeks, those arrested in Crown Entry remained as detainees as the Unionists could hold them for 28 days before entering charges or issuing an internment order. In the midst of all this, the National Council for Liberties published a report (on 23rd May) on the 1935 violence. It stated that the Special Powers Act put the Unionists "…in a position paralleled only by continental dictatorships…". The Unionist Prime Minister, Craigavon, bluntly dismissed it, saying "..no importance should be attached to a document containing such misrepresentations..".[4] However, the timing may have influenced the framing of the charges against the Crown Entry men.

When they were finally charged, it was under the Treason Felony Act of 1847 which was last used against Tom Clarke in 1887.[5] During their hearing, Charlie McGlade had asked why the R.U.C. men's evidence didn't mention that one man (Joe Hanna) had been allowed to leave the building. But he got no reply.

Sean McArdle had tasked Sean McCaughey and Albert Price (both members of the Ginger Group) with investigating the Campbell College raid and Crown Entry court-martial. The R.U.C. had prior knowledge of the Campbell College raid. Charlie McGlade's questions in court had gone unanswered. Why was Hanna allowed to leave by the R.U.C.?

In May gerrymandering had been formalised in Derry and the Ulster Protestant League capitalised on the previous year's sectarian violence by defeating the official Unionist candidate in the Duncairn ward for a municipal seat. Widespread trouble also occurred in Stewartstown in Tyrone when loyalists from York Street in Belfast went on an excursion there. The R.U.C., though, concentrated on raids in Fermanagh and arresting republicans, like William Dorgan from Armagh who was sentenced to three months for possessing a Wolfe Tone engraving inscribed "…to break the connection with England is the aim of Óglaigh na hÉireann."

It also continued to put pressure on the I.R.A. in Belfast. On Sunday 13th July, Richard McIlkenny's house was raided in Parkview Street and the R.U.C. went straight to an arms dump hidden beneath floorboards in the kitchen.[6] This gave added urgency to confirming the informer's identity. As one of the Battalion staff still at large after the raid on Lavery's court-martial, Hanna, as an I.R.A. veteran, would have known what would happen. Someone would put a list together of those who knew about Campbell College and Crown Entry. He knew he would be under suspicion. He would either have to identify the culprit or risk being the prime suspect. The Battalion was also now having to put a new staff together.

The Crown Entry trial started on 21st July. During testimony from R.U.C. witnesses, Charlie McGlade asked to cross-examine his arresting officer. He again asked about the R.U.C. evidence not mentioning "...the fourteenth man?", meaning Hanna, and got no reply. The next day, Wednesday 22nd July, the jury retired then returned in an hour.[7] They found everyone guilty. Killeen as, Adjutant-General, got seven years. The rest of those arrested got two or more years. Others were to join them. Gerry O'Connor and Arthur Corr, arrested for tarring Alexander McDonald in February, both got a year's hard labour a couple of days later.

A sizeable group of I.R.A. prisoners would now be held in Crumlin Road. There was a danger that, under an existing agreement about long term prisoners, those sentenced to more than two years would be sent to Peterhead in Scotland. The Belfast Prison, as Crumlin Road was officially known, was only suitable for prisoners who received sentences of up to two years. The Unionists, rather than spending money on a suitable long term prison, just carried out some modifications of A wing. For decades afterwards, long term prisoners were sent there despite the lack of suitable facilities.

Most of the Crown Entry men had already spent periods of time in prisons, some on both sides of the border. A number had been in Arbour Hill and Mountjoy the previous year. Collectively they brought a depth of republican prison experience to Belfast where there had been relatively few long term prisoners since the mid-1920s.

In late July or early August, Tony Lavery received word from an I.R.A. volunteer nicknamed 'Cruelty' that suggested that the Battalion was making progress in its investigation into the informer.[8] The I.R.A. prisoners in Crumlin Road were also preparing to begin a protest over political status on 18th August. The prisoners' demands indicate what they were defining as political status: to wear their own clothes, use their own razors and toiletries, hold one hour's Irish class three nights a week, be allowed text books, a monthly letter out and in, a monthly half hour visit, two weekly and two monthly periodicals, an improved diet for all republican prisoners and to be allowed to work together. They also regarded any deviation by the authorities from the standard prison rules as de facto political status, whether it was officially acknowledged or not.[9] Apart from Mick Kelly and Tony Lavery, all non-juvenile republican prisoners in Crumlin Road started a hunger strike for political status.[10]

Hunger strikes were not a new tactic in Belfast. Patrick Cavanagh had undertaken a hunger strike the previous year in demand for political status, which lasted five days. The Crown Entry men included veterans of various prison protests including a hunger strike in Arbour Hill only the year before. After four days the Catholic church tried to pressure the prisoners into ending the strike even misinforming them that some had already ended it. The protest began as a thirst strike and the prisoners only took liquids after the fourth day.[11]

By 1st September, day sixteen, Sean McCool and Jim Killeen had come off the strike and only Jimmy Steele remained on hunger strike.[12] Within a few days Steele's condition had weakened sufficiently that his brother Dan was summoned by the prison authorities. He came off on the twentieth day when a deal appeared to have been brokered.[13] However, the deal quickly fell apart.

While there was little public agitation about the hunger strike, it did not mean that everything was completely calm on the streets. On Saturday 13th September, twenty-four year old Rose Wylie was shot in the thigh by a sniper in Trafalgar Street.[14]

Steele went back on hunger strike on the 17th September and finally came off it again on 30th September. The authorities attempts to negotiate with the republicans as a group was taken as a form of political recognition.[15]

---

[1] McNally (1989) mentions that another member of Belfast staff was present but doesn't name him. Charlie McGlade mentioned this person at the trial as well but doesn't name him. Liam Rice did mention that he met Hanna that day in his account. Chris McLoughlin, in a newspaper cutting (from *Irish People* in August 1970) names him as Hanna.

[2] For some reason court reports in the press give the time of the raid as 9.30 pm.

[3] Those arrested were John Fox, Mick Gallagher, Mick Kelly, Jim Killeen, Tony Lavery, Sean McAdam, Sean McCool, Charlie McGlade, Jack McNally, Liam Mulholland, Liam Rice, Jimmy Steele and Mick Traynor.

[4] MacEoin 1997, p372.

[5] McNally (1989, p45) reckons it was around three weeks before they were presented with charge sheets.

[6] *Irish Independent*, 15th July 1936, the arms dump included five revolvers and over one hundred rounds of ammunition.

[7] Various times are quoted, from 50 minutes to 70 minutes.

[8] Tony Lavery's diary (S.737). P.R.O.N.I. HA/32/1/635. 'Cruelty' may be Sean McArdle). An imprisoned ex-I.R.A. volunteer mentioned by Lavery may be Pat McGrath (see page 72).

[9] This account of the strike is based on Jack McNally's memoir, *Morally Good, Politically Bad* and Tony Laverys diary held in P.R.O.N.I..

[10] Some of the press reported the start date as Friday 21st August (eg *Irish Times*, 24th August1936), I am using Lavery's account here.

[11] It isn't entirely clear from the timings in McNally's account whether this was when the first prisoners in A wing came off the thirst strike (as well as hunger strike), or whether he was being lied to by the chaplain who was implying they had given up both the hunger and thirst strike. I'm assuming, given the chronology, that McNally means the phase of the strike when they also refused water. Lavery's account also lacks these details.

[12] *Irish Press*, 4th September 1936.

[13] Given the uncertainty over who was on thirst strike, the speed at which Jimmy Steele's condition weakened would seem to suggest he was on thirst strike for the first five days.

14 *Irish Press*, Monday 15th September 1936.
15 McNally 1989.

Top left: Charlie McGlade (Quinn 1999); top right: Sean McCaughey (Quinn 1999); bottom left: Hugh McAteer (R.U.C. wanted poster, 1943); bottom right: Chris McLoughlin (courtesy of Chris McLoughlin Jr).

the ginger group

While the prison protest was ongoing, in the background, Albert Price and Sean McCaughey were still investigating the security lapses. Sometime in the autumn of 1936, the Battalion was directly ordered not to carry out any armed actions for a few months.[1] Things remained relatively quiet. On Hallowe'en night, a box containing rusted Mills bomb parts and gelignite was found by a pedestrian on waste ground at Trinity Street.[2] A few days before that, a Royal Artillery gunner on leave in Brookfield Street, Daniel Smith, was talking to a woman at the door of a house on the street when six men approached. One told him, "Come with me." They tied Smith to a lamppost and placed a placard around his neck. After the R.U.C.'s follow-up operation, Billy Wiggins and Tommy Morris were both arrested and charged with illegal possession of weapons and assault. A couple of weeks later, on the night of 15th November, six armed men held up the nightwatchman at the York Street Flax Company's Spinning Mills at Muckamore. They took away two old U.V.F. rifles.

In the middle of November, some former Belfast I.R.A. volunteers left for Spain with Eoin O'Duffy to fight on the fascist side. This included Sean Cunningham, a 1920-22 veteran, Peter Jones, Peter Fanning and Brendan Kielty. At least Jones and Fanning were still active I.R.A. volunteers and were tried in absentia by the I.R.A. for abandoning their posts.[3]

On the afternoon of 4th December, Dan Turley was walking along Clonard Street and into Kashmir Road. A car drew alongside him and he was shot four times. When passers-by rushed to his aid they found his hand clasped on a small statuette of the Child of Prague that he carried in his pocket.[4] He died in the Royal Victoria Hospital half an hour later.

Turley himself had written in 1933 that he had concerns that an informer was active and that he was being targeted because of his suspicions (suggesting that he had openly voiced his disquiet among colleagues). His shooting was carried out in contravention of the order for no armed actions in Belfast suggesting it was not sanctioned by the Belfast I.R.A. leadership.[5] Turley clearly had no knowledge of either Campbell College or Crown Entry and the I.R.A. may even have sanctioned his return to Belfast.

Just over a week after Turley's death, some current and former Belfast I.R.A. volunteers like Liam Tumilson and Willie O'Hanlon, also left to go to Spain to fight on the republican side. As with those who had left to fight on the fascist side, the likes of Straney were subject to a disciplinary hearing in absentia (according to Jimmy Drumm, who took part in the hearings, they were just a formality).

In January 1937 the R.U.C. made another significant arms find. On this occasion, fifteen rifles and ammunition were found at a house in Whiterock Crescent. When the sole occupant, Joe Keenan, was brought to court even the judge admitted that he appeared to have been unaware of the arms being present in the house.[6] This discovery may have not been what it seemed, though, and the dump may have been deliberately exposed to test the informer by giving them the opportunity to give away a substantial arms dump. The day after the raid, the I.R.A. disposed of a large bomb by detonating it in the Bog Meadows. A couple of days later, on 15th January, Billy McAllister (the Battalion Adjutant), had his home raided and had to go on the run. Over the next few days, munitions were apparently left out for the R.U.C. to find in a number of locations. There were bullets left to be found in an umbrella in Raglan Street, a rusted Mills bomb on a windowsill in Upper Meadow Street, a hand grenade left beside railings in Townsend Street and four bombs on waste ground in Fox Row off Cullingtree Road. The I.R.A. was apparently off-loading arms they thought had already been compromised to the R.U.C.

Then, at 8 pm on 26th January, Joe Hanna was shot dead. He had left his home in Servia Street to take a walk. He entered a shop and then was followed by two men who had hung around waste ground close to his house all evening. At the corner of Marchioness Street and McDonnell Street, where a street light had been purposely dismantled, he was shot and left in the middle of the road.[7] He had been hit four times, including three times in the face. The shooting was witnessed by women and children who saw two gunmen run off down Ton Street towards Cullingtree Road. Hanna was brought to hospital but died from his wounds.[8] Chris McLoughlin was later to write that Hanna was tried, found guilty and shot as an informer. Charlie McGlade was also credited as the man who worked out that Hanna was the informer, which suggests it was the court evidence that tipped opinion against him.

Harry White contradicts the newspaper accounts as he claims that Hanna had been court-martialled in a club off Bow Street then taken to the waste ground and shot.[9] At this time that whole area around Bow Street, Baker Street and Massereene Street contained a network of I.R.A. safe houses linked by escape routes through entries and back yards.[10] Unlike Turley, no-one seems to really doubt Hanna's guilt.[11]

Following Hanna's death, the R.U.C. raided houses over the weekend, including a series of raids between 7 and 8 am on Saturday morning in Iris Street, Hawthorn Street, Raglan Street and other parts of the city but found nothing.[12] Then, for the next few months, the Battalion quietly dealt with the aftermath of Hanna's death. When a rent strike took place in Ardoyne in February, the Battalion was not involved. One of those leading the strike was Tommy Geehan. The Sheriff's officer who oversaw the evictions (supported by a party of 200 R.U.C. men) was Frank Moyna.[13]

Around 11 am on the morning of the 1st July, 1937, visitors to Milltown cemetery found that the monument in the republican plot had been badly damaged by a bomb (oddly, few people, if any, heard the bomb explode during the night).[14] The bombing brought an outraged reaction from the National Graves Association. That night, John Dunbar was wounded in the Grosvenor Road when twelve shots were fired during trouble in the district. Later on a Mills bomb was thrown which, rightly or wrongly, the R.U.C. took to indicate I.R.A. involvement.[15]

There were ominous signs of trouble. In Spamount Street, close to the New Lodge Road, eight Catholic residents received threatening letters warning them to clear out of their homes by July 11th or be bombed out. The letter ended, "We want the houses for the Loyalists. We want no damned Fenians here. Signed, Billy Boys." Similar letters had been distributed before the violent attacks in 1935.[16] The usual speeches and posturing aside, the Twelfth remained quiet, though.

A British royal visit was also planned for Belfast in late July. The night before, an R.U.C. constable, J.A. Purdy, was on duty guarding flags the authorities had erected at Dunville Park and Falls Library. During the night he was confronted by a number of I.R.A. volunteers (he claimed there were fifteen). They relieved him of his revolver, spare ammunition, notebook and handcuffs. They also removed the decorations and flags. Brian Burns and Hugh McCloskey, who the R.U.C. had searched and questioned once already that day, were pulled in and charged based on identification evidence by Purdy (both eventually got twelve months in prison).[17] Two days after the Dunville Park incident, a bomb exploded blowing out a large hole in the wall of a marine dealer in Devonshire Street, not far from Cullingtree Road barracks. The bomb had been left there by men who had driven into the street and then drove off.[18]

While it is not immediately clear who planted the bomb on Devonshire Street, from at least mid-1937, the Ginger Group was pushing for a more open confrontation with the authorities. There was also a noticeable shift to the use of explosives as units began to sense plans for an English sabotage campaign.[19] At the start of February 1937, Tom Barry (who was now Chief of Staff), Cavan O/C John Tully and two others had reconnoitered Armagh with a view to seizing all the barracks and army posts in the city at Easter that year (it was to be codenamed Operation Mallow). Barry hoped that either de Valera would order the Free State army north to assist them, or, that he could conspire with elements in the Free State army so it would act unilaterally and come to the I.R.A.'s aid (regardless of de Valera's orders). Whether the Ginger Group had some sense of impending action or not isn't clear but when Barry realised that knowledge of Operation Mallow had spread he called it off.[20]

Harry White includes himself, Sean McCaughey and Albert Price, as well as Pat McCotter, Peter Farrelly and John Rainey in the internal Battalion 'Ginger Group'.[21] At the same time as the Ginger Group was starting to agitate, there are hints at other disciplinary issues in the Battalion. Harry White, Jack McNally and Tarlach Ó hUid all record the emergence, during 1937, of practices that were to cause concern to the former staff members locked up in Crumlin Road. A number of I.R.A. volunteers, who became known as the 'belt and boots men', began to use increasingly physical disciplinary measures. Some attacks against non-I.R.A. members over the summer of 1937 may reflect the same trend, such as an ex-soldier, Edward Palmer, who was tarred and feathered outside St Peters, Tommy Doherty, whose attackers beat him with knuckledusters and on the head with the butts of their revolvers and Thomas Martin, who was beaten unconscious by four men.[22] Such attacks by the I.R.A. weren't common place, though. As the Battalion had grown in size over the 1930s, the expansion in numbers increased the security risks. This meant, on one hand, that individual volunteers might be pressured or corrupted into aiding the R.U.C. or political opponents of the I.R.A.. On the other, this also meant needing additional supports, including safe houses for meetings and training, dumps and billets. Each new safe house brought its own risks in terms of nosey neighbours and potential R.U.C. informants. Some issues might also have to be policed locally by the I.R.A. to minimise R.U.C. involvement.

After the incidents during the British royal visit to Belfast, the English and American press had run seemingly lurid tales of bombs and landmines going off in the royals' path. A unionist resolution to Belfast City Council deplored these "…outrageous and libellous statements…".[23] The Unionists' response to the bad press was extensive raids in Barrack Street and Beechmount Avenue, but without finding anything.[24] They did pick up Frank McKenna at his home, though, and brought him to his Falls Road shop where they recovered a number of concealed arms dumps (for which he got three years).[25] Other R.U.C. raids did meet some success as both Hugh Sheppards and Felix O'Neill were arrested after weapons were found in their houses in Ardoyne.[26] There were no raids or arrests, though, when unionists fired shots at William McCafferty's house in Altcar Street off Mountpottinger Road in early August.[27]

That August word also came back from Spain that former I.R.A. volunteers Liam Tumilson and Dick O'Neill had been killed in action.[28] Back in Belfast, unionists bombed St Theresa's Church on the Glen Road on 20th September. Again, there were no arrests or R.U.C. raids. A letter to the parish priest in St Theresa's alleged that communists were involved, prompting Billy McCullough, of the Communist Party of Ireland, to have to deny any connection to the bombing.[29]

On 21st October, four armed I.R.A. volunteers stopped and assaulted James McNulty at the junction of Milford Street and Alexander Street West.[30] This was followed by shots being fired into the home of a widow, Mrs Teresa Wright, in Quadrant Street on the 1st November. Mrs. Wright said that there had been ill-feeling against her in the district and "…Several people had called me an informer when I was passing them on the street.." (implying the attack was carried out by the I.R.A.).[31] The next week, six republicans were sentenced to a year or more on various charges.[32]

In November, the I.R.A. carried out a more significant attack, detonating a bomb inside the navy and marine recruiting office in Donegall Street on the night of 10th November. It destroyed the interior of the building but even though the caretaker was upstairs, he survived unscathed. The blast also knocked pedestrians off their feet and some were wounded by flying glass and bricks.[33] The use of a time delay bomb was a further sign that the I.R.A. was changing tactics.

Raiders that hit an Ormeau Road pawn-brokers shop on 8th December, were presumably the I.R.A. as they only took guns and ammunition. The following Sunday, the R.U.C. and Fianna clashed at a commemoration ceremony for Joe McKelvey in Milltown cemetery leading to Harry White and others being arrested and imprisoned in Crumlin Road.

That New Year saw de Valera's new constitution coming into force in the Free State, now to be known as 'Éire'. The constitution retained a formal claim to the territory of the whole island and there were rumours that the southern army would attempt to march over the border and seize the north. To the unionist *Northern Whig*, it appeared that de Valera wanted to achieve "...the annexation of Northern Ireland - as a condition of political and economic peace between Dublin and Westminster...". Despite de Valera's attacks on the I.R.A. since 1935 this view also stayed the I.R.A.'s hand in a last vain hope that its past investment in Fianna Fáil would finally pay off. His ongoing negotiations with the British over his new constitution had opened up the prospect of the ending of partition as part of the any political deal. The I.R.A. awaited the outcome.

---

[1] This letter was captured by the R.U.C. in Liam McAllister's house in January 1937 (see below).

[2] *Irish Press*, 2nd November 1936.

[3] Quinn 1999, p24-33.

[4] While this story may sound fanciful, Dan Turley's grandson still has the statuette.

[5] As discussed later on, within a few years Turley's guilt appears to have been set aside as the I.R.A. pursued active investigations against others over his original court-martial.

[6] *Irish News*, 13th January 1937 for discovery and *Irish Times* 2nd March 1937 for Keenan's trial.

[7] *Irish News*, 27th January 1937. In MacEoin 1985, White gives a slightly different version.

[8] Based on the *Irish Independents* account of 27th January 1937

[9] McLoughlin's comments appear in his obituary of Jimmy Steele, published in the *Irish Echo*. Harry White's comments appear in MacEoin 1985. Bow Street is only a few streets away from Servia Street, so it is conceivable that he was on his way back to hear the verdict and was intercepted on McDonnell Street at waste ground just past Marchioness Street close to the bottom of Roumania Street. The R.U.C. believed it was McLoughlin himself who shot Hanna.

[10] Adams, G. *Falls Memories*, 1982, p73. In Belfast, an 'entry' is a laneway that runs between back-to-back terraces of houses.

[11] During interrogation of Tarlach Ó hUid, an R.U.C. special branch detective called Davidson claimed that Hanna was guilty and that Turley was innocent. Paradoxically, he was trying to get Ó hUid to work for the R.U.C. rather than be interned.

[12] *Ulster Herald*, 30th January 1937.

[13] *Irish Independent*, 17th February 1937.

[14] *Irish Independent*, 2nd July 1937.

[15] *Irish Press*, 2nd July 1937.

[16] *Irish Press*, 2nd July 1937.

[17] *Irish Press*, 27th November 1937. Brian Burns' brother, Peter, worked for the *Irish Press* in Belfast.

18 See *Irish Press,* 29th July 1937 and *Irish Independent,* 31st July 1937.

19 Eoin McNamee says the London I.R.A. knew by this time (see *Harry*, p180).

20 MacEoin 1997, p639 and p652.

21 In MacEoin 1985.

22 See *Irish Independent*, 31st July 1937 and *Irish Press* 15th September, Palmer and Doherty made claims blaming the I.R.A. See also *Irish News*, August 6th 1937.

23 *Irish News*, 4th August 1937.

24 *Irish Independent*, 5th August 1937.

25 See *Irish News* 5th August 1937 and *Irish Press* 24th August 1937. Of course the raids may have just been a pretext to specifically target Frank McKenna's shop.

26 *Irish Press,* 11th September 1937.

27 *Irish Independent,* 4th August 1937.

28 Quinn 1999, p28.

29 See *Irish News,* 21st September 1937 and *Irish Press,* 14th October 1937.

30 *Irish News,* 22nd October 1937.

31 *Irish Press* 2nd November 1937.

32 Including Robert McCann, Jimmy Drumm, Gerard Harte, Daniel Fitzpatrick, Brian Burns and Hugh McCloskey.

33 *Irish Press,* 11th November 1937.

Top: Frank Moyna with 200 armed R.U.C. carrying out evictions in Ardoyne (*Irish Press*, 17th February 1937). Bottom: The after effects of the 1938 bombing of the republican plot at Milltown by the 'Ginger Group' within the Battalion (*Irish Independent*, March 12th 1938).

THE 'SECOND CIVIL WAR', 1938-46

the English campaign

The growing problem for the Battalion was that it had increased in size but still had no clear outlet for those that had trained for a campaign. Neither was there coherent strategic direction from G.H.Q. and none of the I.R.A.'s political projects had lasted.[1]

In the week after de Valera's new constitution came into force, the Ginger Group tried to kill a hated ex-warder, William Smyth, who worked as a night watchman on Divis Street.[2] I.R.A. volunteers confronted Smyth at work and one opened fire, wounding him four times. Leaving the scene, they aroused the suspicions of R.U.C. Sergeant Latimer and Constable Patrick Murphy in a patrol car although both R.U.C. men were unaware of the shooting.[3] This led to a chase along John Street where shots were fired and ended with Latimer and Murphy, guns at the ready, storming a house to find no-one there. In the end the I.R.A. unit evaded capture.

The same night as Smyth was shot, a sixteen year old called Jack Logue was court-martialled by the I.R.A. then tied to a lamp-post by four men in the Short Strand and had tar poured over him. Another man was reputedly tied to a tree in the Beechmount area. Any possibility of a new republican political initiative receded a fortnight later as the Unionists extended the oath for candidates to all elections. This stated that "I hereby declare that I intend… to take my seat..". The oath meant that republican candidates would refuse to stand as, even if they signed the oath, on being elected they would simply be unseated if they refused to take their seat. A similar oath had been in place since 1927 for elections to the southern parliament (which effectively smoothed de Valera's route to government since his republican opponents debarred themselves from even standing in elections by their abstentionist stance).

The proposed new constitution in the south prompted the foundation of the Northern Council for Unity in 1937 to promote the extension of de Valera's new constitution to all of Ireland. The former Belfast O/C Hugh Corvin was prominent in the group which included a number of individuals from the Nationalist Party. This prompted a public debate about the status of the north and how it should feature in de Valera's ongoing negotiations with the British.

The next election to the northern parliament was due on 9th February. William Smyth's precarious recovery was part of the backdrop during the lead-in to the election.[4] The I.R.A. painted slogans on the gables of houses including 'Boycott the Elections' and ten people were injured in violent clashes between various sets of supporters. When they clashed at the Slate Street polling station on the day of the election the Nationalists (who were to win the seat) sang 'A Nation Once Again' while republicans countered with 'The Soldier's Song', 'Legion of the Rearguard' and 'Lord Craigavon Sent The Specials' before being baton-charged by the R.U.C..

The next action by the Ginger Group illustrated their ruthlessness in what Harry White describes as a "...misdirected attempt to rouse the people".[5] On 11th March, they exploded a charge of gelignite beneath the republican monument in Milltown blowing a sizeable portion of the plinth out of the plot. Nearby in the graveyard, odd graffiti was chalked on the walls "Welcome home Crown Entry 'Victims'" (some of whom were soon due for release). Each letter 'e' in the graffiti was written in the font usually used for text in the Irish language. This aroused the Battalion staff's suspicions. However, Sean McArdle, the Belfast O/C, was still persuaded to respond and a British army recruiting office in Alfred Street was bombed around 11 o'clock that night, doing considerable damage but causing no injuries. The Ginger Group's Milltown bombing of March 1938 seems to have been a pretext to carry out further attacks and demonstrate they could effectively destroy property without causing casualties.

The same month as the bomb attack, the Unionists prosecuted the National Graves Association for failure to pay entertainment duties, fining it £50 (eventually reduced to £12 10s). On the same day, the Ulster Protestant League also appeared on a similar charge and was fined but the magistrate advised it that although 'a sectarian organisation' it would be granted tax exempt status if requested.

The Ginger Group was finally brought back into line by the Battalion staff in the summer of 1938 just as they planned to spring Eddie McCartney from Crumlin Road jail.[6] Sean Russell's elevation to the I.R.A.'s Chief of Staff in April 1938 now offered the prospect of the action they had been demanding (Belfast was represented on the I.R.A. Executive by Jimmy Trainor)[7]. The March 1938 bomb in Alfred Street was the last such Battalion action for some time. Since Tom Barry had replaced Sean McBride as Chief of Staff in 1937, the I.R.A. had been scoping out a new campaign.[8] Barry had begun to look at a northern campaign, but when his concept leaked out among republican circles, he first abandoned the plan, then resigned.[9] Barry's replacement, Mike Fitzpatrick, was basically a stopgap until Sean Russell came in as Chief of Staff and championed a sabotage campaign in Britain. The Ginger Group seem to have been active in the gap between Barry's resignation and Russell taking over as Fitzpatrick had no particular strategy (never mind one focusing on the north).

Critical to the timing here was de Valera's announcement on St Patrick's Day that his negotiations with the British government had failed to secure an end to partition. Opponents of Russell's campaign now stepped away from G.H.Q. and the Army Council, or were nudged out. The remaining critical voices, like Moss Twomey and Jack McNeela, didn't rock the boat or, like Jim Killeen and Sean McCool, were cooped up in Crumlin Road. On his release from Crumlin Road, Mick Traynor relocated to Dublin and finally gave the Battalion an important voice at G.H.Q.. Bob Bradshaw, who had worked at G.H.Q. since he left Belfast in 1933, resigned when Russell became Chief of Staff. Russell had had a secret meeting with de Valera in April 1935 to propose co-operation with the I.R.A. and now had another in 1938. Russell again proposed greater co-operation with Fianna Fáil.[10]

In Belfast, arms raids were now less of a priority than training in explosives so an engineering company was added to the Battalion structure. It was worth noting that the bombings in late 1937 and early 1938 show that explosive training in Belfast was already under way before Russell took over and before de Valera's negotiations failed.

The I.R.A. strategy for the English campaign was to create an atmosphere of uncertainty brought about by varying the target and timing of attacks in England. Damage was meant to be minor and psychological rather than physical. Training classes in explosives were held throughout Ireland with the best known in Killiney Castle.[11] In preparation, some Belfast volunteers now transferred to I.R.A. units in Britain.

In Belfast itself, it was business as usual. The run-up to Easter saw repeated R.U.C. raids and a proposed Easter Sunday curfew on the Falls to prevent a commemoration taking place at Milltown. In the week before Easter, details of commemorations were painted on gable walls and then hurriedly painted over by the R.U.C.. The intensity of R.U.C. raids was so high that the local business community complained that it was killing trade. On Easter Sunday, the I.R.A. played cat and mouse with the R.U.C. while attempting to stage a commemoration. Up to fifty additional R.U.C. detectives had been deployed in the Falls Road to assist in 'comb-outs' of republicans.[12]

In King Street, a number of people in Culley's shop and in the street escaped serious injury when a bomb exploded in Pearse Hall, which was upstairs in the building over the shop. Some people were blown over by the force of the blast. A couple of hours earlier the R.U.C. had raided Pearse Hall which was the I.R.A.'s city center headquarters. The building was wrecked in the blast. The I.R.A. believed the R.U.C. had planted the bomb.[13]

Then there was a disaster at the end of May. In Josephine Brady's house in Leeson Street, Bridie Dolan, of Cumann na mBan, was moving a box containing grenades when she pulled a loose cord to tighten it. Instead it detonated the grenade causing her near fatal injuries. Shrapnel also injured Brady. Brady's husband, Michael, and her brother Henry McNamee, were arrested by the R.U.C.. The R.U.C. found a substantial arms dump, including an array of bomb-making materials, in the room where the grenade exploded. The dump showed the Belfast I.R.A. was receiving deliveries of identical materials as the units in England in May 1938.[14] Bridie Dolan, like her sisters Chrissie and Maureen, had joined Cumann na mBan in 1932-33. She barely survived the injuries she received in the blast.[15]

A raid on the McAreavey's Stratford Gardens home in Ardoyne, on 11th July, gave the R.U.C. another substantial coup. Captured I.R.A. intelligence reports included detailed information on R.U.C. dispositions, senior staff, arms statistics, military barracks, the R.A.F., private houses containing arms, prison warders, electric power stations, members of parliament and freemasons. Since John McAreavey had been away working, no case was made against him. Mary McAreavey got twelve months hard labour.

Unionists then bombed the *Daily Mirror*'s Rosemary Street offices for reporting violence and arrests at the Twelfth of July Orange demonstrations. Just as the Pearse Hall bombing had been ignored, there was no obvious search for those responsible for the *Daily Mirror* bombing over the next couple of days. However, Hubert McInerney and James Woods were both sentenced for possession of seditious literature.[16] In the following days, Josephine Brady's brothers Denis and Henry McNamee (who had just returned from England) were arrested for the arms in her Leeson Street home. The McAreaveys were also charged on 25th July.

Before the end of July, unionists bombed William McKeaveney's house (he had stood in the by-election after Joe Devlin's death). Two weeks later the replacement for the republican monument at Milltown was bombed in O'Neill's sculpting yard in Divis Street. Eye-witnesses saw the perpetrators run off but, again, there were no follow-up searches or arrests.[17] Yet, when the I.R.A. tied James McKenzie to a lamp-post the next day, the R.U.C. mounted a series of raids arresting nine men for questioning. All were eventually released without charge.[18]

In September, a unionist speaker told a public meeting in Willowfield that "...if this church is built I will bring up the artillery...". Not long afterwards, the newly constructed Catholic church which he was referring to, St Anthony's, was indeed bombed. Over the next week the unionist press, particularly the *Belfast Newsletter*, carried a series of articles and letters condemning anyone who might consider blaming the bombing on unionists.[19] Ironically, the Church of Ireland Bishop of Down and Connor, Dr MacNeice, had recently claimed to see 'a new tolerance' in Belfast.

Throughout October and November, the Ulster Protestant League and other unionists made further openly aggressive public calls for bans on all 'disloyal' political activity. They also called on the Unionists to prepare for war claiming Chamberlain would betray them like he did the Czechs. Some even wanted to take over Cavan, Donegal and Monaghan, while others dismissed that as unambitious. R.J. Beattie told the U.P.L. in Belfast in mid-October, "After all, we here are the real Celts, the people in the Free State are only the scum. The Six Counties are too small for us. It makes us feel mean. We would feel big if we had all the country." The U.P.L. decided to run candidates in the upcoming elections. In the week after the St Anthony's bombing, Eamonn Donnelly of Fianna Fáil was due for release after a month's detention for breaching a ban on entering the north (just prior to an election). The Irish Republican Prisoners Defence Association managed to utilise the publicity being given to his detention to draw attention to the current plight of republicans in the north. By mid-September there were some thirty-five republican prisoners being held in Belfast prison.[20] That autumn there was growing concern in the south over the number of republicans being held in northern prisons. Sean McHenry, who was released in September, spoke at a ceili in Dublin to raise funds for the dependents of republican prisoners in Belfast and Armagh.[21] The issue of republicans held in northern prisons was described by McHenry as a 'national responsibility' and was to be raised at many local authorities over the next period.

Around the same time, the Unionist Minister for Finance, J.M. Andrews, was claiming that he had heard rumours of northern nationalists and southern republicans holding conferences to try and adjust their differences and hatch a "… plan for separating them [the unionists] from Britain and bringing them under a central Irish Government of some kind."[22] This was not too far-fetched as Sean Russell had met de Valera again to try and agree a protocol by which the southern government would, at least, not actively oppose a sabotage campaign in England. It was even considered whether to use a different name (than the 'I.R.A.') for the campaign.[23] The Northern Council for Unity was now gently merged into a new campaign, supported by de Valera, reviving the 'Anti-Partition League' name by the end of 1938. It organised prominent meetings in Britain and the United States. To some extent the Anti-Partition League and Russell's S-Plan campaign were inter-dependent, whether consciously or not. If the sabotage campaign was to be effective it needed to rapidly seize and harness any political momentum to open up talks on partition.

In the last week of October the republican monument was finally re-erected in Milltown cemetery. It had even been guarded by the R.U.C. in the days prior to being put back in place. But November was to see further violence in Belfast. The Battalion mounted a co-ordinated action to coincide with a two-minute silence that was being called on Armistice Day, 11th November. It also demonstrated the ongoing development of its capability in building and detonating bombs. Explosive devices were prepared and detonated simultaneously across Belfast in Beechmount, Dunville Park, the Bone, Ballymacarrett and North Queen Street. In the silence the sound of the explosions carried across the city. None of the bombs caused any damage except in Beechfield Street where it blew out windows and damaged the wall of a house.

That night unionists threw bombs at Holy Cross monastery. Then, a week later, Joe Devlin's National Club (in Berry Street) was burnt down. The lack of an R.U.C. response to these attacks again found a stark contrast in a raid on the McKelvey club a few days later that saw twenty-six 16-18 year olds detained (all got fines or short prison sentences).[24] The following week Henry McNamee got three years for the Leeson Street arms dump. Josephine Brady got fifteen months.

After the McKelvey club arrests eight hundred people attended a protest at Peel Street. Jack Brady, on the Battalion staff, attacked the British government over its criticisms of the treatment of minorities on the continent yet ignoring the behaviour of the Unionists. The crowd then carried a tricolour down the Falls Road as far as Hastings Street barracks where they started singing republican songs and broke windows. A baton charge by the R.U.C. moved the crowd into Barrack Street and John Street where further clashes took place.[25] Unionists tried to bomb the McKelvey club the next weekend but managed to blow up the adjoining Rockmount Recreation Hall instead. Forty people were inside the hall and three received significant injuries.[26] Needless to say, the R.U.C. didn't seem to expend any energy on pursuing the perpetrators.

The next morning people also woke up to the news that the I.R.A. had blown up customs huts along the border.

---

[1] The phrase 'Second Civil War' was later used to describe this period by de Valera's Minister for Justice, Gerry Boland.

[2] See, e.g. *The Irish Times* 19th March 1938 and MacEoin 1985, p52.

[3] This account is based on the various accounts given in the press over January, March and April 1938.

[4] In March Patrick McKenna from Glenard Park (in Ardoyne) was picked up and charged with attempting to murder Smyth.

[5] MacEoin 1985, p51.

[6] Ray Quinn dates the rescue plan to mid-1937 but Harry White claims he only aligned with the group after his release from Crumlin Road in May 1938, and it was clearly active in 1938, making the latter year appear to be correct, rather than 1937 as suggested by Quinn. McCartney had been sentenced to 10 years after the Campbell College raid.

[7] MacEoin 1997, p29.

[8] See Dan Keating's account in MacEoin 1997.

[9] This is briefly described in Coogan (1970) and Bowyer Bell (1970).

[10] MacEoin 1997, p329.

[11] Volunteers from Belfast known to have taken part in the English campaign included Dominic Adams, Dympna Bradley, Liam Bradley, Margaret Bradley, James Burns, Michael Campbell, Leo Casey, Pat Doyle, Frank Duffy, Gerry Dunlop, Pat Ferran, Daniel Fitzpatrick, Pat Hannon, Sean Hannon, Jimmy Hasty (using the name Arthur Fitzgerald), Mary Hewitt, Gerry Kerr, Jack Logue, Thomas Magill, Joe Malone, Pat McAleer, Bill McAllister, Robert McCann, Hugh McCloskey, Eoin McNamee (from Tyrone but who was to be connected to the Belfast Battalion), Albert McNally, Billy McNeill, Jimmy Morgan, Maggie Nolan, Willie O'Hanlon, Bridget O'Hara, Tarlach Ó hUid (who wasn't from Belfast but was soon to be attached to the Belfast I.R.A.), Dan O'Toole, Terence Perry, Albert Price and Harry White (various sources).

[12] See *Irish Press,* 12th April 1938 and *Irish News,* 7th April for McKenna's court case.

[13] MacEoin 1997, p405.

[14]The arms included five revolvers, seventy-five rounds of ammunition, thirty detonators plus another full box of detonators, 2 coils of fuse, a bomb case, four thermite bombs, two maroons (a type of flare), forty sticks of gelignite, one bag of paxo (explosives), a German dynamo exploder, a battery testing meter, an electrical clock, a gallon jar and a pint bottle of sulphuric acid, seven slabs of paraffin wax, bomb filling material, a bag of white powder, a coil of electrical wire and republican literature. It was a substantial display of the I.R.A.'s current capabilities. See *Irish Press*, 31st May 1938. The I.R.A. units in England were receiving similar deliveries the same month (see MacEoin 1985, p181).

[15] *Republican News*, 22nd February 1975.

[16] See press on 20th July 1938, eg *Irish Independent*. McInerney got twelve months for a copy of *The Republic of Ireland*, Woods got a month for having *Irish Republican Congress*.

[17] *Irish News*, 16th August 1938.

[18] *Irish Press*, 19th August 1938.

[19] See likes of *Belfast Newsletter* for the two weeks from 7th September 1938 onwards.

[20] *Irish Independent*, 14th September 1938.

[21] *Irish Independent*, 3rd October 1938.

[22] See press, eg *Irish Independent*, on 17th October 1938.

[23] Jack McNally records that this was being discussed at the time (1989, p112).

[24] Joseph Adams, Matthew Bunting, Thomas Cairns, Thomas Gourley, Kevin Barry Hughes, Frank McCusker, Harry McGurk, David McKay, Billy McKee, John McKee, Joseph McKenna, Hugh Molloy, Michael Mullan and John O'Rawe.

[25] See press on 28th November 1938.

[26] Arthur McDonnell (17), Thomas Lennon (16) and John Bell (19). All suffered leg wounds.

internment (again)

The night after the customs posts were blown up, there were more attacks. The I.R.A. had simply been placing bombs with a delayed fuse in suitcases and leaving them 'for collection' at customs huts (a fairly common practice at the time). That same night, at Castlefin in Donegal, three I.R.A. volunteers (none from Belfast) died in a premature explosion.

Immediately there were public calls for the re-introduction of internment. The Battalion anticipated a major swoop and most known republicans stayed away from their homes for some weeks. A week before Christmas, I.R.A. G.H.Q. in Dublin advised them that it was safe to return. Almost immediately, on 22nd December, the Unionists carried out a large-scale swoop, arresting and then interning thirty-four men. Liam Rice claims the R.U.C. received information from Dublin to carry out the round-up.[1] Some of those arrested were held without trial until 1945.

By mid-December, some of the I.R.A. volunteers who had been in Spain had also begun to return to Belfast. Some, like Willie O'Hanlon, returned to Birmingham in preparation for active duty there.[2]

In January 1939, the I.R.A. formally declared war on Britain. Some Belfast I.R.A. volunteers had transferred to units in England but continued unionist attacks meant there was an ongoing need for the capacity to defend districts as it had done in 1935. It also kept a sceptical eye on developments in Dublin from where strategy was directed. The Battalion was to become increasingly uncomfortable with what it could see.

During the night of 18th January, 1939, unionists yet again bombed the republican plot at Milltown. The R.U.C. responded with more raids on suspected republicans that led to fresh arms finds. In a letter to the *Irish Press*, Maud Gonne McBride contrasted the hysteria in the newspapers about the English sabotage campaign with the indifference shown towards the sustained unionist bombing campaign in the north.[3] The same day the newspapers reported how Dawson Bates had gone to London to meet security officials about the I.R.A. campaign and had announced to the press that the R.U.C. had recently discovered an 'execution list' of prominent figures in the north. In London, he lobbied for more money for extra R.U.C. constables and to call up the B Specials.

The arrests had again increased the number of republican prisoners in Crumlin Road.[4] Some of the news brought into the prison began to alarm Jimmy Steele and the other senior I.R.A. men who were held in A wing. Tim Pat Coogan records that, for some time past, I.R.A. volunteers had been complaining that battalion staff officers had been beating them up.[5] Coogan puts this down to some of those now filling Battalion staff roles mimicking the disciplinary practices of continental fascist groups. This included the existing activities of the 'belt and boots' men.

On the weekend of the 4th and 5th February, the British press announced that documents had been passed to Scotland Yard from Belfast containing plans to bomb Buckingham Palace, Windsor Castle, the Houses of Parliament, the Bank of England and to kill the King, Queen and various officials. The R.U.C. Commissioner denied that any such documents had been found to the Irish newspapers but the subsequent panic saw strict security precautions put in place in Britain. In retrospect the hysteria of the weekend of 4th and 5th February was to be the closest the sabotage campaign would come to achieving its aims. Despite a flurry of activity at the end of 1938, the Anti-Partition League only organised meetings erratically in April and May 1939, too late to harness any of the early political momentum of the I.R.A. campaign.[6]

On the night of Tuesday 7th February, the I.R.A. posted up hand bills around Belfast calling for the release of the internees. Hand bills were also posted up at the City Hall and on the walls of newspaper offices. The text declared that "We, the citizens of the Irish Republic, demand the release of the Republican prisoners in Northern jails." Predictably enough, the R.U.C. followed up with raids, particularly in Ballymacarrett where they arrested four men after finding some 'documents'. Attacks by loyalists also continued. At 10.30 pm on February 20th a bomb was thrown at an A.O.H. Hall on Herbert Street in Ardoyne.[7]

At the end of February the first actual Belfast involvement in the English campaign was revealed as Hugh McCloskey, Thomas Magill and Robert McCann were picked up with bomb-making equipment in England. The police claimed that, when they raided the house and searched the men, McCloskey admitted he had been in the Battalion. They also said McCloskey acknowledged that an unnamed I.R.A. volunteer from Belfast had been killed after turning informer and emigrating to Australia. It is not clear if this is a garbled reference to Patrick Woods, Dan Turley or Joe Hanna or another, unknown case.[8] Jack Logue, James Burns and Michael Campbell were also arrested in England.

In April, there was a major confrontation between the R.U.C. and a crowd of 200-300 people in Ardoyne, where an R.U.C. Constable had his revolver taken from him (this was blamed on an I.R.A. volunteer, Robert Magee).[9] Later, it was alleged that five of the seven R.U.C. men involved in the incident were transferred from Belfast for 'lacking moral courage' because they hadn't "…shot all round them…" when given the opportunity.[10] Immediately afterwards the R.U.C. made nine arrests in Ardoyne.[11]

The Battalion was also now attempting to widen its political base by forming a Republican Club. This coincided with the communists pushing for a broad anti-fascist front and provided for some common ground to explore. The steering committee included both I.R.A. volunteers like Charlie McGlade, Jack Brady, Ernie Hillen and Tarlach Ó hUid and Communists, trade unionists and other interested parties like Malachy Gray, Jimmy Johnston and Jimmy Devlin.[12] Over the course of 1939, this could be seen to influence the communist's language as it shifted from talking of a broad 'antifascist front' to opposing Britain's 'imperialist war'.[13]

By now Sean Russell, the I.R.A.'s Chief of Staff, had gone to the United States on a very public tour to raise support and political leverage from Irish America (and, of course, funds). Russell could now do this off the back of a high profile sabotage campaign in England. In his absence, Russell had Stephen Hayes, his Adjutant-General, act as Chief of Staff. Over the course of 1939, Hayes rarely convened his Army Council which now had increased Belfast representation as both Mick Traynor and Dominic Adams were to join during the year. Others like Jack McNeela and Tony D'arcy were proponents of a northern campaign. However, disaffected districts like Cork and Kerry remained aloof from Hayes. Kerry even occasionally antagonised G.H.Q. by carrying out unauthorised attacks such as exploding a bomb at the rear of Hawney's Hotel in Tralee where the British Prime Minister's son, Frank Chamberlain, was holidaying. The Kerry I.R.A. (of course) denied all knowledge of the bomb.

Many senior republicans felt that the I.R.A. needed to shift its campaign from England to the north. Critically, they believed that the I.R.A. was not in a position to overthrow the southern government and was frittering away human resources and political capital in half-heartedly trying to do so. Belfast was to become increasingly disaffected with G.H.Q. in Dublin over the course of 1939. From the spring of 1939 through to the autumn, though, it had a key voice at the top table as Mick Traynor was now I.R.A. Adjutant-General.[14]

For its annual 1916 commemoration, the Battalion decided on a different approach after the Unionists instituted the annual ban. Instead of Easter Sunday, ceremonies were held on the Saturday. An I.R.A. party marched from Sultan Street to Cyprus Street where an I.R.A. statement was read outside Joe McKelvey's former residence. In the Bone, another I.R.A. parade marched to the home of another I.R.A. volunteer who had been killed in 1922, David Morrison. In Ballymacarrett, a third parade marched from Anderson Street to Mona Street to hear the I.R.A. statement outside the former home of another dead I.R.A. volunteer Murtagh McAstocker. Similar commemorations took place in the likes of Derry, Newry and Armagh. A total of twenty-five women and men were charged with wearing Easter Lily emblems including Cuman na mBan leaders like May Laverty and Mary Donnelly.[15]

The threat of conscription also hung in the Belfast air. On the Thursday before the first weekend in May, the I.R.A. paraded on the Falls Road behind a banner saying 'Down With Conscription'. Some two thousand marched, many reputedly carrying hurls or blackthorn sticks. After the parade, an open air meeting took place in Balkan Street and an I.R.A. statement was read out. A similar parade took place in Derry. The statement said, "All the army units in the six Ulster counties are to hold themselves in readiness for an immediate response to orders from headquarters. Arms and equipment must be ready for distribution, and commanding officers are instructed to supervise all details. The civil population, without any distinction of religious or geographical distribution, will be protected from military interference by Britain, and the machinery of the social services will be maintained unimpaired. Enemy preparations of a military nature, whether in the way of propaganda or pretended precautions against attack, must be ignored and the policy of complete non-co-operation enforced. The strength, discipline and unity of purpose of the I.R.A. have made Britain withdraw the threat of conscription and rallied the majority of thinking civilians behind our leadership. We must increase that strength, maintain that discipline, and unite for the decisive struggle which is approaching."

There was then a call to join the I.R.A. followed by cheers and the crowd sang 'The Soldiers Song'. When the R.U.C. appeared at the end of the meeting, those armed with hurls formed a protective ring and prevented the R.U.C. from interfering with the crowd which then dispersed without incident.[16]

A couple of days later the R.U.C. picked up James Regan of Beechfield Street in Ballymacarrett and charged him with reading the I.R.A. message to the crowd. Regan was quickly processed by the courts and given two years. He didn't recognise the court and, on being sentenced, shouted "Suas leis an Phoblacht." (Up the Republic). A few days earlier, Samuel Walker from Malcolmson Street, received two years for possession of I.R.A. documents, training manuals and other papers.[17]

In May, unionists carried out further attacks. In the first, a bomb went off at St Paul's Recreation Hall near Beechmount Avenue. It badly damaged one end of the hall. Afterwards, the R.U.C. would not publicly confirm that the bomb had been planted outside the hall mischievously leaving open the possibility that the bomb had been inside and gone off prematurely.[18] The next week there was a large explosion during the night at a house in Dunville Street. Robert and Margaret Stockman, who lived in the house, had no political connections but a bomb was left on their windowsill that destroyed the front of the house. The Stockmans and their families escaped unharmed. It was assumed the bomb had been intended for the Michael Davitt G.A.A. club a couple of doors away from the Stockmans. Despite these attacks by unionists, the R.U.C. again made no attempt to arrest or question potential perpetrators.

At midnight on the 23rd May, the I.R.A. punished two volunteers from Clonard and two from North Queen Street. They were beaten and left unconscious in Raglan Street. Cards left with the men stated that they had been "Dismissed with ignominy from the I.R.A." and "Found guilty by Republican courts of cowardly conduct." On the discovery of the four men, the R.U.C. immediately began raiding the area.[19] In the same month Charles Mulvenna, an ex-serviceman from Ashton Street (near the top of the New Lodge Road), was found with a bullet wound in his leg at Deerpark while a revolver was found lying nearby. Mulvenna claimed that he wasn't connected to any organisation but that he had found a revolver in an arms dump and accidentally shot himself in the leg. In September, when he had recovered, he was given three months.[20] It is possible Mulvenna was an I.R.A. volunteer who had been shot as a punishment.

The I.R.A. then mounted its largest operation in Belfast in some time. At 7 pm on Tuesday 30th May, across various districts in the city, including Clonard Street, Milan Street, Leeson Street, North Queen street, New Lodge Road and the Short Strand, the I.R.A., Fianna and Cumann na mBan knocked on doors, called for people to hand over their gas masks and told them to tune their radios to the 450m wavelength. Over sixteen hundred gas masks were thrown into piles and burnt at fifteen separate locations. A mysterious blast in St James Crescent at 5.30 pm appears to have been a decoy to distract the R.U.C. who flooded the area.

A short time later, the Battalion made its first, fifteen-minute, radio broadcast across Belfast. It included a statement saying that the final stages of military intervention in England would be carried with even more vigour than had been necessary to display in the past. As for the gas masks, it was reported that "These gas masks are supplied by England to wean the people over to her side if she happens to be involved in a conflict. Ireland's only enemy has always been England." The station went on to criticise what it described as the agent-provocateurs who had carried out recent bomb explosions in Belfast to "...cause strife and bitterness between Catholics and Protestants in Belfast. We appeal to all Irish men and women, irrespective of creed or class, whether they be from Shankill, the Falls or Sandy Row, to unite, as their ancestors did in 1798 in the final onslaught to rid our land of the English invader." The broadcast was also critical of the Special Powers Act and made reference to republican prisoners in Belfast jail. At the end, following 'The Soldiers Song', the announcer stated, "This is the end of the programme and we will be heard again shortly." The R.U.C. and radio engineers attempted to locate the source of the broadcast, but to no avail.[21]

The next day there was an explosion at the New Victoria Cinema in London. Joe Malone, who had moved from Belfast to London in January, was arrested after he received arm and wrist wounds when the bomb detonated prematurely.[22] Fortunately for Malone, the bomb was small as it had been designed to cause minor damage with the intended value being psychological and for propaganda rather than actual destruction. By the end of June there had been 127 attacks causing one fatality and over fifty serious injuries. Some sixty-six individuals had been arrested and charged over the campaign.

By the end of June the British and Irish press were speculating about discussions between Scotland Yard and the Home Office over applying for Sean Russell's arrest in the U.S. and extradition to London to face charges. When Russell was then arrested in Detroit, seventy-six members of Congress informed President Roosevelt that they intended to boycott a reception for the British king (who had just arrived). Russell was quickly released on bail pending a deportation hearing.[23] The mobilisation of Irish American opinion in Congress strengthened the idea that it could be used to exert political pressure on the British over partition. Russell continued to make public appearances in the U.S. but there were persistent rumours that he had arrived back in Ireland (each time prompting R.U.C. raids in the north).

The same day Joe Malone was arrested in London, back in Belfast, a shot was heard in an entry between Clonard Gardens and Cawnpore Street. An hour later a bomb left on a window sill detonated badly damaging the front of a house in Clonard Gardens. The R.U.C. offered no explanation but did not carry out raids or make arrests.[24]

The next weekend, fourteen of those sentenced over the Easter commemorations were released. A dance in the Johnston Memorial Hall on the Falls Road was organised to mark the occasion. The R.U.C. then decided to raid the hall at the end of the night as 'The Soldiers Song' was being sung. Two baton charges followed and a number of people were detained.[25] A few days later the republican monument was again re-erected in the

Harbinson plot in Milltown, alongside an announcement by the National Graves Association of a scheme for expenditure of money on the preservation of republican graves in the Six Counties. The announcement coincided with the banning of another republican paper, *The Sentry*, by the Unionists.

A week later, the I.R.A. radio station broadcast again. Members of Cumann na mBan, Fianna Éireann and the I.R.A. went door to door in nationalist districts selling tricolour paper flags with the inscription "Damn Your Concessions, England – We Support The Men Who Fight Our Battle" on the Sunday afternoon. They also advised people to tune their radios again that evening. The broadcast included 'The Soldier's Song' played on a gramophone record. A message was read saying "Since our last broadcast, agent provocateurs of Britain have been responsible for a number of explosions in Belfast. These explosions are meant to cause strife and bitterness between Catholic and Protestant." It went on to explain that the R.U.C. had recently intensified their campaign of terrorism by frequent raids and that people had been warned by the R.U.C. not to report incidents to the newspapers. "The obvious reason for this is that the British Government do not want the world to know of their dictatorship in North-East Ulster." On the Monday night, another broadcast was picked up in London which claimed to be from the I.R.A.'s station in Belfast. It included an item in Irish, the recorded version of 'The Soldier's Song' again, an item on the recent bomb attacks in Belfast (which were blamed on the British government) and an appeal to all Irishmen to unite in the cause of freedom. The R.U.C. could still not locate the source of the broadcasts.

At the end of the month, the Unionists decided it could no longer afford the cost of the continuing mobilisation of the B Specials and they were stood down. The announcement was sarcastically welcomed by some of the press which suggested that the mobilisation of the Specials to patrol the border and other disturbed districts had mainly been a measure to provide jobs and contain unionist discontent at high unemployment. The coincidental bombing campaign against nationalists was also drily noted.[26]

That weekend, de Valera banned the I.R.A.'s Bodenstown commemoration just as it was about to take place. But a five hundred strong Belfast contingent had already arrived in Amiens Street. After an unsuccessful attempt by the Gardaí to surround them and remove their banners at the train station, Sean McCaughey rallied the Belfast republicans and a series of clashes followed.[27] At the G.P.O. J.J. O'Kelly addressed the crowd as did Jack Brady of the Battalion staff. Charlie McGlade then produced a Union flag which was burned.

Ironically, Christy Quearney claims that the clash between the Belfast I.R.A. and Gardaí was the best thing that could have happened that day. Elements of the Dublin I.R.A. were so incensed by de Valera's political police that they had gone out armed intending to open fire once given the provocation. As there were clashes between Gardaí and republicans at most venues across the south, there was a real chance that it may have sparked significant violence. As it happened, de Valera passed an Offences Against The State Act, anyway, in mid-June to make it easier for him to arrest and imprison suspected I.R.A. members and supporters.

August began with more rumours of Sean Russell's return (and more R.U.C. searches) even though he was still making public appearances in the likes of Chicago until the middle of the month when he finally had his passport returned by the U.S. authorities. In Chicago he told his audience that de Valera and his government "...deal with the enemy, but our fight is not with them. Our fight is with the British, not with our own people."[28] But Russell's strategy of a campaign in Britain, avoiding the north, co-existence with de Valera and leveraging Irish-America was coming unstuck.

At the end of August, an I.R.A. operation in Coventry went badly wrong. A bomb meant for a power station was abandoned in a street in Broadgate. It exploded killing five people and injuring fifty. Liam Bradley, from Belfast, was taking part in a separate operation in Birmingham, detonating fire bombs in mail boxes. One bomb detonated in Bradley's pocket. He was seen throwing burning material from his pocket onto the street, quickly arrested and held for trial.

In mid-July, the British parliament had passed a Prevention of Malice (Temporary Provisions) Bill which effectively allowed for deportations which took place over the next few weeks. In the south, de Valera went a step further and created a special criminal court and arrests of I.R.A. volunteers began to increase in September. By October, the R.U.C. also began its own second intensification of internments.

In Belfast, the I.R.A. mounted another large co-ordinated operation just before the British declared war on Germany. On the 30th August the Battalion carried out a mass burning of gas masks, on this occasion in the Cullingtree Road area. The same night, inscriptions were written up on gable walls and roadways saying "A.R.P. for British slaves, I.R.A. for Irish braves" and "Republican prisoners badly treated in English jails".[29] Within a couple of days the second world war had broken out and anyone interned by the Unionists now ran the risk of being held 'for the duration'.

---

[1] Quinn 1999, p65.
[2] *Belfast Newsletter*, 16th July 1940.
[3] *Irish Press*, 21st January 1939.
[4] It now included the likes of John Gilmore, Art McGivern and Michael Walsh, see *Irish Press*, 18th January 1939 and 28th February 1939 and *Irish News,* 22nd February 1939.
[5] Coogan 1970 *The I.R.A.*, p182, certainly (if newspaper reports are anything to go by) the occasional case where there is a claim of I.R.A. involvement in either beatings or tarring and feathering were being reported each year from the mid-1930s. Some very clearly were the work of the I.R.A. (e.g. where someone had a placard place around their neck). In other instances, the evidence is uncertain. Matters are complicated by compensation claims arising from the incidents. If an individual was attacked by the

I.R.A. and so was injured by an 'unlawful assembly' they could take a claim against Belfast Corporation for damages. This meant that the authorities had an incentive to challenge claims of I.R.A. involvement since it would incur the expense of the compensation on the Corporation. At the same time, the possibility of compensation gave an incentive to those who wished to claim I.R.A. involvement.

6 Correspondence in February between Cahir Healy and Eamon Donnelly (who represented the north on the F.F. Executive) shows they were so surprised by de Valera's lack of action they assumed he had made a deal of some sort with Chamberlain (Newry and Mourne Museum, Eamon Donnelly Collection).

7 *Irish Independent,* 21st February 1939.

8 I haven't yet identified anyone from Belfast murdered in Australia in the 1930s who might fit this claim. Jack Logue had been court-martialled the previous year.

9 See *Irish News* and *Irish Press* on 6th April 1939.

10 See press on 28th June 1939 and Stormont debates on 27th June 1939.

11 This included Eamon Ó Cianáin, John Kelly, Cornelius Fox, Frank Walsh and Edward Greenan, who all got a year or more in Crumlin Road, as well as four Fianna Éireann youths (who got a month in jail each).

12 See Ó hUid, T. 1960, *Ar Thóir Mo Shealbha,* p182. Subsequently, the likes of Malachy Gray and others have not mentioned this initiative in their own memoirs but there is no reason to doubt Ó hUid.

13 Swan, S. 2008 *Official Irish Republicanism, 1962 to 1972*, p93.

14 Traynor had been arrested at Crown Entry back in 1936.

15 Those charged were May Laverty, Mary Donnelly, Kathleen Quinn, Jeannie Ryan, Bridget Corr, James Leddy, Charles Harty, John Austin, Philip McCullough, John Morrissey, Felix Kelly, Robert Donaldson, Helen Hayes, Winifred Simmington, Barney Boswell, Joseph Morgan, Mary McMahon, Patrick McKeown, Patrick Hickie, Edward Quinn, Sarah Jane McCartney, Thomas McLoughlin, Patrick McVicker, Patrick McConville and Charles McCann (eg see *Irish Independent,* 11th April 1939). Most were fined although some took the option of imprisonment.

16 Excerpts from I.R.A. proclamation published across various papers, *Belfast Newsletter, Irish News, Irish Press, Irish Independent* on 5th May 1939.

17 The sentencing of Walker was reported in the press on 10th May 1939 (eg *Irish News*).

18 *Irish Independent,* 6th May 1939.

19 *Irish Independent,* 24th May 1939.

20 *Irish Press,* 12th September 1939.

21 *Ulster Herald,* 3rd June 1939.

22 Harry White explains how the bombs were manufactured in Quinn 1999, p58. The details of Joe Malone's arrest are taken from reports in the *Irish Press* and *Irish Independent* over the first week of June 1939.

23 This is covered in the *Irish Independent* over the 4th to 9th June 1939.

[24] *Irish Independent*, 1st June 1939.
[25] *Irish Press*, 3rd June 1939.
[26] *Strabane Chronicle*, 24th June 1939.
[27] MacEoin 1997.
[28] *Belfast Newsletter*, 14th August 1939.
[29] *Irish Press*, 2nd September 1939.

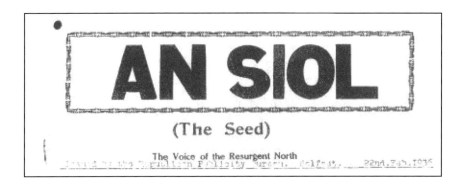

Newspapers: *An Síol* (1933-1938), *Republican News* (1941-1945), *Faoi Glas* (hand drawn in prisons, 1940s, see Ó hUid 1985).

agitating for a northern campaign

The Battalion continued to lobby for action in the north. By early September 1939 it was being argued that the English campaign had spent itself and that the September declaration of war would finally finish it off. The feeling amongst the Battalion and others was that there should now be a switch in emphasis and direction towards a campaign in the north. It was proposed that this be discussed at the next command meeting but it wasn't as Peadar O'Flaherty (on the Army Council), Paddy McGrath, Willie McGuinness (Director of Intelligence) and Larry Grogan (Quartermaster General) were all suddenly arrested in a Garda raid in Rathmines. The Gardaí also recovered $8,000 and letters to Sean Russell calling for him to return to Ireland (ironically, Russell by now was out of contact with G.H.Q.). Apparently, all four were strong supporters of the proposed northern campaign.[1] At the time, Belfast influence at G.H.Q., through Mick Traynor (as Adjutant-General) and Dominic Adams (Director of Training) was pushing for a return to weapons training and away from explosives, in preparation for a northern campaign (and to recognise the failure of the absent Russell's sabotage campaign). Other Army Council members like Jack McNeela and Tony D'arcy also backed the idea.

In October the number of internees increased dramatically as the R.U.C. carried out a series of co-ordinated arrests in Belfast. In total, another thirty-four were arrested, including Seamus 'Rocky' Burns, Paddy Morrison, Jack McCluskey, Jimmy Drumm and Liam Burke. Added to the original thirty-four from December 1938 and the ten or so who had been interned since, almost eighty internment orders had been served in less than a year.

That same month the Unionists allowed internees to apply for release. For various reasons, some made submissions. By late October fifteen were out on bail having accepted the conditions of their release with just over sixty internees left inside. The internees themselves thought that the process was intentionally divisive. By the end of October they began mounting protests inside the prison. Then on 7th November, they were notified that they were to be moved to an unnamed destination (which was Derry Gaol).

Production of *War News* had restarted with the sabotage campaign and now commenced in a Belfast edition from where it was being distributed to other districts under the Northern Command. In November 1939 it was recorded as far away as Derry and Letterkenny.[2]

There were also more arrests as Billy McAllister was picked up in London in July, while Dominic Adams (under a false name, James O'Connell), Liam Rice (using the name Ryan), Sean McCaughey (calling himself Dunlop), Pat McCotter, Hubert McInerney and Paul Walsh were all detained at a weapons training camp just outside Dublin in December.[3]

In mid-December, despite not being directly involved, Peter Barnes and James McCormick were sentenced to death in England for the Coventry bombing which had caused the biggest loss of life during the English campaign to date.

Then, just before Christmas the I.R.A. had a major coup when it emptied the southern government's arsenal in Dublin's Magazine Fort, capturing thirteen lorry loads of ammunition (over one million rounds). What is often overlooked is that a simultaneous raid on its weapons store in Islandbridge didn't come off and G.H.Q. was left with an abundance of ammunition but not the weapons to fire it. The southern government was acutely embarrassed even though the bulk of the ammunition was quickly recovered.

Given the predictable extent to which the raid aggravated the southern government, not everyone within the I.R.A. had supported the proposal and some like, Dominic Adams, were unsure about the timing. His arrest in early December had removed an opponent of the plan. It's not clear, though, if his opinion reflected a broader misgiving amongst the Belfast I.R.A. about continuing to antagonise the southern government. Clearly the Magazine Fort raid was far too early for an, as yet unplanned and unorganised, northern campaign. There are also claims (made later in Stephen Hayes 'confession') that there was also an active lobby within the southern defence forces for a northern campaign but these are hard to verify. Hayes suggested that conspirators in the Free State army had plans for four mobile units, each a thousand strong, to invade the north. This vision of a militant lobby within the Free State army also had influenced Tom Barry's proposed seizure of Armagh in 1937. Joe Cahill records an episode, apparently around the end of 1939 or start of 1940, in which he was sent out one night with other units from South Down to guide invading Free State army units over the border. They never arrived and Cahill never heard the full story of what happened.[4] Certainly, in the latter half of 1939 and early 1940 the I.R.A. was indeed trying to induce the Free State Army to provide assistance independent of the wishes of the southern government.[5]

True or not even the rumour of renegade Free State army columns may have influenced the decision to prematurely strip out the Magazine Fort hoping to force the conspirators into the open. While all this may seem implausible, the Spanish fascists had just won a civil war that started with a military coup so this underlying rationale would have seemed eminently plausible in 1939.

Inside Derry Gaol, which mainly housed Belfast internees, tensions over the distance from their families and the conditions of their detention all came to a head. On Christmas morning the prisoners delivered a statement to the governor protesting their continued internment. They then took the warders captive and put them into the cells. The internees then broke the windows and put out banners and flags to draw attention to their protest. When the R.U.C., B Specials and British army entered the prison, the Derry fire brigade brought in their hoses to assist the authorities to re-take control. The internees were then pushed back within the prison and were eventually overcome by weight of numbers. The B Specials and R.U.C. then delivered some ferocious beatings with lead pipes, rifle butts and boots (in particular to Paddy Adams and the former Battalion O/C Sean McArdle).[6] The week of the Derry Gaol mutiny, the Unionists proscribed a series of republican publications. They then took issue with the BBC for reporting that they had "...banned a number of opposition papers." Dawson Bates wanted 'opposition papers' amended to 'those periodicals which advocate sedition' (the BBC duly obliged). The list of publications then banned by the Unionists was extensive, including *An Phoblacht* (and any variations on that title), *The Irish World and American Industrial Liberator, Fianna, Republican Congress, An Síol, Saoirse Éireann Wolfe Tone Weekly, Irish Freedom* and *The Sentry*.

Ironically, *War News* wasn't officially banned (although possession of it was regarded as seditious). It effectively replaced *An Síol* and was issued as a Belfast edition in 1939 (issued from the 'Irish Republican Publicity Bureau in Belfast'). While *War News* largely reported on the progress of the English bombing campaign, it retained elements of the conventional republican publications and included poetry and other items. In Belfast it was produced by Charlie McGlade (a compositor by trade), then Tarlach Ó hUid, who worked out of various addresses in College Square, the Markets and the Pound. Each print run was collected by women who usually hid them under babies in prams and then distributed them across the city. While some content was shared, in reality, separate editions of *War News* were produced in Belfast, Dublin and other centres (Ó hUid states that a chunk of the 'news' was just made up by McGlade). There was no real attempt to align issue numbers between the different local editions.

In Dublin, de Valera's government made a concerted attempt to crack down on the I.R.A.. It captured the I.R.A.'s Dublin radio station and transmitter along with key I.R.A. G.H.Q. and Army Council staff such as Jack McNeela, Jack Plunkett (brother of Joseph Plunkett), James Byrne and James Mongan. In January another senior figure, Tomás MacCurtain, shot dead a detective who was trying to arrest him in Cork. As the son of the mayor of Cork who was shot dead by the R.I.C. in 1920, MacCurtain's family name was too much for even de Valera to conjure with and he was to escape execution by the narrowest of margins, having a death sentence commuted.

In January the Belfast Industrial Workers Conference of the Trades Council and Trade Unions protested at conditions in the north. This protest was probably co-ordinated by the joint I.R.A./Left Republican Club. As British fortunes in the war were deteriorating, anti-imperialist sentiment appeared to be on the rise.

At the start of February, the British government confirmed that the executions of Peter Barnes and James McCormick was to proceed. While both had been involved in I.R.A. operations in the area, neither had been directly involved in planting the bomb in Coventry where orders had been to specifically avoid civilian casualties.[7] There was little that could be done in the way of an effective reprieve campaign. The same week, in England, Liam Bradley from Carrickhill got ten years while Bridget O'Hara was found not guilty (but deported).

When Barnes and McCormick were hung in Winston Green prison on Wednesday 7th February 1940, there was a wave of protests in Belfast. On the day, a meeting in

Smithfield to protest the executions was banned by the Unionists and many people were injured in clashes between the R.U.C. and protestors. At one stage, there were fourteen R.U.C. baton charges on the Falls Road. A crowd of around five thousand marched from the Falls Road to Smithfield and then returned to Peel Street where two speakers addressed the crowd in English and Irish from the roof of a shed. Further violent clashes and baton charges took place in Peel Street, Ross Street, Milan Street, Lemon Street, Derby Street, Milford Street, Leeson Street, Alma Street and Mary Street. There was also trouble in Seaforde Street in Ballymacarrett.[8] That Friday there was a two-minute silence and the flying of black ribbons in nationalist districts.

On the Saturday night after Barnes and McCormack the Battalion had a huge publicity coup when it raided the large British Army installation at Ballykinlar. Sean McCaughey had been infiltrating men into camps like Ballykinlar for some time before 1940. By then some four hundred and thirty civilians were employed on construction and related works within the camp. Four I.R.A. volunteers including Billy Graham and Billy McWilliams entered the camp in a limousine stolen from Leeson Street.[9] They were dressed in canvas overalls and wore service caps. While the timing of the raid was, presumably, to raise morale following the executions, it appears that it had not been fully approved at Northern Command and Battalion level. But that was not immediately an issue given the initial reaction to the success of the operation.

Once inside the camp, the I.R.A. unit took the sentry hostage and began clearing weapons out of the armoury. The number of rifles captured by the I.R.A. is variously put at between thirty and one hundred. The fallout from the Ballykinlar raid was considerable. The I.R.A. unit held the sentry overnight and released him on the Shankill Road. Ten days later, the British Military Authorities in Belfast were forced to issue a statement following the raid that stated "…it has been established that 43 rifles, of which 41 were serviceable, were stolen from Ballykinlar Camp on the night of February 10-11."[10] The I.R.A.'s radio station then broadcast for twenty minutes a few days later, on the 24 metre wavelength at 3 pm. According to press reports the announcer had a northern accent, which suggests this dates to before Tarlach Ó hUid became the main announcer (Ó hUid had an English accent). On air, the I.R.A. claimed that two hundred rifles and twenty Bren guns had been taken from Ballykinlar. It also denounced the executions of Barnes and McCormick in England.[11]

In Dublin, proposals for a northern campaign were again to be brought before a command meeting on 17th February. In this case, though, it was a mixture of the Northern Command, Western Command and G.H.Q.. Mick Traynor, as Adjutant-General, was present, while Joe Deignan represented the Battalion. According to Stephen Hayes, the meeting was to re-organise the Western Command as a prelude to a northern campaign. But all sixteen of those present at the meeting in the Meath Hotel were arrested when Free State troops and police surrounded the building.[12] Each got three to six months in prison.

Traynor and the others quickly discovered that they were to be treated as ordinary prisoners in Mountjoy, with no political status. In 1939, a number of I.R.A. figures that were imprisoned had regained their freedom by going on hunger strike, pressuring the southern government into releasing them.[13] But, by early 1940, that attitude had hardened. A speech by Gerry Boland, the Minister for Justice, in January had indicated that the southern government was now going to be even more ruthless in dealing with the I.R.A..[14]

Against that backdrop, seven of the I.R.A. volunteers imprisoned in Mountjoy went on hunger strike on 25th February, including Mick Traynor. The other hunger strikers included names that evoked a huge emotional draw, such as Tomás MacCurtain (son of the murdered Cork mayor), Jack Plunkett (brother of Joseph Plunkett), Jack McNeela, Tom Grogan, Tony D'arcy and John Lyons. McNeela and Plunkett were due to appear in court on the 1st March and the I.R.A. prisoners tried to prevent them being taken to court, barricading themselves into D-wing until they were forcibly and violently subdued. Over the course of March, the hunger strikers were removed in ones and twos to Arbour Hill, then moved to the adjoining military hospital, St Bricins.

While that was happening in Dublin, the Unionists were trying to pressurise the Battalion. After various close shaves, on the 4th March, 1940, an R.U.C. raid found a duplicator and copies of *War News* at the address used by Ó hUid in College Square North. A business man, Harry Beasant, was subsequently fined £7 10s for supplying the typewriter and paper used in the production of *War News*. Nearby, 15 Christian Place, off Albert Street, was also raided. Between the two locations the R.U.C. recovered a Thompson submachine gun, thirteen revolvers (including three Webleys, seven automatics and two Colts revolvers), five hundred rounds of ammunition, a Mills bomb casing and, at College Square North, another Gestetner duplicating press. Henry McGrogan, Francis O'Regan and Hughie Kerr were all arrested.[15] The weapons in Christian Place were mostly dumped on the floor awaiting repair. One revolver was defective while the Thompson was missing a spring. The R.U.C. found two Webleys concealed, along with some powder, beneath the floor boards. A dump of documents and training manuals were found with the weapons.[16]

During early March a broader republican strategy became visible in appeals to Irish America and the U.S. government. The high profile tour of Sean Russell in the U.S. the previous year brought some pressure on the U.S. government to refuse to assist Britain in its war efforts. The argument was put forward that Ireland demonstrated the hypocrisy of Britain claiming to be at war with Germany over the freedom and independence of the peoples of Europe. The hope that Irish America could be leveraged to deploy U.S. political pressure on the British government was a tantalising one as prominent Irish Americans, like Congressman James O'Connor, demanded that U.S. support for British war efforts should be conditional on a favourable settlement in Ireland.[17] As military catastrophes overwhelmed the French and the early British war efforts, it became clear that U.S. acquiescence, if not outright assistance, was needed for the British government to continue to prosecute its war efforts. So to some extent, the expectation that Irish American political power could deliver a united Ireland began to fill the void left by the disappointments of de Valera and Fianna Fáil.[18] Either side of St Patricks Day, two small bombs exploded ineffectually in London. They were to be the last of the English campaign.

In mid-March the Ballykinlar raid continued to make the news as the British War Secretary, Stanley, was forced to make a statement on the raid to the House of Commons. This included a brief exchange in which the Minister was asked if slackness and neglect had made the raid possible.[19] There was also, by now, some unease in the Battalion and Northern Command about the raid. The camp was being prepared for a raid that was to capture machine guns, such as Stens and Brens, rather than rifles. The repercussions now made it certain that security would be tightened at the camp. In another follow-up R.U.C. raid an arms dump was recovered in Patrick Cunningham's house in Etna Drive in Ardoyne. The R.U.C. discovered eight revolvers, two automatic pistols, a Mills bomb and ammunition wrapped up in parcels in the attic. Cunningham managed to leave his house during the search and went on the run. A deportee from the English campaign, Tim Collins, was arrested in Lincoln Street on March 2nd in possession of an I.R.A. communication which was in code. Collins had previously been imprisoned for possessing republican documents while in the Free State army in 1933. He was given two years in prison on 20th March.[20]

Easter in 1940 was early, falling in late March. With the Unionists as intent as ever on banning all public commemorations, the Battalion carefully planned how to circumvent the ban just as it had done in 1939. On Good Friday, with the R.U.C. expecting the commemorations to fall on Easter Sunday itself, the I.R.A. mobilised in a significant show of strength in the city.[21] Concentrated into four districts (the Falls, the Bone, North Queen Street and Ballymacarrett), the I.R.A. formed up and paraded on the streets early on the morning of Good Friday. Some volunteers openly carried weapons, while others took up defensive positions in case of an appearance by the R.U.C. Officers wore Sam Brown belts and revolvers, giving commands to the ranks of volunteers. In each district, the parade culminated in a meeting where the officers read statements from G.H.Q. in Dublin and the Northern Command. The meetings ended with prayers said for the two executed volunteers in England, Barnes and McCormick. On Easter Sunday itself, tricolour flags were flown in nationalist districts and Easter Lilies were openly worn while prayers were said for the republican dead at Easter Sunday church services. That evening the I.R.A.'s radio station broadcast a special commemorative programme. People had found the time and frequency of the radio broadcast written in chalk on the pavements in nationalist districts. The only arrests were four young men in Ardoyne.

The radio broadcast (by Tarlach Ó hUid) mentioned a U.S. fact-finding mission and stated that "If Roosevelt is sincere he will specify Ireland, India and Palestine as republics. If Roosevelt wants to make peace he should make peace in a united Ireland first." The broadcast also mentioned the recent riot by republican prisoners in Dartmoor Prison.[22]

A fortnight after Easter, an Irish Press van making deliveries of the newspaper on the Falls was stopped as it turned into Derby Street (heading towards St Peters). Six armed I.R.A. volunteers told the driver and despatch men to take them along Ross Street to Cape Street. They then set fire to their Dodge lorry and its contents. By the time the fire brigade had arrived both were completely destroyed. The two men were told the attack was a protest against the *Irish Press*.

---

[1] See N.L.I., MS 47,650. This is contained in a copy of the Stephen Hayes confession. While evaluating the utility of the confession is complex, the general emphases must reflect contemporary perceptions of various trends within the I.R.A. in the period from 1939-41 for Hayes to be able to pass it off to senior I.R.A. figures. While details may be disputed, the general observations must have carried some ring of truth about them (such as the claims about a northern campaign proposal in September 1939). In this case, McCaughey must have known that there was a proposal in September 1939 and that it was going to be considered. He probably had an idea who supported it too. The calls for Russell to return were clearly to deal with the decisions that needed to be made on the English and northern campaigns and to use his personal influence to smooth over matters with de Valera.

[2] *Donegal News*, 25th November 1939.

[3] See *Irish Press* on 6th and 15th December 1939.

[4] Anderson 2002, p26-9. Reputedly senior Fianna Fáil TD Frank Aiken, from south Armagh, may have supported the idea.

[5] See likes of O'Callaghan, S. 1956 *The Easter Lily*, p129-31. Henry Morgan, a Tyrone IRA volunteer was arrested for giving seditious leaflets to the Free State Army in October/November 1939.

[6] MacEoin 1997, p442-443.

[7] MacEoin 1997, p643.

[8] See press on 12th February 1940 for accounts of the trouble in different areas.

[9] Exactly two years previously, to the day, the staff of Ballykinlar had awoke to find a tricolour flying from the main flagpole in the camp.

[10] *Irish Press*, 12th February and 22nd February 1940.

[11] *Irish Press*, 26th February 1940.

[12] See *Irish Press*, 20th February and Hayes confession (N.L.I., MS 47,650) where he states that the meeting was to re-organise the Western Division. The Northern Command representation suggests it was part of the preparation for a northern campaign as does Tim Pat Coogan, who also interviewed some of those present, in *The I.R.A.*.

[13] Apart from Seamus Burke who had managed to get himself freed from internment under a writ of *habeus corpus* and, by doing so, had all internees in the south released. Afterwards he was only ever known in republican circles as Habeus Corpus Burke.

[14] See Oireachtas debate on the Offences Against The State (Amendments) Bill on 5th January 1940.

[15] *Irish News*, 5th March 1940.

[16] *Irish Press*, 19th March 1940.

[17] See quotes from Roosevelt's letters in Hastings, M. 2011 *All Hell Let Loose*, p190.

[18] For instance see the account in *Irish Press*, 11th March 1940 of calls for U.S. Ambassador to visit the north.

[19] *Irish Press,* 13th March 1940.
[20] *Belfast Newsletter,* 20th March 1940.
[21] See the various newspaper reports of 23rd-25th March 1940.
[22] *Belfast Newsletter,* 25th March 1940.

the Belfast Battalion in Dublin

In the background, the hunger strike in Dublin had also been reaching its climax. Tony D'arcy died on the 16th April, while Jack McNeela died on the 19th April. Mick Traynor and Tomás MacCurtain were both in a critical condition when, on the day of McNeela's death, they were advised by the I.R.A.'s Acting Chief of Staff, Stephen Hayes, that their demand for political status had been met and to abandon the strike. As they recovered, Traynor and the others discovered that, despite what Hayes had told them, their demands had not been met as they were given internment orders or long prison sentences. The subsequent inquests deeply embarrassed de Valera, Boland and the government, particularly the cross-examinations by Sean McBride that were widely reported in the press (the jury even found that political prisoners should be accorded appropriate status).[1] However, the impact of this was significantly lessened when the I.R.A. carried out reprisals, bombing Dublin Castle early on the morning of 25th April and then wounding two policemen in Holles Street. The policemen were carrying dispatches to the British government representative. Belfast I.R.A. volunteers carried out both operations. Joe Atkinson and 'Black Dan' O'Toole had planted the bomb in Dublin Castle, supported by Frank Duffy, while all three were involved in Holles Street where O'Toole was wounded in the leg.

The first Belfast casualty in a number of years also happened on the evening of the Dublin Castle bombing when Sean Martin was killed in a training accident. Martin was a member of a new I.R.A. auxiliary force formed by Sean McCaughey. While giving instructions on the use of grenades in Willie John McConnell's house on Anderson Street, he realised one of the grenades was faulty and had just been activated. Apparently Martin was unable to throw the grenade out the door as there were children playing outside so he shouted at the rest of his class to leave. He gripped the grenade to try and contain the explosion but it blew off his right hand and most of his left. He also received two broken legs and serious facial injuries. The force of the blast blew out the windows and caused significant damage to the kitchen of the house. Martin died en route to hospital, while McConnell was arrested by the R.U.C. (he was given three years in July for possession of the bomb in his house). Martin was thirty-four and an unemployed father of four. He lived opposite the house in which the bomb had exploded. Thousands came out in another show of support for the I.R.A. as his funeral procession made its way along the Falls Road to

Milltown. At the gates of the cemetery a tricolour was placed on the coffin but the R.U.C. didn't attempt to intervene.

Martin was an auxiliary in the Battalion, a section created by Sean McCaughey to allow some volunteers to remain exempt from the more rigid Army Orders and as a response to internment. He carried out other restructuring of the Battalion, with companies (and units within the prisons) reporting directly to the Northern Command (which had a staff officer assigned the role of Belfast O/C, often the O/C or Adjutant of Northern Command). In I.R.A. documents after this date Belfast appears to be designated Area No. 4 (Northern Command) with 1st Battalion as the Belfast Battalion and 2nd Battalion as the prisoners in Crumlin Road.

In May, Eoin McNamee was released from Crumlin Road (he had been on active service in England before being arrested in Tyrone in June 1939). He gives an idea of the extent of Battalion control in some districts in Belfast. He stayed in a side-street off the Falls which he says the Battalion used as a barracks. From there armed volunteers left on various operations. It turned out he was under arrest by order of the Northern Command, but the issue was quickly resolved and he returned to his native Tyrone.[2] After a while he was to come back to Belfast as Adjutant of the Battalion.

At the start of May, de Valera went on Radio Eireann and made a broadcast echoing comments made elsewhere by Boland about how the I.R.A.'s current strategy meant "…civil war would be the inevitable consequence." And how the government's "…policy of patience is over…" and "…the law will be enforced against them [the I.R.A.]. If the present law is not sufficient it will be strengthened. And in the last resort, if no other law will suffice, then the Government will invoke the ultimate law - the safety of the people."[3] The next day Fine Gael committed to unquestioning support for Fianna Fáil against the I.R.A. Over the next few months, constant raiding and more than twenty armed confrontations with state forces in the south became the main preoccupation of the I.R.A.'s G.H.Q..

Meanwhile, the Battalion fulminated, having repeatedly seen proposals for a northern campaign come close to fruition, it now observed the near collapse of G.H.Q. in Dublin as it fought an unwinnable battle with the southern government. Since the early 1930s the Battalion had brought itself up to a significant size (relative to the R.U.C. in Belfast) and created and trained units, all in readiness for a campaign that was long delayed. When the campaign did take place, it was in England, not in the north. The problem the Battalion faced through the late 1930s and into the 1940s was sustaining itself until it was to go into action in Belfast.

At the same time, prospects for the I.R.A. seemed remarkably bright. The allied armies were under serious pressure in France and Belgium at the end of May and Irish America might manage to trade a favourable Irish settlement for U.S. support for Britain's war efforts. The increasing Battalion control in nationalist districts in Belfast was evident in the Unionists being forced to mount a further wave of arrests and internments. This happened during the collapse of the allied forces and their evacuation from Dunkirk. The significance of the timing lies in the general expectation that the internees would be held 'for the duration' of the war. There was a real chance that the war might be rapidly concluded with a peace settlement. This was not likely to be on favourable terms for Britain and, if Irish-American pressure was realised, could throw the Irish question into the mix.

Whatever the motivation for the timing, a further seventy-six men were picked up in swoops across the north including forty in Belfast (mainly from the Falls, Ardoyne and Ballymacarrett). All seventy-six were brought to Derry Gaol and interned there, bringing the total to around one hundred and twenty internees in Derry. In Dublin, Belfast volunteers were also finding their way into the custody of the southern government such as Billy McCorry, Assistant Adjutant-General, who was arrested along with Tony Magan (who had taken over from Traynor as Adjutant-General).

In the summer of 1940, having completed the short prison sentence he was given in the south in 1939, Sean McCaughey had replaced Charlie McGlade as O/C Northern Command who became Adjutant.[4] Others on the staff included Tyrone men Pearse Kelly and Eoin McNamee (both English campaign veterans), and John Graham from Belfast, a golfer and Protestant divinity student. Jimmy Steele, released in May after his treason felony sentence, joined the Northern Command as Director of Training.[5] The Battalion was also in line to receive arms being shipped to the north from Dublin, although some, if not all, were intercepted in Swords in July.[6] The press was also reporting that Sean Russell, the absent Chief of Staff who was out of contact with G.H.Q., was actually in Hamburg.[7]

The fallout from the Ballykinlar raid still rumbled on in May with Tommy Sturgeon and John Austin arrested and eventually sentenced to four years for trying to procure weapons and information from British soldiers for the I.R.A.. They were accused of trying to persuade or force a number of soldiers to help them obtain Bren guns and anti-tank weapons. On at least one occasion soldiers were abducted and held in a house in the Markets district in an attempt to pressure them. The casual access to weapons afforded through pressurising or bribing soldiers at Ballykinlar was fading.

To some extent, the opportunities lost in the Ballykinlar raid and the repercussions were now beginning to outweigh the success. While opportunities to acquire weapons hadn't suddenly disappeared, they came with greater risks, such as a confrontation on the Whiterock Road where I.R.A. volunteers managed to take weapons from two soldiers. However, it led to the arrest and imprisonment of Ned Maguire who was picked up and got six years for assaulting a soldier and robbing him of his rifle and ammunition. Other intelligence gathering operations were also being uncovered by the R.U.C. Two I.R.A. volunteers, Leo Casey and Thomas McLoughlin, were given two years for collecting and recording information on a telephone kiosk, fire alarms and electricity boxes.[8] A formula for the manufacture of explosives was also found on Casey.

Ten year prison sentences were also becoming the norm. R.U.C. raids in June saw that penalty given to Robert Donaldson for possessing five revolvers, a rifle, grenade, ammunition and I.R.A. documents, while James Kane was given it for possessing thirteen rounds of ammunition and documents.[9] Not that sentencing policy was consistent. Around the same time Patrick Cunningham got five years for the arms dump found in

Etna Drive earlier in the year, while John McCoy got seven years for possession of five bullets.[10]

While the Battalion was employing various tactics to acquire arms, it was also under significant financial pressures due to the large number of prisoners now requiring some financial support. Earlier in the year, the I.R.A. had issued a statement advising account holders to withdraw from certain banks that were supporting economic activity in the north. Given the failure of Sean Russell's U.S. tour to drum up sufficient funds to sustain a campaign, the Battalion resorted to bank raids and targeted those particular banks. On the morning of 28th June, three were raided simultaneously. Armed I.R.A. units entered the Munster and Leinster Bank and the National Bank on the Falls Road and the Northern Bank on Divis Street at 10.35 am. In total around twenty-five I.R.A. volunteers took part in the raids, armed with revolvers and, in some cases, Thompson submachine guns. One of the revolvers was left in a doorway beside Dunville Park and picked up by the R.U.C. in a follow-up search. At the start of the robbery of the Munster and Leinster Bank a number of shots were fired and a cashier was wounded. Eye witnesses indicated that some I.R.A. volunteers escaped on foot while others used getaway cars.

The three robberies had netted a total of £3,200. Full-time volunteers like Tarlach Ó hUid cost the I.R.A. around £2 a week and the Battalion and Northern Command had maybe twenty full time volunteers in 1940.[11] There were also more than one hundred internees and more than fifty sentenced republican prisoners by this time. The Unionists refused any state aid, even to dependents of internees. If the I.R.A. managed to support them with £1 each, the 28th June robberies only provided sufficient finance for about ten weeks. If the internees and prisoners' family's only got 10 shillings a week, the money would still only last thirteen or fourteen weeks. In either event, none of the money would be available for equipment or arms. The Green Cross, which took on supporting prisoners' dependents, estimated that, by December 1942, it needed some £210 per week (the number interned and sentenced had increased by then).[12]

The R.U.C. response was another round-up, this time forty men from across Belfast. After the searches the R.U.C. reported it had recovered £800 which it believed had been taken in the raids. So prisoner numbers continued to increase, including fifteen volunteers of D Company captured at a meeting in Getty Street in mid-August.[13]

Other incidents are ascribed to the I.R.A. at this time and appear to be attempts to disrupt British war efforts. On July 12th, five armed men entered the Ministry of Food stores in Great George Street, cut the phone line and held the staff up while they sprinkled petrol around the building then set it on fire. During a compensation hearing in 1941 the I.R.A. was blamed for the fire.[14]

The same week, Belfast I.R.A. volunteers Jimmy Hasty, Willie O'Hanlon and Terence Perry were sentenced to ten, eight and six years at Birmingham Assizes for possession of twenty sticks of gelignite, fourteen detonators, rubber balloons, powder, two revolvers and over one hundred rounds of ammunition.

A day later, after chasing a man in Baker Street, five R.U.C. constables drew their revolvers and tried to storm a house. A crowd formed outside and then I.R.A. volunteers at the top of the street opened fire on the R.U.C. More R.U.C. constables then joined in and up to sixty shots were exchanged. In the end R.U.C. needed reinforcements to extract the party from Baker Street. Further R.U.C. raids were then carried out in the area leading to twelve arrests.[15] Almost one hundred Belfast men were arrested or interned over the summer of 1940. In Dublin, a raid in Rathgar had led to the death of two Special Branch men. Two of those arrested, the I.R.A.'s Director of Training, Paddy McGrath and Tom Harte (from Lurgan) were executed in September by the Fianna Fáil government. Despite McGrath being a 1916 and War of Independence veteran, the media depicted the shootout in Rathgar as a scene from one of the American gangster movie that were then in vogue and there was little public outcry. McGrath was replaced as Director of Training by Joe Atkinson from Belfast.

Unbeknownst to pretty much everyone, the absent I.R.A. Chief of Staff Sean Russell had died on 14th August on a German U-boat that was trying to land him back in Ireland. In Dublin the Acting Chief of Staff Stephen Hayes remained in charge.

In September, the R.U.C. carried out more large raids, this time across the Markets, Ballymacarrett and Ardoyne on the morning of the 4th September, detaining (and mostly interning) over forty men. This brought the total number of detainees and internees to well over one hundred and eighty (there were now one hundred and fifty in Derry Gaol and a small number left in D wing in Crumlin Road). A few days later the Derry Gaol internees were brought 130 miles to Killyleagh and rowed out to a prison ship, the Al Rawdah, anchored in Strangford Lough. Some internees protesting their innocence, staged a brief hunger strike in October 1940 which did eventually lead to William Barrett being released.

In the weeks before the Al Rawdah was brought into use as a prison the I.R.A. continued its campaign of disrupting British war efforts in Belfast. A number of air raid shelters were bombed during August and September, mostly with a nuisance effect rather than causing any major damage. The Belfast Battalion and Northern Command also needed funds again. On 20th September at 10.15 am, the Battalion co-ordinated a series of robberies across Belfast involving over thirty volunteers. Units entered the National Bank on the Falls Road, the Munster and Leinster Bank on the Falls Road, North Queen Street post office, Edenderry post office, Alliance Avenue post office, Falls Road post office and Grosvenor Road post office.[16] The results were chaotic.

The Alliance Avenue post office raid was a debacle. The I.R.A. unit was foiled by Mary Cunningham, the postmistress' sister, who chased them out at knife point. At nearby Edenderry post office, the post-mistress, Maria Davison, tried to raise the alarm and was shot twice in the arm. As the I.R.A. unit left a passer-by tried to grapple with one volunteer who had to brandish his revolver to escape. However, by then the R.U.C. had been alerted and the unit was chased along Butler Street and tried to escape through a house into Chatham Street. As in previous encounters in John Street (in 1938) and Baker Street earlier in the summer, the R.U.C. drew their guns and immediately stormed the house. The I.R.A. opened fire as the R.U.C. burst in and R.U.C. Sergeant James Lynch was shot in the head while I.R.A. volunteer Thomas Byrne was seriously wounded in the stomach and back. Both survived, though.

At the National Bank on the Falls Road, the I.R.A. unit ran into the R.U.C. on the way out after the raid. The I.R.A. opened fire with a Thompson submachine gun and revolvers. While bullets struck windows and walls, the R.U.C. hid in an air raid shelter and no-one was injured. One eye-witness claimed nineteen I.R.A. volunteers were present on the Falls Road during the gun battle.

In total the raids netted a further £2,165. While the R.U.C. didn't recover the money, follow-up searches uncovered arms dumps in Cairns Street and Bow Street including a Thompson, four rifles, eight revolvers, four grenades and almost five hundred rounds of ammunition.[17]

All this time, the Northern Command O/C, Sean McCaughey, was agitating with Stephen Hayes for a formal campaign to begin in the north. As the 20th September raids showed, the capacity developed by the Battalion needed resourced and couldn't be maintained indefinitely in the absence of a specific plan of action. Hayes prevaricated, putting various obstacles in McCaughey's way. Hayes feared the impression given by the bank raids in Belfast also resonated with the southern government's depiction of the I.R.A. as 1930s cinema gangsters.

The Army Council had circulated a statement in July 1940 which outlined the official position:[18] "The Army Council are frequently asked to state the Republican attitude to the European War and the powers taking part. Here are some points which should help to clarify the position. As the immediate objective of the I.R.A. is to drive out the British Army and to break the grip of the British power and control over the whole of Ireland, we are not waiting to be invaded. We already have invaders on our territory, and until we have dealt with them we need give no heed to other possible enemies. It should not be necessary to remind the Irish people that the Government of the Republic declared war on England on January 12, 1939. As the conditions demanded in the ultimatum remain unfulfilled the war still goes on. The weapons we use to pursue the war to a successful conclusion are of our own choosing. The present crisis caused by the intervention of Germany and Italy and the success of their campaign makes our job the easier. The enemies of England are, by that fact, the friends of Ireland. We are no more Nazis and Fascists than Connolly and Pearse were imperialistic by seeking the aid of Imperial Germany in 1914."

Politically, the I.R.A./left Republican Club now bore some fruit as Jack Brady published an article in *Red Hand*, the Communist news-sheet, on how the Irish had never had qualms about seeking foreign support in pursuit of an Irish republic (particularly from England's enemies). This was effectively a justification for some future acceptance of aid from Germany or the Soviet Union (Hitler and Stalin still being mutually tolerant of each other in 1940). Communists Billy McCullough and Betty Sinclair were arrested and given lengthy sentences over the publication of Brady's article in *Red Hand* (which the Unionists now banned).[19] In the end their sentences were reduced and they only spent a few weeks in prison.

For some considerable time the Northern Command staff had been hearing the stories of Battalion officers beating up volunteers and in October the issue came to a head. Tim Pat Coogan recounts how, as punishment, one or two volunteers had reputedly been shot in the leg whilst others were stripped and made to walk home.[20] Tarlach Ó hUid recounts an example of the 'belt and boots' men in action. He tells how they abducted a suspected informer, brought him to somewhere secluded, alternately beat him and consoled him, plied him with drink, then finally extracted a confession. He was escorted from Belfast and told that he was never to return.[21]

Jimmy Steele had started recording the stories while imprisoned in Crumlin Road. Released on licence in May, he immediately returned to activity duty on the Battalion staff but he continued compiling his dossier. Then in October, as Tim Pat Coogan describes it, he "… had the entire battalion staff court-martialled in a little hall in a 'loney' off the Falls. It was a strange business and while it was being held Belfast was like an armed camp, with armoured cars, ordinary police cars and foot patrols four and five strong on every side of the street in the area. Evidently the R.U.C. had word of some impending activity, but didn't know what it was to be."

The issues extended beyond the disciplinary practices. A number of Belfast I.R.A. officers, including Jack Brady and Dan Doherty, were accused of subverting the authority of the Northern Command O/C Sean McCaughey. As a former member of the Ginger Group, McCaughey thought he recognised similar dissent. The evidence given against them included the Ballykinlar raid, which appears to have gone ahead without the appropriate approval of Northern Command. The court heard evidence for several days, with Ó hUid as the notary, Steele appears to have been the prosecuting officer and Billy Coogan (F Company O/C), was President of the Court. Those that gave evidence included the likes of Arthur Corr (an I.R.A. Intelligence Officer).[22] Ó hUid claims that the prosecuting officer said the accused deserved the death penalty for mutiny during wartime but instead they were all reduced to the ranks.[23]

That autumn Ó hUid ended up in Crumlin Road. His radio bulletins (the I.R.A. station called itself 'Raidió Phoblacht na hÉireann') led to the press calling him 'Ireland's Haw-Haw'. He also produced the Belfast edition of *War News*. Jimmy Steele seems to have taken over the editorship when Ó hUid was arrested.[24] The R.U.C. raids on nationalist districts also continued, sometimes accompanied by further violence. For instance, an R.U.C. constable shot and wounded a woman inside a house in Servia Street on the 29th October.

On 18th November, word came that Battalion veteran Jack Gaffney had died on the prison ship Al Rawdah. The official cause of death was given as cerebral haemorrhage, put down to high blood pressure. However, Gaffney had been knocked unconscious falling out of a hammock and received no treatment. He never recovered. After his funeral in St Johns, his remains were brought to Milltown with several thousand mourners closely watched by the R.U.C. in armoured cars. The tricolour used for Joe McKelveys funeral was produced and placed on his coffin in the church and again at Milltown. Gaffney was a popular veteran of the Battalion's McKelvey G.A.A. club which had folded the previous year. His funeral also, in effect, marked the club's demise.

On Friday 6th December, now Belfast O/C, Jimmy Steele was captured in North Queen Street.[25] He had a loaded .380 Webley revolver and spare rounds hidden in the pocket of an overcoat and £100 in Irish pounds in an envelope that was to be distributed to dependents of the men on the Al Rawdah. He also had I.R.A. documents in his pocket.[26] Unusually, Steele was kept in solitary confinement in C Wing and Liam Rice took over as Belfast O/C. His wasn't the only arrest that Christmas. Early in January Billy Shannon got five years for possessing over one hundred rounds of rifle ammunition. He had been stopped in the Whiterock Road with a second youth (Thomas Delaney). When the R.U.C. demanded to search them, only Shannon was found with a parcel containing ammunition. Delaney was found not guilty.

Despite the tensions that must have lingered after Jack Gaffney's death on the Al Rawdah, the atmosphere inside Crumlin Road was still relatively calm in early 1941.[27] Tim Pat Coogan suggests that relations between the I.R.A. prisoners and the warders tended to wax and wane with the fortunes of the British and Germans in the war.[28] This is corroborated by Tarlach Ó hUid. His memoir, *Faoi Ghlas*, was named after a hand-written newsletter that circulated among the internees.[29] This contained historical articles, items on the republican movement and a light-hearted page (similar to the formats from *An Síol* through to the *Republican News* of 1970 onwards). The sentenced prisoners also had a hand-written newspaper, called *Saoirse*.

By the end of 1940, concerns had been developing in the south over the possible threat that it might be invaded by the British, particularly in light of various large scale field exercises by the British Army close to the border. After making contact through Moss Twomey (now retired from the I.R.A.), Sean McCaughey and Charlie McGlade met first with Special Branch in Dublin then senior officials from the office of Defence Minister, Frank Aiken, about the I.R.A. collecting intelligence on British plans to invade the south.[30]

Meanwhile, another Battalion arms dump was captured by the R.U.C. in February 1941, in Unity Street, including ten rifles, two revolvers, grenades and thousands of rounds of ammunition. As the house had been previously occupied by Liam Bradley, who had been imprisoned in England the previous year, the current occupier, Arthur McCann avoided conviction.[31] On the last day of February, Owen Callaghan, a twenty year old aircraft worker from 11 Lemon Street, was shot dead in Servia Street during the black out. Three men had called to his Lemon Street home on the Wednesday night and Callaghan left with them saying he would only be a few minutes (at the inquest it was said they left in a car). He was not seen again until the Friday night when he was shot three times in the stomach and left in Servia Street. The R.U.C. believed he had been held at a secret hideaway in Belfast. He had also been beaten around the head. In the previous November, Callaghan and his wife had been prosecuted on false identity card charges but were let off by the judge. His widow, Sarah, denied he had been involved with the I.R.A. but she claimed the I.R.A. had killed him.[32]

The next week the R.U.C. surrounded a recreation hall off the Falls Road and arrested thirty sixteen to nineteen year olds. The R.U.C. subsequently issued a press statement which claimed they had been drilling (illegally) in the hall but no-one appears to have been charged or processed through the courts. Two weeks later another major arms dump was found in a factory building on the Crumlin Road. At least one rifle, twenty-one revolvers, a machine-gun, other weapons and parts and fifteen hundred rounds of ammunition were found. No arrests were made. Kevin Barry McQuillan was also arrested in March and charged with possession of two revolvers and ammunition found in a house in Currel's Place.

The end of March saw a further armed raid, this time on McAlevey's bookmakers in Berry Street. Six I.R.A. volunteers entered the bookmakers and got away with around £1,000 in notes and coins. Two of the clerks in the shop grappled with the I.R.A. volunteers as they were leaving including one carrying a suitcase containing some £900. In the struggle two shots were fired but the suitcase was dropped and left behind, as was a bundle containing £50 in coins. In the prisons, the internees began to threaten to go on hunger strike over the use of wire netting to separate them from family and friends during visits.[33]

At the start of April, the Belfast I.R.A. made its usual attempt to circumvent the ban on commemorating the Easter Rising by holding brief, clandestine, ceremonies at a number of locations.

Since December 1940, the Unionists had been publicly acknowledging the presence of German aircraft over the north and noted that that tended to be a forewarning of a substantive air attack. Some bombs were randomly dropped in the countryside the same month without causing any damage. Flyovers by German aircraft were again reported in the press for 9th, 10th and 11th and January but there was still no urgency about 'public discipline' (with reference to the blackout) and preparation of anti-aircraft defences. The first major German bombing of Belfast then came on 7th April when thirteen were killed. Having exposed the inadequacies of the air defence system, a massive German air attack followed on Easter Tuesday (15th April) and Belfast suffered dreadfully. Over 900 died, 55,000 homes were destroyed and some 100,000 were left homeless. The Unionists were even forced to telegram Dublin for assistance (which was provided immediately). Another substantial raid causing a further 150 casualties occurred on the 4th-5th May. There is no evidence from the time that the I.R.A. even considered providing assistance to the Germans bombing Belfast, or in German archives recovered after the war (although that claim is still occasionally made).[34]

According to Tim Pat Coogan, the Belfast I.R.A. did use the cover of air raids to conceal four killings of informers. Given that a large number of bodies brought to the temporary mortuaries at St George's Market and Falls Baths were never identified and had their deaths all assigned to the air raids, it is plausible. However, it would have required the Battalion to react during the air raid, issues orders to units, then locate and kill the informers and leave their bodies in an air raid or fire damaged property. Which makes it all sound much less plausible. Those known to have been killed in the blitz that had connections to the I.R.A. were Mary Donnelly, of Cumann na mBan and the brother and mother of Arthur and Bridget Corr. There is no reason to believe any of them were killed by the I.R.A. (it should be noted that at one inquest for fifty victims of the blitz, on Saturday 21st June, it turned out that six of those named were actually still alive).[35] Instead what Coogan refers to may be the likes of Owen Callaghan and others who were shot by the I.R.A. around this time, often during the blackout. Another is probably 40 year old

Daniel Connolly, from Rodney Drive who was shot dead with a single bullet to the head on the Falls Road opposite Rockmount Street on the night of 6th June 1941.[36]

German air raids on Belfast in early 1941 were also causing friction inside Crumlin Road. When sirens went off, prisoners and warders were packed into a tunnel linking two parts of the prison. As well as the main blitzes, there were numerous smaller air raids and alerts. In May, during a night-time air raid, internees and ten juvenile sentenced prisoners were together in an air-raid shelter, separated only by prison staff. A warder, Duffield, ordered one juvenile back for getting too close to the internees leading to a row. Afterwards, thirty warders attacked the ten juveniles and batoned them back towards their cells, including up three flight of stairs. Two juveniles were badly beaten about the head but allowed to lie bleeding in their cells all day without attention.[37] On another occasion, German planes dropped bombs all around the prison. According to Joe Cahill and Tarlach Ó hUid, some vehemently anti-Catholic warders got particularly rattled and urged the prisoners to say rosaries to save them.[38]

Over in England, the I.R.A. volunteers captured and sentenced in 1939 and 1940 (some to terms as long as twenty years) were not accorded any form of prisoner of war or political status. Deliberately scattered around wings of prisons to limit their capacity for association, there were ongoing protests and conflict with the authorities in the likes of Dartmoor and Parkhurst. Joe Malone, imprisoned in Parkhurst since 1939, was among the I.R.A. prisoners under O/C Conor McNessa who refused to do work or conform to the prison regime. This culminated in a hunger strike in protest at the conditions starting 16th January 1941. English prison policy was to force feed prisoners from the fifth day. This involved immobilising a prisoner, force his mouth open with a clamp then introducing a tube to the stomach through which liquid food was passed. On the second day of force feeding, Malone passed out during the force feeding. When he regained consciousness half an hour later he was alone in the cell, spitting blood. McNessa, who was in the adjoining cell, immediately ordered him off the hunger strike. Slowly the prison authorities accorded recognition to the I.R.A. prisoners in Parkhurst and Dartmoor.[39]

With so many I.R.A. volunteers in Crumlin Road there was at least the distraction of talk about escapes although not everyone wanted to try to escape. In 1941, when Gerry Doherty and Eamon Ó Cianáin were preparing an escape attempt from D wing, which housed the internees, Ó Cianáin was approached by a 'well known Belfast republican' who lectured him for having the cheek to try to escape when it might "…lose all the privileges enjoyed by the internees".[40]

Doherty and Ó Cianáin first made an escape attempt at the end of May 1941. They failed but avoided the attention of the authorities. They made a second attempt on the 6th June. Liam Burke, Phil McTaggart and Liam 'Bildo' Watson joined this escape attempt which simply involved breaking through a fence into the C wing yard and then throwing a grappling hook and rope (made from prison sheets) over the wall. It was a simple and effective plan. Escaping through the adjoining convent and St Malachy's College, with no pre-arranged get away vehicles or safehouses, all five got clean away and managed to find friendly houses and made their way to Dublin.

The remaining internees got great mileage from the escape constantly taunting the prison staff (who were investigated to identify failures that might have permitted the escape). This included singing the song 'Five Internees' (to the tune of Parlez-vous/The Back of the Bus is in the Huff/Three German Officers):

> "Five internees went over the wall, Barney-Boo,
> Five internees went over the wall, Barney-Boo,
> The rest of the lads were playing football,
> When five internees went over the wall,
> Inky-pinky Barney-Boo.
>
> Five internees went over the wall, Barney-Boo,
> Five internees went over the wall, Barney-Boo,
> The Prison Officer Johnston stood aghast,
> He didn't know men could climb so fast,
> Inky-pinky Barney-Boo.
>
> Five internees went over the wall, Barney-Boo,
> Five internees went over the wall, Barney-Boo,
> Then Thompson cried "Now come back, here!"
> But Doherty smiled and said "No fear!"
> Inky-pinky Barney-Boo."[41]

---

[1] See the likes of *Irish Examiner* 23rd April 1940.

[2] Coogan 1970, p181.

[3] See newspapers, eg *Irish Press* and *Irish Examiner* on 9th May 1940.

[4] There is no implication in any account that this was anything other than McGlade's idea, but the coincidence with internal disciplinary proceedings, even if not against McGlade, suggest upheaval and the changes may have been forced by an atmosphere of discontent, see Shane MacThomais' biographic sketch of McGlade in *An Phoblacht* 7th September 2006.

[5] A number of sources such as the biographical piece on Jimmy Steele by Pat McGlynn in *An Phoblacht,* 29th August 1985, MacThomais' article on McGlade *An Phoblacht* 7th September 2006 and *Belfast Graves* have Steele as Adjutant, Northern Command, but this doesn't appear to have happened until 1943 (when Steele was Adjutant of Northern Command, then replaced Liam Burke as Adjutant-General). This may stem from an ambiguity on the subject in the obituary written for him in *Republican News*, Vol. 1. No. 3, August 1970.

[6] Referenced in *Irish Press,* 20th June 1940.

7 *Belfast Newsletter,* 24th June 1940.

8 *Irish News,* 22nd June 1940.

9 See press on 22nd June and 30th July 1940

10 See *Irish News* and *Irish Press,* 6th September 1940.

11 Based on the size of the Northern Command staff reported in Quinn and the addition of some local O/Cs.

12 *Irish Press,* 5th December 1942. The Green Cross estimate was to support 171 families (roughly £1 5s a week on average). Only those deemed breadwinners were given any substantive support.

13 Those arrested were Terry Benson, Eddie Dalzell, Kevin Harrison, Frank Hicks, Gerald Higgins, John Maguire, Sam McComb, Charlie McCotter, Patrick McGuinness, Billy McKee, Joseph McKenna, Joe McManus, Thomas McMenemy (who was shot and wounded trying to escape), Dan Rooney and James Weldon. All were charged with treason felony.

14 See press reports on 15th July 1940. A flax stores was burnt in April and a coal store in November.

15 *Irish Press,* 17th August 1940.

16 Around 13 weeks after the previous set of raids.

17 *Irish Examiner,* 23rd October 1940, Anthony McMenemy was arrested for the Cairns Street find, Edward Doherty and James Kane for the arms found in Bow Street.

18 A copy was captured in Tyrone and read out in court in November 1940, see *Belfast Newsletter,* 20th November 1940.

19 Swan 2008, p93.

20 Coogan 1970, p182.

21 Ó hUid 1960, p203.

22 Ó hUid names Brady, Corr, Doherty and Coogan in *Faoi Ghlas* (1985, p66).

23 The same court-martial is recounted by both Ó hUid in *Faoi Ghlas* and Coogan in *The I.R.A.* (1970, p176).

24 *An Phoblacht,* 29th August 1985.

25 P.R.O.N.I., BELF/1/1/2/124/7.

26 *Irish Freedom,* February 1941.

27 Memo, O/C 2nd Batt to Adjutant, Northern Command, I.R.A., 30th January 1941. Among documents recovered from 6b Devonshire Street on 6th March 1943 and now held in P.R.O.N.I. (no current reference number).

28 Coogan 1970, p186.

29 Joe Cahill quoted by Pat McGlynn in *An Phoblacht* 29th August 1985. *Saoirse* was definitely the name given to the hand-written paper circulating among sentenced prisoners in the 1950s but the name is supposed to have been taken from its predecessor started by Jimmy Steele. Tarlach Ó hUid 1985 *Faoi Ghlas.*

30 MacEoin 1997, p847.

[31] *Irish Press,* 28th February 1941.
[32] *Irish News,* 1st March 1941; *Belfast Newsletter* 5th December 1941.
[33] See Stormont *Hansard,* 27th March 1941.
[34] See the likes of Lane, J. 1972 *On the IRA: Belfast Brigade Area.* Cork Workers Club.
[35] Coogan (p179 in the 2000 edition of *The I.R.A.*). I contacted him to ask if he still has the names but he can no longer find them. I can identify at least four possible killings Owen Callaghan (as mentioned earlier), Dan Connolly, Joe Kearney and Robert McAlister (see below). No names on the late 1930s I.R.A. suspect lists match recorded Blitz victims.
[36] The R.U.C. interviewed sixty people after Connolly's death. Neither at the inquest or compensation hearing was the I.R.A. blamed.
[37] The juveniles were called Coleman and Collins.
[38] Anderson 2002, *Joe Cahill: A Life in the I.R.A.,* p.99. Cahill must have heard this story at second hand as he was not imprisoned until 1942, and spent his time in A wing not D wing. It seems to be the same story as recounted by Ó hUid (1985, p89).
[39] This is based on an account by MacNessa in *An Phoblacht,* 17th May 1974.
[40] MacEoin 1997, p694. I suspect this may have been Jack McNally.
[41] Based on version given by Ó hUid in *Faoi Ghlas* (1985, p98).

the Belfast takeover of G.H.Q.

The escapers added to the sizeable Battalion contingent already in Dublin joining Sean McCaughey, Charlie McGlade, Joe Atkinson (whom McCaughey had replaced as Adjutant-General), Dan O'Toole, Frank Duffy, Liam Rice and other Belfast volunteers. The northerners among the I.R.A. leadership, McCaughey (as Adjutant-General) and Charlie McGlade (as Quartermaster-General) now had sufficient support on the ground from Belfast to operate independently of the Dublin I.R.A. units. They were also unknown to the Dublin Special Branch men.

McCaughey used this support to target the man he thought was responsible for the problems befalling the I.R.A., Acting Chief of Staff Stephen Hayes (it was not yet known that Sean Russell was dead). Hayes was low-visibility and unpopular. McCaughey had probed around (as Northern Command O/C) and had a discussion with Garda Special Branch about the clashes between the I.R.A. and their officers when he met them early in 1941. He also met a Clare TD close to de Valera to tease out talk of co-operation on the I.R.A. and the ongoing monitoring of British military activity in the north. McCaughey also offered that the information that was collected be given to the German spy Goertz.[1] McCaughey had also tried to recruit the former blueshirt leader, Eoin O'Duffy, as an intelligence agent. McCaughey appears to have been using the meetings to form a view of the I.R.A.'s problems as seen by outsiders. His conclusion was that the problem was Stephen Hayes.

McCaughey and McGlade must be the I.R.A. volunteers from Belfast described by Herman Goertz, the German Abwher agent close to Stephen Hayes, as "…a few young I.R.A. fanatics…They did not understand me and wished to compel me to act according to their wishes". Goertz recounts that they brought him the information and he promptly burned it. Despite the various lurid claims, those encounters with Goertz in Dublin seem to be the extent of Belfast I.R.A. involvement with German agents.[2] Various people outside Belfast articulated the I.R.A.'s attitude towards the outbreak of another world war. One volunteer, Joe Dolan, states that they were "…not pro-Nazi, we just had the hope that England would be brought to her knees and that we would get freedom for our country when the war was over".[3]

Having suspected for some time that the alcoholic Hayes was 'counter-attacking the I.R.A.', he was detained at his flat in Coolock on 30th June by McCaughey, Liam Rice and Charlie McGlade.[4] Joe Atkinson was also present but not party to McCaughey's plan.

They then questioned and prosecuted Hayes in front of the Army Council. McCaughey taking on the role of (Acting) Chief of Staff.[5] After being sentenced to death, Hayes offered to write a confession and began a lengthy period of writing. Pearse Kelly transcribed the confession.

The 'confession' written by Hayes and transcribed by Kelly is a confusing document. One theme pursued by McCaughey was to explore who had previously been I.R.B. members and whether, as an organisation, it continued to exist. There seemed to be a fear among the Battalion that the I.R.B. had been used to resurrect old allegiances between an older generation of I.R.A. volunteers who were now spread around outside the I.R.A., in the southern government, Fianna Fáil and elsewhere and that it included the likes of Stephen Hayes (and possibly even Sean Russell). Russell's and Hayes' strategy is also depicted in the confession as deliberately aligned with Fianna Fáil's interests.

A couple of days before Hayes was arrested, shots were fired at an R.U.C. constable on the corner of Cupar Street and the Falls Road (leading to Arthur Daly, George Daly, Joe O'Neill and John Cox being charged with attempted murder). All four were innocent. What had really happened was that James Murphy and Terence Donegan had been involved in stealing a car with three other Battalion volunteers. They had been drinking and had a revolver taken from an I.R.A. dump which they used to fire shots at the R.U.C.. They had missed and wounded Mary Teer instead.[6]

Pearse Kelly had taken over as Battalion O/C in May when Liam Rice left for Dublin. Previously, he had set up a republican police in Dungannon to stop anti-social behaviour. One of the complications of creating such a large organisation like the Battalion was that, without the start of a northern campaign to work towards, there always a risk that it had attracted some who would get involved in petty crime or anti-social behaviour, particularly as they got bored waiting for a campaign that never started. So Kelly had Murphy, Donegan and three others court-martialled on 5th July, expelled from the I.R.A. and deported from Belfast. The I.R.A. then sent the findings and sentence of the court-martial to the Unionist government. Even though two of those charged (the Dalys, O'Neill and Cox) were I.R.A. volunteers, the Unionists accepted the finding of the I.R.A. Northern Command court-martial and dropped the charges again all four on 22nd July. By then, Kelly was on his way to Dublin to assist in the interrogation of Stephen Hayes. Kelly had also been lucky while based in Belfast – a British staff officer left an envelope in a chemist that was passed to Kelly. It was found to contain the British Army code ciphers for the next week. The chemist passed it to Kelly who had copied and returned before the officer realised it was missing.

In July, the I.R.A. made another attempt to raid McAleveys in Berry Street. Again a six-man I.R.A. unit took part. When they gained entrance to the office at around 7 pm, the takings were being counted but staff managed to raise the alarm. Two B Specials appeared as the I.R.A. unit were about to leave empty-handed and opened fire. One volunteer got away, but Robert Dempsey sustained stomach wounds, while Thomas Marley, Gerry Watson, Gerry McAvoy and Bobby McGuinness were all arrested. They hadn't fired a shot but all got ten years in prison.[7]

The Nazi invasion of Soviet Russia on 22nd June now created a further problem for the Republican Club. The left wing delegates felt they could no longer support the I.R.A. since the British were now an ally of the Soviet Union. To some in the I.R.A. this shift in policy by the communists was seen as being directed externally - essentially that the local party had taken its direction from the Comintern. After June 1941, the communists found that abandoning Irish republicanism and weighing in behind the British war effort was allowing it to build up support among the Protestant working class.[8] At best, future relations between the I.R.A. and the local Communists in Belfast were fractious.

On the night of 4th August, a seventeen year old hairdresser, Joseph Kearney, was found shot through the heart close to his Verner Street home. He was supposed to have been at the cinema earlier that evening but little is known about the incident in which he was shot. Kearney was an Irish language enthusiast but his father insisted he was not connected to the I.R.A. or Fianna.

That August, four internees went on a brief hunger strike protesting their continued imprisonment.[9] Meanwhile, disaster struck in Dublin. First, at the start of September, Sean McCaughey was captured on a tram. Then, a lapse in security allowed Stephen Hayes to escape from a house in Castlewood Avenue in the centre of Rathmines in Dublin on 8th September. After Hayes' escape, McCaughey was sentenced to death by the Special Criminal Court on 18th September. The I.R.A. trod carefully after September 18th as it waited and hoped for McCaughey's death sentence to be commuted. Joe Atkinson had also been picked up in Dublin, leaving a house in Raheny. He was unarmed but was carrying I.R.A. documents and received seven years. Pearse Kelly took over from McCaughey as Chief of Staff.

McCaughey's sentence was finally commuted on the 4th October and he joined those in Portlaoise prison who were refusing to wear prison uniforms and wanted their political status recognised.[10] Two Treason Felony men from Crown Entry, Mick Traynor and Liam Rice (who was seriously wounded while being arrested), were to end up in Portlaoise with McCaughey.

It may be coincidental, but on the day McCaughey finally had his sentence commuted, Robert McAlister was shot by two men in Cyprus Street in Belfast. He had been kidnapped and was missing for a week when shots were heard in Cyprus Street. He was found to have been beaten around the head with the butt of a revolver and then shot several times in the leg. The leg wound was so severe he died in hospital. At the inquest it was stated that the shooting was believed to 'be political'.

Having delayed any action until McCaughey's case was resolved, Eoin McNamee, Hugh McAteer and John Graham again moved against the 'belt and boots' faction in the Battalion. McAlister's death (and possibly Kearney's) may have been the actions that again brought the issue to a head. The Northern Command leadership confronted the Battalion staff in a well prepared manoeuvre. H Company (a special unit mostly staffed by Protestant I.R.A. members) was mobilised under John Graham and McNamee had I.R.A. units from outside Belfast brought in to the city to provide additional support to the Northern Command. The scene was set for a major, and possibly violent, showdown.

When McNamee, and his Adjutant Hugh McAteer, walked into a Battalion staff meeting, it was immediately obvious that there was a problem. While the various sources do not specifically name individuals, Hugh Matthews was the Belfast O/C at the time and one of his staff, Patsy Hicks, is named by Tim Pat Coogan as being the figure who managed to defuse the situation.

Having dealt with the issues in the Battalion and with Pearse Kelly as Chief of Staff, the I.R.A. encouraged Helena Moloney and Liam Lucas to evolve a social and economic programme and fill the political gap in I.R.A. strategy.[11] Arrests continued in Dublin, though, as Charlie McGlade had to grapple with a Special Branch detective who intended to shoot him. McGlade was then shot in the leg trying to get away and was arrested. Kelly was also quickly arrested when he tried to visit the sole remaining German spy at large in Ireland, Herman Goertz, to encourage him to go back underground. Kelly was replaced by Sean Harrington at a hurried Army Convention in Dublin which also now, finally, agreed in principle to focus on a northern campaign.[12] Eoin McNamee moved from O/C Northern Command to Quartermaster-General. Sean McCool, not long out of Crumlin Road, was now Adjutant-General. Harrington, too, was rapidly arrested in Dublin and McCool took over as Chief of Staff.

---

[1] Bowyer Bell (1970) gives an account of McCaughey's meetings.

[2] Stephani, E. 1963 *Spies in Ireland*.

[3] MacEoin 1997, p485.

[4] According to Billy McKee this is how Hayes was described to I.R.A. Volunteers.

[5] Both McKelvey and McCaughey were born in Tyrone.

[6] This story and the other information about Pearse Kelly is given on pages 168-171 of the 2002 edition of Tim Pat Coogan's *The IRA*.

[7] *Irish Press* and *Irish News* 24th July 1941.

[8] Swan 2008, p94.

[9] *Irish Times*, 20th August 1941.

[10] A strip strike is a prison protest where the prisoners refuse to wear prison clothes (normally as they have been convicted of political crimes). An account of the strip strike is given by Uinseann MacEoin in *The I.R.A. in the Twilight Years* (1997).

[11] Bowyer Bell 1970, p216.

[12] MacEoin 1985, p92.

I.R.A. Memo, from Chief of Staff to Director of Publicity, Northern Command, 13th June 1942 (P.R.O.N.I.).

G.H.Q. comes to Belfast

In early 1942, on foot of the command decision for a northern campaign, the Battalion re-grouped into four companies, A-D (with a headquarters company attached to Northern Command).[1] Documents captured later in 1942 give some idea of how individual companies in the Battalion area operated. Over the end of 1941 and 1942 the company (Headquarters Company)[2] recorded names and addresses of any individuals who had weapons, including the types and ammunition held. It also recorded that an Italian was offering to act as a middle man for British soldiers in Aldergrove who were willing to sell on weapons. The names and addresses on the list, B Specials and military, are mainly around the Antrim Road suggesting that this is where the company was based. The minutes of a company staff meeting show that the company met on Tuesdays for physical drill and Thursdays for drill, lectures or a first aid class. On Fridays staff officers only attended and got lectures on all gun types, close and extended order drill, urban and rural warfare and practice in giving and taking commands. I.R.A. volunteers who had an issue to raise with the staff could do so at the general parade on a Sunday night.

The company staff included an O/C, Adjutant, Quartermaster, Intelligence Officer, Publicity Officer, Finance Officer, Training Officer, 1st Lieutenant and 2nd Lieutenant and it had a building that it used as a headquarters. It was developing plans to make the building look like a gymnasium and recreation hall for which it intended to organise a dance to raise money. The company also had a deliberately constructed arms dump and a smaller dump, including a Webley with 59 rounds and a .303 rifle with 79 rounds and five clips. The weapons in the smaller dump were specifically for training. Other events organised by the company were 7-a-side tournaments in hurling, football and camogie.

The Battalion leadership was also changing repeatedly. Jimmy Steele had been O/C for only a few months at the time of his arrest in December 1940. Liam Rice, who took over from Steele in January 1941 left to join G.H.Q. in Dublin during May and was replaced by Pearse Kelly who also left for Dublin in July. Hugh Matthews, Davy's brother, took over as O/C after Kelly's departure. At Company level changes were frequent too. One Company O/C was court-martialled in January 1941 after going missing for several weeks (he claimed illness but was dismissed anyway).[3]

Inside the prisons, there were now constant tensions between the prisoners and the authorities. The beating of prisoners by the prison staff was even raised by T.J. Campbell in Stormont.[4] The Minister for Home Affairs, Dawson Bates denied that any prisoners were injured or batons used although certain 'obstreperous' prisoners were moved away from their cell windows where they were creating disturbances. He said that some prisoners were punished for disobedience of orders and disorderly conduct. Jimmy Steele, now O/C of the prisoners, was reporting that the prisoners wanted the I.R.A. to take action against some of the prison staff. They also began a mass hunger strike on Monday 19th January.

While that hunger strike was taking place an I.R.A. unit staged a daring robbery in Academy Street on Wednesday 21st January. The proposed northern campaign needed resourcing and the failed raids of the previous summer meant that the Battalion was in debt to various people who had looked after I.R.A. volunteers on the run. The target of the raid was the delivery of the payroll cash into Civil Defence Headquarters. A car was commandeered and timed to arrive with the payroll outside the offices on Academy Street. The unit was led by Patsy Hicks and included Bob McMillan. McMillan opened fire with a Thompson as the wages clerk carrying the payroll, Scott McLeod, tried to enter the building. McMillan shot McLeod three times and wounded himself in the foot, but still managed to escape. The raid netted the Battalion a much needed £4,688. McLeod lost a leg due to his injuries.

The same day as the raid, Joe Malone died in Parkhurst prison. The stomach injuries he had sustained during the force feeding the previous year had not healed and an operation in December 1941 had failed to deliver any meaningful improvement. His remains were at least brought home to Belfast for burial.

The mass hunger strike in Crumlin Road had only been planned to last for one week and finished on 26th January. But the demands for action from prisoners was growing louder and louder. There were now reports of three or four warders entering cells and handing out beatings. Seamus 'Rocky' Burns, an internee in D wing, was canvassing for direct action to be taken against one particular warder.[5]

The day after the hunger strike ended, John McQuillan and John Crean entered a shop on the Ravenhill Road and tied up the owner. The R.U.C. (led by District-Inspector Henry Geelan), though, were lying in wait in a back room of the shop and emerged, killing McQuillan with a single shot to the heart. He was eighteen. His brother, Kevin Barry McQuillan had been arrested with two automatic pistols the previous year. John McQuillan is not usually listed as an I.R.A. volunteer, although his death is mentioned in an I.R.A. memo that states "The McQuillan shooting was very unfortunate. Let me have a report of the court of inquiry later."[6] This reference seems to imply that he was an I.R.A. volunteer although the proposed 'court of inquiry' suggests he wasn't acting in an official capacity. Geelan's presence also appears to indicate that the R.U.C. believed it to be political. McQuillan was carrying a Spanish Webley (a weapon the I.R.A. was known to possess based on later arms finds). At John Crean's trial at the end of February, the court was told by the R.U.C. that Crean was in the I.R.A. but he only received a twelve month sentence for the robbery. The I.R.A. has never officially acknowledged McQuillan as a member.

The next day the I.R.A. buried Joe Malone in Milltown. His coffin was dressed in green, white and orange and his wreaths included one from 'his I.R.A comrades in Parkhurst and Dartmoor', another from the Army Council and G.H.Q. and another from the internees in Belfast. After the burial there were clashes in Milltown as the R.U.C. tried to make arrests with Prionsias MacAirt eventually charged with illegal drilling.[7] McQuillan's death, then Malone's and the clashes at the funeral contributed to an ugly mood. In Dublin, over the same week a high profile I.R.A. case in front of the Military Tribunal was leading to a debate on legislative changes to, basically, make it easier to convict and execute I.R.A. volunteers.

The following Friday (6th February), a prison officer, Thomas Walker, was cycling along Durham Street on his way over to work in Crumlin Road. A number of men got out of a waiting car and fired a burst from a Thompson gun at him, hitting him twice in the chest. He was brought to the Royal Victoria Hospital but died of his wounds.[8] He was thirty-eight years old and had been married two years. R.U.C. swoops that weekend detained twenty more republicans. While Walker did work in Crumlin Road and had been on the Al Rawdah, he was apparently considered harmless by the prisoners and had been mistaken for the real target, another warder called Robinson.[9] The killing had some effect in forcing a change in attitude of the prison staff towards the republican prisoners.[10]

That weekend, in the aftermath of the three deaths, the Catholic hierarchy, made a point of only condemning the killing of Walker at St Peters Church, with Bishop Mageean (of Down and Connor diocese) saying: "The supreme public authority is the state, and this authority alone has the power of life and death. This particular murder was not perpetrated in the heat of sudden passion. It had no extenuating circumstances; it was cold and calculated."[11] The following Monday, the R.U.C. raided the Belfast-Dublin train and arrested Henry Lundborg, an attendant and ex-Free State soldier who was carrying despatches between Belfast and Dublin where they were usually handed over to Peter Lawlor.[12]

On the 9th March the Battalion suffered a major blow as Rex Thompson and William Smith of Headquarters Company were arrested. From Protestant backgrounds, their detention revealed a broadening of the Battalion's range of active personnel. They were charged with possessing four revolvers, a grenade, ammunition, intelligence documents and I.R.A. publications, all captured in Thompson's garage and house. Printing equipment was found at Smith's house. Both had come to the I.R.A. through Denis Ireland's Ulster Union Club. They were charged under the Treason Felony Act. The documents captured with Thompson and Smith give some idea of the types of activity the I.R.A. was carrying out in 1941 and 1942 (see the start of this chapter).

In early 1942 the Battalion was advised that an Army Convention would be held and so a Battalion Convention was called to propose motions and deal with any outstanding business.[13] This appears to have happened after Thompson and Smith were arrested. The motions approved by the Battalion Convention must presumably reflect the issues facing them in Belfast over recent years. The motions (numbered as they appeared on the Army Convention agenda) were: 4. "That if German forces should enter Ireland with the consent of the Provisional Government of the Irish Republic that Óglaigh na hÉireann should assist the German forces."; 5. "That the political squad of the C.I.D. be executed."; 6. "That members of Óglaigh na hÉireann guilty of mutiny or incitement to mutiny render themselves liable to the death penalty."; 10. "That Óglaigh na hÉireann should conscript the wealth of the country." 11. "That all members of Óglaigh na hÉireann be given adequate firing practice."; 12. "That enemy raiding parties should be attacked."; 13. "That this Convention agrees with the policy of the Northern Command."; 17. "That members of Óglaigh na hÉireann be allowed to sign statements to the effect that they will not join Óglaigh na hÉireann." Motion 5, in particular, looks like a response to John McQuillan's death in January.

On Tuesday 24th March the I.R.A. held a Convention in Belfast to make preparations for the agreed northern campaign and, apparently, doubled up as an Extraordinary or General Army Convention as it elected an Army Executive. It was chaired by Hugh McAteer as Adjutant, Northern Command, who had been recently released from Crumlin Road. Bowyer Bell states that the Battalion O/C (Hugh Matthews), his Adjutant Sean Dolan and the Intelligence Officer, Gerard O'Reilly, Patsy Hicks, Dan McAllister, John Graham and Tom Williams were all present (the Battalion was now designated No. 4 Area of Northern Command). The records of the convention state that there were only 4 delegates from No. 4 Area present so that list also includes the delegate from Command Headquarters, and the Northern Command's Director of Intelligence (John Graham), who addressed the Convention.

As Eoin McNamee took over as I.R.A. Adjutant-General, the Convention confirmed McAteer as O/C Northern Command and O'Reilly became his Adjutant. John Graham was Director of Intelligence and Publicity. It was agreed that a campaign in the north should be a priority and that a properly constituted Executive should be elected to oversee the campaign. In Belfast, though, this was too little too late as the Battalion's capacity had been frittered away since the late 1930s, and now stood at three hundred active volunteers, around 30-40% of where it was as recently as 1939-40.[14]

The motions brought by the Battalion were dealt with at the Convention. Motion 4, enabling the 'Provisional Government of the Irish Republic' (i.e. the Army Council) to decide on whether to join forces with the Germans if they invaded was passed after a counter motion (from No. 2 Area) was withdrawn. An earlier motion agreeing to accept help from countries at war with Great Britain, neutral countries and Irish America had been proposed by No. 2 Area and approved unanimously. Motion 5 was passed unanimously. Motion 6 was passed with an amendment from No. 2 Area so that the approved wording read "That members of Óglaigh na hÉireann guilty of mutiny or incitement to mutiny render themselves liable to the death penalty. Pending the resumption of hostilities that death penalty be carried out only on mutineers in direct contact with enemy forces." Motion 10 was proposed and seconded by the Belfast delegates, then withdrawn after discussion and an alternative wording was passed unanimously: "That Óglaigh na hÉireann should float a war loan immediately." Motions 11 and 12 were both passed unanimously, as was Motion 13 although it was both proposed and criticised by the No. 4 Area delegates. Motion 17 was also proposed and seconded by the Belfast delegates and had a counter-motion proposing that members specifically be prohibited from signing statements proposed by a Belfast delegate but the Motion was passed by 11 to 6.

The Convention also elected a new twelve man Executive and a twelve man substitute Executive. The election was delayed by Battalion delegates disputing the composition of the panels from which they would be elected. Only a General Army Convention could elect the Executive (under the I.R.A.'s Constitution as approved in 1932). The March 1942 Belfast Convention is described as a 'Northern Command Convention' in the minutes but it must have been deemed an 'Extraordinary Army Convention' to also elect the new Army Executive. In effect the Northern Command was the only remaining organised command capable of being represented at a Convention and Sean McCool, as Chief of Staff, had to spend most of his time trying to rebuild the other commands.

The Battalion immediately acted on the approved resolution "That the political squad of the C.I.D. be executed."[15] Within a few days, William Fannin, one of the R.U.C. Special Branch who was prominent in arrests of republicans, was cycling up the Falls Road towards Springfield Barracks when a car drove past him and three shots were fired at him. He was hit in both the arm and thigh. The car had been taken at gun point from the Malone Road. As a crowd gathered around Fannin, the I.R.A. returned and fired two shots over their heads to disperse them. The R.U.C. immediately responded with more arrests.

---

[1] Tarlach Ó hUid dates this re-organisation to the end of 1941 and start of 1942 (in *Faoi Ghlas*).

[2] H Company, as described by Anderson (2002) and others, included the likes of John Graham, Rex Thompson and William Smith (see below).

[3] P.R.O.N.I., Belf/1/1/2/128/6.

[4] *Stormont Hansard* 10th February 1942.

[5] Ó hUid 1985, p130.

[6] Memo, Army Council to Adjutant Northern Command, 6th February, 1942 (reported in *Belfast Newsletter*, 20th March 1942).

[7] *Belfast Newsletter*, 29th January 1942.

[8] See *Irish Times* and *Irish News*, 9th February 1942.

[9] Ó hUid 1985, p130.

[10] P.R.O.N.I., Belf/1/1/2/129/8.

[11] *Irish News*, 21st February 1942.

[12] See Lundborg's trial in March (eg *Belfast Newsletter*, 20th March 1942).

[13] Company and Battalion Conventions would have been a fairly regular occurrence from the 1920s to 1960s culminating in an Army Convention. The capture of documents relating to the 1942 Conventions provide an insight into the processes that, while not

represented in surviving documentation, would have happened on multiple occasions. The documents are in P.R.O.N.I., Belf/1/1/2/129/8.

14 Bowyer Bell 1970, p219-220.
15 P.R.O.N.I. file, Belf/1/1/2/129/8.

Top left: Harry White (Quinn 1999); top right: Liam Burke (MacEoin 1985); bottom left: Tom Williams (McVeigh 1999); bottom right: Chrissie Dolan (*An Phoblacht*, 22nd February 1975).

Cawnpore Street

For the 1942 Easter Rising Commemorations, the Battalion decided to stage a diversionary attack on the R.U.C. in Kashmir Road. The plan was for a C Company unit, under it's O/C Tom Williams, to fire shots over one of the R.U.C. cage cars that constantly patrolled the district. The R.U.C. would rush forces from elsewhere into the area for a substantial search. The C Company unit would retreat before the R.U.C. saturated the area and the Battalion would hold its main commemorations elsewhere in peace.

Everything went to plan until the R.U.C. decided to pursue C Company into Cawnpore Street. The Convention in March had passed the Battalion's own motion "That enemy raiding parties should be attacked." So, as the R.U.C. tried to storm the house in Cawnpore Street, Williams had opened fired. There was then an exchange of gunfire during which Williams was wounded and R.U.C. Constable Patrick Murphy killed. Murphy seems to have been following an R.U.C. policy of aggressively pursuing I.R.A. volunteers when there was a confrontation. He had been one of those who previously tried to storm a house at gun point in John Street when William Smyth was shot in 1938. With Williams badly injured, the I.R.A. unit delayed any attempt to escape and surrendered to the R.U.C. who descended on Cawnpore Street. Williams subsequently claimed responsibility for Murphy's death even though he had not fired the fatal shots. While he did so hoping to save the rest of his unit (and the Army Convention had passed a motion permitting volunteers to sign statements anyway), he had also been led to believe his own wounds were fatal. In the aftermath of Murphy's death, the Battalion kept a lower profile.[1]

Elsewhere, McCool and McNamee had tried to help a German spy, Gunther Schuetz, (who had escaped from Mountjoy) by organising a boat home to Germany with a request for equipment to assist the I.R.A.'s northern campaign. McCool was arrested, though, before the project could be completed. While trying to arrange Schuetz's escape, the newly elected Army Executive met to elect an Army Council which followed up on the Battalion motion passed at the Convention determining that "...as a prelude to any co-operation between Óglaigh na hÉireann and the German Government, the German German Government explicitly declare its intention to recognise the Provisional Government of the Irish Republic as the Government of Ireland in all post-war negotiation affecting Ireland." Throughout 1942 the I.R.A. also obsessed about the arrival of U.S. troops in the north, seeing it as an infringement of Irish sovereignty. Odd as this view may seem, de Valera took a similar position, saying the deployment of U.S. troops in Ireland should have required consultation with (and the permission of) his government and he protested to the U.S. State Department.[2]

Then, at the end of April, a courier was picked up on the Belfast-Dublin train with documents that gave the Schuetz scheme away. McNamee took over as Chief of Staff with McAteer as his deputy. He lasted until the 23rd May when McAteer had to step up as Acting Chief of Staff with Charlie Kerins, from Kerry, as his deputy.

In the first week of July, in Parkhurst Prison, Terence Perry died. Perry was an I.R.A. volunteer from Belfast and, like most of the others that died in prison, or shortly after leaving, the conditions of his incarceration and the care he received (if any) were widely believed to be contributing factors to his premature death.

An Army Council meeting on 19th July confirmed McAteer as Chief of Staff and he remained O/C Northern Command for the purposes of the upcoming campaign. Charlie Kerins remained as McAteer's deputy in Dublin while I.R.A. headquarters relocated to Belfast. Clashes with Special Branch in Dublin continued though and proved to be an unwanted distraction over the coming months (one led to Brendan Behan having to go on the run to Belfast).

At the end of July, to considerable shock, a court sentenced all six C Company volunteers to hang for Murphy's death. Their executions were scheduled for 18th August. Under McAteer, a response was considered if the executions went ahead. This is often mistaken for the proposed 'northern campaign' which was to be an extension of the I.R.A.'s English campaign which began in January 1939 and was still, officially, being undertaken although the last attack had been in March 1940. As part of the preparations for a future northern campaign arms dumps had begun to be assembled at various strategic locations, some close to Belfast. Campaign plans were being drawn up but with the six executions scheduled for 18th August, Northern Command looked at various possible ways to make a violent response on 20th August and this caused some confusion over whether this should then also become the start of the new campaign. McCool, while travelling around and re-organising various local commands, had personally assembled arms dumps needed for any future northern campaign. Harry White, interned in the Curragh with McCool, memorised the locations, re-signed from the I.R.A. and signed out. He then re-joined the I.R.A. and recovered the dumps. White eventually took over as O/C Northern Command.

Initially, the new campaign was intended to adopt guerrilla tactics with the element of surprise, attacking where the Unionists would not expect them and deploying unusual tactics such as snipers taking single shots at the R.U.C. and then moving location. Simultaneous attacks would take place at Antrim Road and Andersonstown R.U.C. barracks plus a third location to be decided closer to the time. Individual volunteers would be dispatched to locations with a single hand grenade to throw and then leave, all intended to confuse the Unionists as to the focus of attack. High profile targets and individuals (such as Detective Inspector Denis Cremin) were to be attacked as early as possible. Cinemas would be widely attacked as a prelude to the campaign.[3]

As an appeal was scheduled for 20th August and delayed the executions the proposed I.R.A. response was temporarily shelved by McAteer. When the appeal itself was dismissed, the new date for the hanging was now set for the 2nd September and all six were moved to a temporary death row in C wing. A reprieve campaign then gathered momentum. Ironically, it included members of the Fianna Fáil government that had executed four republicans in the previous two years. On 29th August, the pressure finally bore fruit and the Unionists consented to a reprieve. However, the reprieve was for five, not all six, condemning Tom Williams to be hanged on the 2nd September.

On Sunday 30th August, the I.R.A. issued a '*Special Manifesto*' that restated the "…National principles actuating the Irish Republican Army…". Notably, the manifesto goes as far as making reference to the "…resumption of hostilities between Great Britain and the Irish Republic…" indicating a tacit acceptance that the military campaign against Britain that had been declared in January 1939 was effectively dormant since 1940. Indeed, symbolically, by the summer of 1942, '*War*' *News* was now being published as '*Republican*' *News*, an even more overt recognition that the British campaign was over. Hugh McAteer had also been critical of the poor quality of the Dublin edition of *Republican News*.[4]

The *Special Manifesto* also saw McAteer re-address the attitude of the I.R.A. to Germany stating that "…the Irish Republican Army, being essentially a national organisation, cannot be used, nor will it be used, as a pawn in the hands of foreign Powers." Furthermore, it notes that the I.R.A. would "…regard the invasion of any part of Ireland by any other foreign power against the wishes of the Irish people…" and that the "occupation of any part of Ireland by any foreign Power for its own ends, whether in the guise of a protector or of a deliverer, is a usurpation of Ireland's national integrity." As June had been dominated by reporting of former I.R.A. Chief of Staff Stephen Hayes trial, there had been references to the involvement of the I.R.A. with German agents. McAteer clearly wanted to put distance between the I.R.A. and Germany (at a time when the Germans were not yet on the backfoot in the war). He was also highlighting the I.R.A.'s continued opposition to the presence of U.S. troops in the north (a position, as noted earlier, shared with de Valera).

The text was written by John Graham and Hugh McAteer. The '*Special Manifesto*' is presented as a proclamation and treated as the beginning of a 'northern campaign' (eg see Bowyer-Bell's *Secret Army*) even though the actual text doesn't support that interpretation. True, arms were being moved into dumps in the north in anticipation of a future campaign, but that was as a much a reflection of the I.R.A.'s centre moving to Belfast and a shift in priority from opposing the southern government to removing partition. The Belfast O/C, Rory Maguire, was also at the border with other Belfast I.R.A. volunteers such as Harry White, Liam Burke and Frank Duffy, readying for a reprisal action in the event that Williams' execution proceeded. Maguire's absence clearly shows that a 'northern campaign' was not about to kick off in Belfast.

By now, arms recovered by Harry White and others had been transported to Northern Command dumps being assembled at Jack McCaffrey and Eddie Jordan's adjoining farms at Budore, near Hannahstown. Many weapons were there to be repaired before redistribution. The day after the *Special Manifesto* was published, the R.U.C. raided the dumps. Jerry O'Callaghan was surprised by an R.U.C. search party and shot dead. The circumstances are unclear as the R.U.C. claimed he had a weapon but admitted that it wasn't working. Charles McDowell, who was also arrested at the scene, was completely shell-shocked by the gunfire from the R.U.C. and unsure as to what had actually happened. The claim has persisted that O'Callaghan was killed out of hand. This was all against the already grim backdrop of Williams' imminent hanging.

The full inventory of what was recovered is extensive but gives an idea of the eclectic weaponry available to the I.R.A. It included four Lewis guns, eight Thompsons (plus magazines) and ammunition, nine rifles and nine thousands rounds, fifty-six revolvers and pistols and two thousand rounds, a tear gas pistol, a wide variety of weapons parts and miscellaneous ammunition. There were also explosive materials, fuses, grenade parts and gunpowder.

Other weapons had already been distributed to Newry, Camlough, Lurgan, Pomeroy, Dungannon, Belfast, Armagh, Mayobridge, Crossgar, Kilkeel, Hilltown and Omagh including a Lewis gun, seven Thompsons, twenty-five revolvers, three thousand rounds of ammunition, grenades, mines and over two hundred pounds of explosives.[5] The R.U.C. had captured three tons of weaponry but at least twelve tons had been assembled and shipped north.[6]

John Graham (as Director of Publicity) and David Fleming (Northern Command Adjutant) immediately began to investigate the raid. They drew up a list of those who both knew the dumps were there and that Graham and Fleming were supposed to have been there when the raid took place (the O/C Headquarters Company appears to have been the main suspect). They also considered springing Eddie Jordan from custody but McAteer cautioned against it.

The huge reprieve campaign for Tom Williams, in both Belfast and Dublin, was to be in vain. From 7 a.m. the R.U.C. had closed Crumlin Road for a quarter of a mile on either side of the jail. Trams bringing workers to factories were prevented from stopping. Crowds, mostly women, had gathered at Carlisle Circus and the Old Lodge Road. The atmosphere inside Crumlin Road itself was dreadful. The republican prisoners had agreed to fast for the day and Catholic prisoners were attending mass at 8 am to coincide with the time set for the execution. After 8 am when Williams' was led through the adjoining door of his cell into the execution chamber, the chaplain had arranged that a key point in the Catholic mass, when the communion host is raised up, would coincide with the exact time of Williams execution. It broke up many of those present. Afterwards, one of those present, Arthur Corr, wrote the well-known song called 'Tom Williams' in his cell.[7]

In Belfast, pubs and shops closed for the day in nationalist districts. Transport workers and dock workers also downed tools in Belfast in protest. Many factories and businesses close to nationalist districts also closed all day, more in anticipation of trouble than out of sympathy. The R.U.C. continually patrolled nationalist districts in armoured cars. Outside the prison, the crowds clashed after the execution. As they moved off from the prison, there were minor disturbances in the city centre.[8] The R.U.C. broke up groups of people that gathered anywhere in nationalist districts to prevent crowds forming. In the south most businesses, shops, manufacturers, offices and transport companies closed from 11 am to 12 pm on the day of the execution. Many people went to church services at 11 o'clock, while some buildings flew flags at half-mast. One shop which did not close on O'Connell Street in Dublin had its window broken. Most Dublin cinemas stayed closed until 6 pm. The outpouring of emotion no doubt reinforced a sense within the I.R.A. that there was still general sympathy for it's aims and motivated it's leadership to keep going.

That evening, the I.R.A. mounted an attack near the border in Armagh in which a number of Belfast I.R.A. volunteers participated. After the relative calm since the execution, from the next day the R.U.C. carried out a huge wave of raids and arrests, detaining over two hundred men and women. Some people were chased through the streets before being arrested. The continuing R.U.C. raids led to armed confrontations where shots were fired at the R.U.C. and B Specials as the I.R.A. continued to observe the Convention policy on attacking and resisting raiding parties.

A sixteen year old I.R.A. volunteer, Gerry Adams (senior), was wounded by the R.U.C. when he opened fire at them with a revolver in Sultan Street. In Leeson Street, a B Special patrol encountered an I.R.A. unit and a B Special, firing from behind the cover of an air-raid shelter, shot James Bannon who had been armed with a Tommy gun. Bannon collapsed to the ground and his unit had to give covering fire so they could carry him away. He was later arrested with wounds to his arm and stomach.

More and more arrests followed. In Servia Street, an R.U.C. follow up search recovered a revolver that had been dropped in James Lynam's house. Both Lynam and John McNally were arrested. Gerald Hodgson (Grosvenor Road) was also picked up and charged with possession of illegal documents, while Joe Quinn and Tom Collins were arrested over the finding of a revolver, ammunition and three Mills bomb in Distillery Street. Patrick Tolan and Michael Morris were also charged with possession of arms.

Jerry O'Callaghan was buried in Milltown on the 4th September. The R.U.C. drove armoured cars into the funeral procession prompting a large scuffle but it eventually proceeded to Milltown. It was also announced that the Unionists had prohibited the coroner from holding an inquest into O'Callaghan's death.

The I.R.A. actions in the days after Williams' execution didn't conform to the proposed actions drawn up in August and so were clearly a response to the R.U.C. raids. In Dublin, clearly using the cover of the sympathy aroused by Williams execution, I.R.A. volunteers shot dead a Special Branch detective who had defected from the I.R.A. in 1933, Dinny O'Brien.[9] This was to have repercussions in Belfast and the southern government included Harry White, Liam Burke, Hugh McAteer and Frank Duffy among the suspects. The R.U.C. also tried to sustain the pressure in Belfast. On 10th September it raided 463 Crumlin Road, the I.R.A.'s Northern Command publicity bureau headquarters. Shots were exchanged on the stairs but eventually David Fleming and John Graham surrendered. The R.U.C. discovered a trapdoor into a hidden room where they also recovered the September issue of Republican News, a duplicator, typewriter, radio broadcasting equipment, six revolvers and ammunition. Graham, in particular, was a big loss to the I.R.A.. The R.U.C. also recovered publications on the *Constitution and Governmental Programme of the Republic of Ireland*, the *Constitution of Óglaigh na hÉireann*, fifty copies of the *Special Manifesto*, a memo on the Hannahstown Arms Raid, a report on the Convention held in March 1942, proposals for the northern campaign, the text of a proposed radio broadcast, one hundred recruiting posters and headed notepaper entitled 'I.R.A., Northern Command Headquarters, Belfast'. Within twenty-four hours, to make a point, the Battalion had the issue of *Republican News* captured on 10th September, re-printed and six thousand copies distributed onto the streets. The tenant of 463 Crumlin Road, a radiographer in the Mater Hospital called Sean Dynnan, was also arrested.

That issue of *Republican News*, the first following Williams' execution, stated that "…neither the passions of the people, nor the fiery demand for action of the Volunteers, will make the Army authorities enter into hasty or unplanned action." This seems to confirm that there was no formal 'northern campaign' planned for the immediate future. At the time, the loss of Graham and other members of the Headquarters Company, the special intelligence unit, was believed to be down to treachery. Specifically, it was alleged that the Belfast communists who had worked with the I.R.A. in the Republican Club from 1939 to 1941 were now assisting the R.U.C. to target the I.R.A.. They claimed the Battalion planned to shoot a number of them, only to be denied permission by Hugh McAteer.[10] If nothing else, even as a rumour, it shows the depth of the tensions between the I.R.A. and communists in Belfast.

The Battalion's attempt to kickstart a northern campaign came a month later. On the night of 30th September, I.R.A. volunteers opened fire on two plainclothes R.U.C. constables on patrol at the junction of Whiterock Road and Britton's Parade, wounding one in the foot. The R.U.C. returned fire. The I.R.A. unit eluded the R.U.C. follow-up raids in the district.[11] However, Mick Quille, from G.H.Q. was picked up in North Queen Street on 2nd October. He was promptly shoved over the border to the Gardaí. They wanted to bring him in front of the Special Criminal Court over the shooting of Dinny O'Brien. If Quille refused to recognise the court, he was almost guaranteed to be executed.

That first week of October saw a series of attacks by the I.R.A. across Belfast that are more consistent with the operations originally proposed in August.[12] On the Tuesday night (6th October), a bomb in Raglan Street injured three R.U.C. constables and two children.[13] On the Wednesday night, the I.R.A. threw a bomb on Cullingtree Road, then detonated a second at the entrance to Cullingtree Road Barracks.[14] A seventeen-year-old was injured in the side by splinters from the bomb.[15] The next night, an R.U.C. constable was shot and wounded when the I.R.A. opened fire on an R.U.C. patrol in the Cullingtree Road. The same night a bomb was thrown at an R.U.C. patrol between Upper Library Street and Kent Street. The bomb fell behind an air raid shelter onto waste ground. The R.U.C. then fired shots at the I.R.A. volunteers who threw the bomb but no-one was injured.

On the Friday afternoon Dawson Bates, as Minister of Home Affairs, put part of the Falls Road under curfew from 8.30 pm to 6 am. The curfewed area was delimited by the Grosvenor Road from Durham Street to the Falls Road itself, from there down Divis Street as far as the Barrack Street junction, then along Barrack Street and Durham Street to the Grosvenor Road.[16] The R.U.C. continued to raid within the curfew area over the

Friday night and Saturday morning, detaining nine people. On the Friday night a bomb was thrown at Shankill Road R.U.C. Barracks, outside the curfewed area. It shattered the windows but caused no injuries.

That night the I.R.A. Chief of Staff, Hugh McAteer, had arranged to pay a visit to an old school friend, who was an R.U.C. constable, to see if he could be of any use to the I.R.A.. Instead, the constable had informed his colleagues and McAteer and his Director of Intelligence, Gerard O'Reilly, were picked up by the R.U.C. McAteer felt particularly foolish at the circumstances of his arrest.

On the Saturday night there were two further bomb attacks. In Raglan Street (inside the curfewed area) a bomb was thrown at an R.U.C. patrol just as the curfew started. The blast broke some windows but there were no injuries. The R.U.C. opened fire with revolvers at the I.R.A. unit involved but did not manage to hit them or detain them. The predictable searches followed within the curfewed area and seven arrests were made.

A couple of hours later an I.R.A. unit threw a bomb at Donegall Pass R.U.C. Barracks. The bomb fell short and detonated in the middle of the street shattering windows in the barracks and surrounding shops. Five people received minor injuries, including three women. The crowd in adjoining Shaftesbury Square then scattered as the R.U.C. Constables ran out of the barracks and fired off shots. This alerted B Specials on patrol on Botanic Avenue. More shots were fired as the men who threw the bomb were believed to have run up Botanic Avenue. One passer-by who saw the bomb exploding said he didn't see anyone except the R.U.C. fire shots and it isn't entirely clear if the I.R.A. returned fire.[17] Whoever fired the shots, two B Specials, James Lyons and Joseph Jackson, were seriously wounded. Jackson was shot in the side while Lyons was shot in the chest and died in hospital during the night. Following Lyons death and with McAteer in the hands of the R.U.C., the I.R.A. attacks more or less ceased in Belfast.

A series of arms finds were made in Ardoyne in mid-October, the first near Ligoniel Barracks on Monday 11th, two in Etna Drive on the Thursday and at a garage the next day, then at Belsheda Park and Holmdene Gardens the following weekend. More arms were found in Clyde Street later in the month. By mid-October the further raids, arrests, internments and sentenced prisoners had pushed Crumlin Road beyond bursting point and two hundred and fifty internees were shipped off to the eighteenth century dungeon of Derry Gaol.

At the Communist Party's congress in Belfast at the end of the month, Billy McCullough launched an attack on the I.R.A. claiming it was assisting 'the enemies of progress' and 'condemning in the strongest possible terms acts of terrorism by the I.R.A.'. Coming in the wake of Williams' execution, the widespread R.U.C. raids, several hundred arrests and the curfew, McCullough's comment could only further sour relations between the I.R.A. and the communists in Belfast.[18] Earlier the same month the communists had also criticised workers for going on strike.

Unionists also continued to mount attacks without fear of arrest. On Wednesday 28th October, a bomb was thrown at St. Brigid's Parochial House in Derryvolgie Avenue. It struck the roof and rolled down onto the ground at the front door where it detonated. It damaged windows and doors and blew debris into the house. The two resident priests were inside but were unhurt. The bomb was a homemade canister. This seems to have been the last such attack for some time.[19]

On the 30th October, I.R.A. attacks resumed in Belfast when a bomb exploded outside the Harbour Police Station in Corporation Square. Two men had been seen placing the bomb beneath a recruiting poster. The R.U.C. fired shots after them but were unable to apprehend them. Separately, the R.U.C. challenged two men in Herbert Street in Ardoyne who dropped a Mills bomb as they ran off, injuring nine people. That same day, the Unionists had moved the writ for a Falls by-election to replace Richard Byrne.

Eamonn Donnelly, who had been Fianna Fáil's director of elections and had been sent north as an envoy of the Belfast Reprieve Committee in August, stood as a 'republican' (the I.R.A. believed that, ironically, Fianna Fáil was trying to capitalise on the sentiment aroused by William's execution). Donnelly signed the oath committing him to sit in Stormont if elected. The reprieve campaign had cost the I.R.A. £500 and some £70 more had been raised but the I.R.A. struggled to keep it out of the hands of Donnelly and Fianna Fáil.[20] John Glass, the candidate for Labour in 1938, stood again, while George McGouran was to be the Nationalist Party candidate. Donnelly's backers included a prominent G.A.A. figure in Sean McKeown and Dr John Harrington (who had driven Liam Burke away in his car when he escaped from Crumlin Road in 1941).

Two days later, a bomb was thrown over the wall of a British army billet but did no damage.[21] The Falls by-election took place on Saturday 7th November and Eamonn Donnelly won comfortably. Donnelly then announced that, despite the oath, he would not take his seat.

---

[1] On 26th May, a former British soldier (and Dunkirk veteran), John Smith, was taken from his bed in Osman Street by five armed men, dragged across to Varna Street and beaten around the head with revolvers butts. He was so badly injured he spent ten days in hospital. At a later compensation hearing, Smith didn't blame the I.R.A. though (*Irish Examiner*, 21st October 1942).

[2] *Irish Examiner*, 20th June 1960.

[3] P.R.O.N.I., Belf/1/1/2/129/8.

[4] Memo, Chief of Staff to Director of Publicity, Northern Command, I.R.A. 21st June 1942. P.R.O.N.I., Belf/1/1/2/129/8.

[5] P.R.O.N.I., Belf/1/1/2/129/8.

[6] Bowyer Bell 1970, p225.

[7] See McVeigh, J, 1999 *Executed: Tom Williams and the I.R.A.* Williams signed cards on the day of his execution that listed his unit as C Company, 1st Battalion, Belfast Brigade. The five who had their sentences commuted were Joe Cahill, Henry Cordner, Sean Oliver, Billy Perry and Patrick Simpson. Madge Burns was also arrested at Cawnpore Street and imprisoned.

[8] James O'Hara and William O'Sullivan got three months for riotous behaviour.

[9] A memo dated 29th September 1942 and later captured by the Gardaí indicated that this was an official I.R.A. operation (*Evening Herald,* 2nd October 1944).

[10] See Milotte 1984 *Communism in Modern Ireland*, p203-4 and Swan 2008, p92-3.

[11] *Strabane Chronicle,* 3rd October 1942.

[12] Harry White indicates that the planned northern campaign was to start in the autumn (MacEoin 1985, p95).

[13] *Irish Press,* 7th October 1942.

[14]*Irish Independent,* 8th October 1942.

[15] There is nothing to suggest that Alexander Mawhinney (the youth who was injured) was the person who threw the bomb.

[16] *Irish Press,* 10th October 1942.

[17] See accounts in *Irish Press* 10th October and *Sunday Independent* 11th October 1942. The latter contains an eye-witness report that suggests only the R.U.C. opened fire. The issues of *Republican News* around that date do not appear to make any claim that the I.R.A. shot Lyons. The file on his inquest is still closed to the public (see P.R.O.N.I., BELF/6/1/1/7/81).

[18] See Milotte 1984, p203 and N.L.I., 10a/1061.

[19] *Irish Press,* 29th October 1942.

[20] Memo, Chief of Staff to GHQ, 1st October 1942 (see *Irish Press*, 5th October 1944).

[21] *Irish Press* 3rd November 1942.

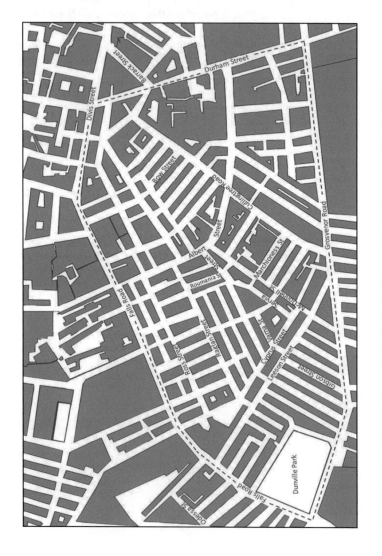

Map of curfewed district (lower Falls, Divis, Cullingtree Road, Grosvenor Road), 1942.

1943

In November 1942 the Government of Ireland Act was amended to allow the Unionists to stay in power an additional year without an election. It also continued to hand out what the December issue of *Republican News* described as 'very vicious sentences…', including fifteen years for Hugh McAteer, twelve for John Graham and David Fleming, and nine and eight year sentences for others.

Sporadic I.R.A. attacks also still took place. A bomb was detonated at Talbot Street electrical substation.[1] A few days later (on December 4th), Northern Command O/C Harry White wounded a B Special who stopped him in College Street.[2] In early January, a post box was blown up on the Oldpark Road and there were further arrests after a street confrontation with the R.U.C. in mid-January. Arms finds also continued to be made, such as one in Hamill Street in December and another in a Falls Road A.R.P. post in January.[3] I.R.A. volunteers Eddie McGeough and Roddy Hassan were also arrested with weapons in December. However, the attacks were sporadic and continued to lack any real strategic coherence.

Meanwhile, an unnamed member of the Battalion staff was taken to Swatragh in Derry and court-martialled over the loss of the I.R.A. dumps during the year.[4] He was sentenced to death but it wasn't carried out as, it being January, the ground was frozen.[5] The I.R.A. then dithered over what to do with their prisoner until they were forced to return with him to Belfast following an encounter with the R.U.C. (the suspected informer was then exiled).[6] At the same time, others on the staff were assisting with Mick Quille's defence in Dublin (he managed to get off as Cumann na mBan girls provided him with an alibi). According to Joe Cahill, just before Christmas in 1942, an I.R.A. prisoner had noticed an unlocked trapdoor in the ceiling of the washroom on A3, the top landing in A wing (it had been left open to inspect a leak in the roof). A line out to Harry White was activated but got no response as he was at the court-martial.[7] So an escape attempt proceeded without outside help.

The escape team largely selected itself. Jimmy Steele and Ned Maguire were in cells on A1, the ground floor. Steele had best knowledge of the immediate geography close to the jail. Maguire, also a prison orderly, was a roofer and younger brother of the Belfast O/C. Pat Donnelly, now O/C in the prison, was on A2. Hugh McAteer was on A3. A second team, of Joe Cahill on A1, John Graham on A2 and David Fleming on A3 were to ask for permission to visit the toilet as soon as the daytime staff appeared to open their cells at 9 am.[8] John Graham told others to take their chances and follow the second team.[9] On the morning of the 15th January, the first escape team assembled in the roof-space then escaped through the roof, descended three storeys by rope then climbed over the wall and, by 8.30 am, were out of the prison and away. Hugh McAteer was afraid of heights and so was the last man in the first team. He twice fell off the rope ladder at the outer wall. The first time was back into the prison but the second time he fell outside the prison. He was spotted by the son of a warder, Lancelot Thompson, but he didn't manage to raise the alarm in time to prevent McAteer's escape. He was in time to prevent the second team attempting to escape though. McAteer, while injured falling from the wall and unsure of that part of Belfast, eventually managed to find the safe house in Trainor's Yard in Lancaster Street with the others.

The morning of the escape R.U.C. raids took place across Belfast. McAteer reckoned, if they had used cars, the particular safe house they would have used was raided and they would have been re-captured within 24 hours. Not only had that pitfall been avoided, the pattern of the R.U.C. raids was now revealing the depth of their intelligence regarding Battalion safe houses. House-to-house searches took place on the morning of the 15th in North Queen Street, Carrickhill, the Oldpark, Ardoyne, Ballymacarrett, the Short Strand, the Whiterock and the Falls. The roads in and out of Belfast were blocked by armed policemen, while trams and buses were stopped and searched. Even bread vans and other covered vehicles came under police surveillance.[10] Under their noses, the I.R.A. used a fire service tender to move some of the escapers over to Beechmount (to Amcomri Street), while the others hid elsewhere.

On the outbreak of the world war in 1939, there had been a conscious move on the part of the I.R.A. to get involved in the Auxiliary Fire Service on the Falls to be seen as taking a meaningful role in looking after the community there.[11] As the A.F.S. had acquired the right to issue official identity cards and replace ration books, the Battalion were able to accommodate the escapers with official documents (and ferry them around the city).

On the day after the escape, a reward of £3,000 was offered for information leading to the arrest and re-capture of the escapers. Dawson Bates, the Home Affairs Minister, literally took to his bed. In Crumlin Road, there was a further alert on the Monday night when a warder thought he saw someone on a landing. Spooked by the escape, the Unionists moved some prisoners to Derry Gaol.[12]

The time the escapers spent cooped up in safe houses was turned to producing *Republican News* as Jimmy Steele took over production. The Swatragh court-martial's decision was brought to Charlie Kerins (now Chief of Staff), Hugh McAteer and Steele for their comments. They determined that there was sufficient doubt of the suspect's guilt that the death sentence wasn't warranted. Instead, they recommended exile. Liam Burke, as Adjutant-General, agreed with the findings.[13]

The value of the escape to the I.R.A. was both in the return of McAteer, Steele, Maguire and Donnelly and in the huge propaganda value. In *Ulster Idyll*, Vincent McDowell has the protagonist explain how, in late 1942, the I.R.A.'s main strategy was focused on achieving sufficient publicity among the Irish-American community that a post-war

Versailles type conference would place Irish unity on the table (clearly with an eye on the scale of protest in Congress on Sean Russell's behalf in 1939).[14] From early 1943, the Axis powers had been pushed back and the Allies had been increasingly calling for the unconditional surrender of Germany. The possibility of a post-war conference was now receding and with it, the hope that Ireland could be forced onto the agenda. Ironically, the January escape coincided with the Casablanca Conference which articulated the doctrine of unconditional surrender. McAteer drew the lesson that the I.R.A. now needed to go back underground and concentrate on actions that would lift morale while events played out on the world stage.

Liam Burke later wrote that the escape of Jimmy Steele and Hugh McAteer was a great boost of morale and that it prompted a dispatch from Charlie Kerins to Burke, instructing him to organise an I.R.A. Convention in Belfast. With that in mind it was decided to hold a staff conference on Sunday 14th February.

This took place in Seaforde Street in Ballymacarrett. Those in attendance included Hugh McAteer, Charlie Kerins, who had come up from Dublin with Archie Doyle (the Quartermaster General), Harry White (O/C Northern Command), Liam Burke (Adjutant-General), Jimmy Steele, Hugh Matthews, Jimmy Clarke (South Donegal), Jim Toner (O/C Tyrone), Frank Duffy, Ned Maguire, Bob McMillan and Louis Duffin.[15]

Charlie Kerins and Archie Doyle were kitted out with valid identity cards, complete with the requisite photographs, which meant they could spend two weeks in Belfast before returning to Dublin. Kerins stepped down to Deputy Chief of Staff and McAteer was restored as Chief of Staff. Liam Burke remained as Adjutant-General. Steele became Belfast O/C and Northern Command Adjutant. Harry White remained as O/C Northern Command and Ned Maguire was appointed as Quartermaster..

The I.R.A.'s Standing Order 8, forbidding military actions in the south was re-affirmed and a resolution was passed calling for: "A political arm to be formed representative of the whole country, whose constitution shall be based on the Constitution of the Republic proclaimed in arms in 1916 and ratified by the free vote of the Irish people in 1918."[16] But much of the day was taken up with the I.R.A.'s current reality: discussions of prisoners, issues in the prisons, dependants and prospects. There was also some discussion of re-establishing relations with Clan na Gael in America and the possible use of publicity and radio transmitters again to challenge the orthodoxy of a media controlled by the I.R.A.'s political opponents.

The Convention also had a major surprise. Since October 1942, in a plan devised by Billy Graham and Eddie Steele, a tunnel had been started in the cell of Harry O'Rawe and Jimmy O'Hagan in the Derry Gaol.[17] A fifteen foot shaft had been sunk and then an eighty foot tunnel burrowed out towards a house in Hardinge Street. Communication in and out of the jail was by secret text between the lines of letters to Annie Hamill from her fiancé, Paddy Adams, who was O/C of the prisoners (she was also a sister of another internee, Sean Hamill). The tunnel was now nearing completion having gone through all manner of problems including water-logging, a collapse (nearly killing Billy Graham), and even having to dig under a coffin. The excavated soil from the tunnel also clogged the drains and had to be cleaned out but didn't arouse suspicion.

Finance for the escape had been procured in a hold-up in Strabane on February 2nd by Jim Toner, O/C Tyrone, and his Adjutant, Joe Carlin. It netted £1,500 but Toner and Carlin had not been informed of the intended use for the money.[18] The outside operation would be staffed by the likes of Liam Burke, Harry White, Jimmy Steele, Ned Maguire and Louis Duffin. Toner and Jimmy Clarke would help organise back-up. Word was sent in that the escape was to take place on the Saturday morning, 21st March, at 8.30 am.

Twenty men were to attempt to escape, supported by the waiting I.R.A. units in Derry and across the border in Donegal. Selection was based on those who would commit to reporting back for duty to Northern Command after the escape. Once the twenty had passed through the tunnel, any other internee was free to follow them and make their own way to safety.

On the morning of the escape, the prisoners found that the mouth of the tunnel had been blocked. As time wound down to the escape the idea had begun to take hold that the authorities' failure to uncover the tunnel was a ruse and the plan was simply to shoot the internees as 'escapers' as they emerged. So, on discovering the tunnel blocked, they assumed the escape was over. Outside, Liam Burke and Jimmy Steele, waiting with a furniture lorry to remove the escapers, were unaware of any of the dramas inside the prison as the agreed time of 8.30 am approached. By now, the prisoners had realised that the tunnel was blocked by two bags of coal which were then transported back through the tunnel and into the prison clearing the way for the escape.

The prisoners then began to emerge from the tunnel and, much to the Logue family's shock, ran through the house into the road. Kevin Kelly remembers that Joseph Logue had stood with one leg in his trousers in the parlour as they ran through. When he reached the street he saw Liam Burke and Cathal McCusker and, even sixty years later, remembered the feeling of elation and how fresh the air was after being inside (Derry Gaol was notoriously dark and damp). Kelly himself says "You could never describe the feeling."

Liam Burke handed Kelly a revolver and directed him towards the van in Abercorn Place where Steele was still sat in the front with the driver. Back in the Logue's house, Sean Hamill was keeping watch over them as the other members of the escape team emerged from the tunnel. He remained there until the last man came out, even then delaying to make sure no-one else was going to emerge.[19] Meanwhile, Kelly had jumped into the back of the lorry while others delayed in Abercorn Place. To free up space Steele and Burke were going to stay in the city and return on a train the next day, rather than leave with the lorry. Maguire took over in the lorry's cab with the driver.[20]

By the time the warders discovered the tunnel, twenty-one men had passed through it and escaped. Fourteen of them climbed onto the lorry. Some didn't go on the lorry and made their way to Letterkenny on foot. Sean Hamill had remained in the Logues to prevent them raising the alarm. By the time he left the house, the lorry had already driven off. But he knew the city and was able to make his way across the border. Brendan O'Boyle was the last official escapee, while Jimmy O'Rawe, the last through the tunnel, was the only non-official member to get away.[21]

The lorry drove off, making the four and half mile journey to Carrigans with the intention of linking up with a waiting I.R.A. unit on the other side of the border.[22] The journey was pretty uneventful and the apprehension and tension among the escapers in the back exploded in a yell of triumph when they crossed over the border. They travelled on to St Johnston to meet another lorry. Instead, pursued by Free State soldiers and Gardaí, they ended up surrendering and were re-interned, this time in the Curragh.[23]

Some, like Kevin Kelly, believed the timing of the escape was all wrong and they should have gone out in the evening to take advantage of the blackout and then night-time. Within a week only three of the 21 were still at liberty. Some of the lessons learned in May 1941 and January 1943, like not using getaway cars, had been ignored.

The disappointment of the recapture of the escapers brought home the futility of the current campaign. By mid-April, according to McAteer, the I.R.A. staff had acknowledged internally that the possibility of the I.R.A. succeeding in its northern campaign was out of the question for the moment. Liam Burke had been picked up by the R.U.C. and Jimmy Steele had taken over as his Adjutant-General. Recognising the propaganda value of the Derry escape, McAteer realised that the pattern of their work was clear. Their immediate object was now to 'preserve the spirit of the movement' and that was to guide how they would plan and execute their next actions.[24]

According to Harry White, it was Joe Doyle and Dan Diffin who came up with the next idea, of using armed volunteers to take over a cinema or dance hall to stage a public Easter commemoration that year. The idea was dismissed as impractical on security grounds. In reality, McAteer and Steele were very enthusiastic about the idea and only dismissed it to maintain as much secrecy as possible.

Initially the plan had been to simply flash up a slide on screen that said "Join The I.R.A.", but the concept expanded until it became a full dress commemoration.[25] White had been staying at the house of a projectionist in the Broadway Cinema on the Falls Road, Willie Mohan, whose brother Jerry was an internee. Mohan's uncle, Frank, was also the manager of the cinema. Typically, the projection box was kept locked, but normally the projectionist went for a smoke between films which gave the I.R.A. a short window in which to go and take control of it.

The plan that developed was relatively simple but was loaded with symbolism. The public reading of the 1916 proclamation in 1943 in Belfast during a world war was clearly meant to echo the reading of the original proclamation in Dublin in 1916 during the first world war. Symbolically, Easter 1943 also emphasised the shift in the I.R.A. campaign to the north. McAteer, writing in 1951, clearly saw the parallels between 1916 and 1943.[26]

The R.U.C. were expecting some form of Easter commemoration to take place. According to the Irish News, they had turned the Falls Road into an armed camp with hundreds of uniformed and plain clothes police, armoured cars, whippet cars, patrol cars and cage cars patrolling the district. Still, sixteen armed I.R.A. volunteers accompanied McAteer and Steele to Broadway cinema where they staged the commemoration.

A slide was flashed up on screen then Steele, in full dress uniform, appeared on stage and read the 1916 Proclamation of the Irish Republic. McAteer then read a statement from the Army Council on I.R.A. policy. The resonances with 1916 were clear. While the

"…cause had not yet triumphed" he told them, "Ireland is being held within the Empire by sheer force and by force alone can she free herself. Now with Britain engaged in a struggle for her very existence, we are presented with a glorious opportunity." McAteer finished to applause. He then called for two minutes' silence to commemorate those who had died for Ireland.

In Dublin, *The Irish Times* even reported that no commemoration took place.[27] In Belfast, though, *The Irish News* enthusiastically reported on proceedings which were recounted in news bulletins as far away as Germany.[28] The Unionist Prime Minister, J.M. Andrews, who was already under pressure as being perceived as a moderate, resigned on the Friday after Easter. He was replaced by Basil Brooke. The Belfast communists issued a statement welcoming the change.[29]

But the net was now closing around the remaining I.R.A. leadership in Belfast. There were further big raids on the Falls Road on Tuesday 4th May. Harry White records whole streets being sealed off during the raids (in his biography *Harry*). He and Steele were in a safe house in Amcomri Street. On 20th May the R.U.C. arrested a large group drilling in the brickfields off the Springfield Road after an exchange of gunfire.[30]

Then, on the night of 28th May, a large body of armed R.U.C. cordoned off a number of houses at the top of Amcomri Street and captured Steele. White had left just days beforehand.

[1] *Irish News,* 30th November 1942.

[2] *Irish Press,* 5th December: this appears to be the episode recounted by White in MacEoin 1985 *Harry.*

[3] See *Evening Herald,* 7th December 1942 and *Irish News,* 7th January 1943.

[4] See account in Quinn 1999, p120.

[5] White, who provided an account of the incident, was laid up with food poisoning and wasn't present at the abandoned execution. The intention appears to have been to shoot and bury the alleged informer in an unmarked grave. It isn't clear from White's account whether others had been executed by the I.R.A. and disposed of in a similar way – it is implied by Tim Pat Coogan but he can no longer recall the source of the claim.

[6] MacEoin 1985, p132.

[7] Quinn 1999, p106.

[8] Anderson 2002 , p88-90.

[9] John Graham gave this advice to Billy McKee.

[10] Quoted in English, R. 2008 *Armed Struggle: The History of the I.R.A..* Pan Macmillan.

[11] As described by Joe Cahill in Anderson (2002).

[12] *Belfast Newsletter,* 18th January 1943.

[13] See Liam Burke in Quinn 1999, p120.

[14] McDowell (a former internee) intended the novel to be historically accurate (according to his daughter). He did intentionally obscure some names, in particular that of John Graham. In the novel Graham is named 'John Grey' as McDowell did not wish to draw attention to Graham's past.

[15] The account and positions assigned at the I.R.A. convention beginning February 14th are drawn from Bowyer Bell and Harry White's book (MacEoin 1985).

[16] Bowyer Bell 1970, p232.

[17] There are various accounts, including in *Harry* and *The I.R.A. in the Twilight Years*, also an episode of the TG4 series, *Ealú: To Hell and Back*.

[18] MacEoin 1985, p133.

[19] Information as related by Sean to his son Féilim. The *Republican News*, April 1943, names the twenty official escapees as: Paddy Adams, Sean Hamill, Liam Graham, Albert Price, Seamus P. Traynor, Seamus Burns, Alfred White, Brendan O'Boyle, Hubert McInerney, Harry O'Rawe, Cathal McCusker, Liam Perry, Thomas M'Ardle, Seamus O'Hagan, Sean McArdle, Frank McCann, Daniel McAllister, Kevin Kelly, Hugh O'Neill and Seamus McCreevey. As he hadn't been part of the official escape party, Jimmy O'Rawe's name was not included on the list, even though he did actually escape through the tunnel. The individual named as Alfred White's was actually Alphonsus White and was more usually known as Alfie 'Shuffles' White.

[20] Based, in part, on Hugh McAteer's account (*Sunday Independent* 13th Mary 1951).

[21] Coogan 1970, p185.

[22] According to Liam Burke's account in *The I.R.A. in the Twilight Years*, the driver and Ned Maguire took the lorry to the border, himself and Jimmy Steele apparently staying in Derry city. This isn't clear, though.

[23] The *Belfast Newsletter* (25th March 1943) claimed that, on arrest, the internees asked to be returned to Derry Gaol as it was much more comfortable than the Curragh.

[24] This is referenced in the 1947 film adaptation of FL Green's of his novel *Odd Man Out,* written in 1944 and published in 1945. It is a composite of characters and details of the Belfast I.R.A. Green clearly had excellent sources.

[25] This account is largely based on the accounts in MacEoin's *Harry* (1985, p136), Coogan's *The I.R.A.*, (1970, p186 – based on interviews with Jimmy Steele) and McAteer's own account in *Sunday Independent,* 20th May 1951.

[26] In the *Sunday Independent* articles mentioned above.

[27] *Irish Times*, 26th April 1943.

[28] Coogan 1970, p186; *Irish News* 26th April 1943.

[29] *Belfast Newsletter*, 7th May 1943.

[30] Those arrested included Des Brady, Joseph Doyle, William Doyle, Hugh English, John Ferran, William Gough, Bobby Hughes, Daniel Liddy, Joseph Magee, Sam McCotter, Eugene McKeown, James Mooney, Robert O'Neill, James Reilly, Thomas Russell,

Edward Sherlock and Arthur Steele. Joseph Doyle and James Mooney were wounded by shotgun pellets during the confrontation. The two Doyles, Mooney and Steele were ordered to receive 12 strokes of the whip as part of their prison sentences, which were lengthy (Joseph Doyle and Steele got twelve years, while Liam Doyle and Mooney got ten). See *Belfast Newsletter* 24th May and 4th August 1943.

Top: 1942 *Special Manifesto*; Bottom: Northern Command memo (P.R.O.N.I.).

the prisons

With few operations taking place in Belfast and *Republican News* only appearing erratically, the main focus of the Battalion now shifted to the prisoners and the dreadful condition in the prisons. Harry Diamond told Stormont in May 1946: "...seven of those young men who got out died almost immediately as a consequence of the treatment they received, and that others were taken off to lunatic asylums absolutely insane owing to the conditions they endured."[1] No-one on the Unionist benches disputed this.

Those men were released so they would die at home rather than in the prison, included Richard Magowan, Dickie Dunn, John McGinley, Tom Graham, Mickey McErlean and Bernard Curran.[2] There were confirmed cases of tuberculosis including Richard Magowan. James Doyle also died of tuberculosis shortly after his release. Jack Gaffney had died aboard the Al Rawdah. Diamond's figure of seven appears conservative, as at least twelve such deaths are known. Two other Belfast I.R.A. volunteers, Joe Malone and Terence Perry, died in Parkhurst Prison.

According to Billy McKee, after the escape in January 1943, the warders selected for duty in A wing, in particular, were chosen for their physicality and brutality. Prisoners could expect rough treatment, were placed on punishment for anything and had their cells searched and tossed at least twice a week, every week. Tossing the cell – throwing everything onto the floor in a heap – served no purpose other than to humiliate the prisoner.[3] The use of solitary confinement and the number one diet (a fifth of the recommended calorie intake) was commonplace after January 1943. Official punishment also meant receiving marks that counted against remission. Some prisoners were also given the birch (or whipped).

In June 1943, six prison staff were sacked over the January escape. This also triggered what Joe Cahill refers to as Lancelot Thompson's 'reign of terror' that lasted three years. In June 1943 there were 491 sentenced prisoners and internees, 366 of whom were from West Belfast alone.[4] In the late spring and summer that year, there was continued debate within the I.R.A. in A wing over how to challenge prison authorities and how to mount a suitable protest. The escape had ended a policy of unofficial recognition of the political status of the prisoners outside D wing. John Graham, as O/C, and others on his staff, like his Adjutant David Fleming, were unhappy with the idea of a hunger strike.

Graham and Fleming thought the Unionists would not back down, would disregard any negative publicity or external pressure and happily let prisoners die. This was likely based on their experience of the authorities' attitude towards the individuals who had already died due to conditions in the prison, and the way the Unionists had resisted pressure not to execute Tom Williams.

As the authorities effectively recognised the political status of the internees in D wing, the I.R.A. prisoners in A wing thought that political status was an achievable goal. During June 1943, a level of political status was given to the small group of I.R.A. prisoners in Portlaoise. They had been refusing to wear prison clothing since 1940. As they had been sentenced by a military tribunal, they claimed they were political prisoners not convicts. The punishment regime was severe and was also believed to be directed straight from the Fianna Fáil government and de Valera.[5]

The, admittedly limited, achievement of the two years long Portlaoise campaign suggested a strip strike had some merit to it and it started on 16th June.[6] The prisoners demanded that "On behalf of all sentenced Republican prisoners in this prison I demand that we be given the treatment usually accorded to prisoners of war. For justification of this demand, if any be needed, I refer you to the Hague Convention of 1899 which defines the rights of a guerrilla army, and to the convention of 1907, at which 44 nations re-affirmed the definition. If this demand is not acceded to we shall, by every means in our power, fight against the routine of criminal treatment. As part of our right we demand that we be allowed the full exercise of our native language, i.e. the writing and receiving of letters in Gaelic, that our confiscated Gaelic books be restored, that Gaelic periodicals be allowed into the prison, and all other rights which are at present denied to us. David Fleming, Adjutant."

The initial prospects of a deal with the authorities looked bleak. John Graham, the prisoners O/C, had to get medical attention for a broken knee-cap.[7] In mid-August he returned and there was a difference of opinion on whether his medical condition meant he should re-join the strike (he had lost so much weight in hospital he was tested for tuberculosis). In the end he did return to the strike. His knee gave way again and, since they had got no publicity or momentum, he appears to have pushed for the strike to end.[8] He, optimistically, requested that the prison authorities permit him to meet five other prisoners to discuss the strike. The authorities agreed. In effect, despite the Unionist's public position, facilitating Graham's staff to meet was effectively recognising their political status. The I.R.A. staff overlooked this point and ended the strike. Jimmy Steele writing about the strike ten years later said, "Even if it is only a small thing you have a feeling you have beaten them". The prison authorities believed their own tactics were a success. Later, speaking in Stormont as Attorney-General, William Lowry said "…we broke the strike."

By September 1943, there were also confrontations between the authorities and the women (many from Belfast) in Armagh Gaol. A commemoration to mark the first anniversary of Jerry O'Callaghan and Tom Williams was cut short by the prison staff turning jet hoses on them and five of the women prisoners were injured. Again publicity, outside *Republican News*, was almost non-existent. Even *Republican News*, still being issued erratically by Harry White and Dan Turley Jr, was really too infrequent to be of any use in raising awareness of the issues the women faced. White, at the time O/C Northern

Command, left Belfast to spend a couple of weeks in hiding in Altaghoney in County Derry, posing as an invalided merchant seaman.

Arrests saw more and more men ending up in the prisons. Amongst other arrests, Louis Duffin was searched while carrying a loaded revolver in June. Thomas McArdle, one of the Derry escapers, was picked up in Belfast in September. In August, a dump being moved was given away and two women (Agnes McLaughlin and her daughter Mabel) were arrested along with Dan Diffin. Diffin got seven years, the McLaughlin's both got two years. The local priest had discovered the dump was being held for emergencies in the local parish hall and had demanded it be moved.

Funds were non-existent again. An I.R.A. raid on a payroll delivery at Clonard Mill in Odessa Street on 1st October went badly wrong. A three man unit tried to intercept money being carried back to the office by a company clerk, accompanied by an R.U.C. constable, Patrick McCarthy. Discovering that the money had been deposited in the safe, they attempted to gain entrance. When McCarthy tried to pull his gun, he was shot in the chest. He was rushed across the road to the Royal Victoria Hospital but died before he got there.[9] The R.U.C. claimed that the three men involved were supported by up to ten lookouts and they carried out intensive raids holding more than twenty men immediately afterwards.

Then, on 20th November, Hugh McAteer was spotted by the R.U.C. on the Falls Road and arrested. In Dublin, Charlie Kerins, who was Deputy Chief of Staff, took over from McAteer while White was recalled to Belfast from Altaghoney.

Meanwhile the Armagh internees had decided to go on a hunger strike, which started the day after McAteer's arrest. The physical condition of the prisoners prior to the strike was already poor. Madge Burns and others had to abandon it as they were in such poor physical shape. Two had already had to drop out by 1st December. Censorship ensured there was no external support campaign, while the I.R.A. was also re-organising following McAteer's arrest. This was brought home when Teresa Donnelly, who had a weak heart, was so ill that she was given the last rites. After twenty-two days, on 13th December, starved of publicity and having weighed the risk of a fatality against the likelihood of success, word appears to have been sent in to call off the hunger strike. The only positive outcome from the strike was that, after an interval, the authorities allowed the women to share cells. Some lessons from the hunger strike were also learned by the male prisoners (while some lessons were not learned).

Now back in Belfast, Harry White was passed further information by Frank Moyna on the loss of the dump that had led to Dan Diffin's arrest. Moyna had received the information from the same R.U.C. sources who had advised him about Dan Turley. On this occasion, Moyna passed on the news that the Sheriff Street dump had been given away by Hugh McAteer. White investigated what he had been told. An I.R.A. inquiry discovered that a local in Sherriff Street had found out about the dump then followed the McLaughlin's when they moved the arms. Afterwards he gave all three away to the R.U.C. for a small sum of money. As he had T.B., the I.R.A. didn't take any action against him. White had also sent the information from Moyna about McAteer in to Jimmy Steele in Crumlin Road for an opinion. He laughed at it.

[1] *Stormont Hansard*, 21st May 1946.

[2] McGuffin 1973, p75. Details on Curran were also given by Harry Diamond in Stormont on 30th October 1945.

[3] McGuffin, J. 1973 *Internment*, p139.

[4] *Belfast Newsletter*, 16th June 1943 (this appears to be when the prison population peaked).

[5] At a later stage, de Valera was receiving daily reports on hunger strikes.

[6] Eg see *Republican News*, No. 13, July 1943. The initial participants were James Bannon, Pat Corrigan, Robert Dempsey, Dan McAllister, James McCusker, Henry O'Hara, (all from Belfast), Sean McMahon, Edmund Tennyson. Frank Morris and Sean Gallagher. Dempsey and Bannon had both sustained serious wounds at the time of their arrest. By the end of June, Thomas Marley, Seamus McParland, Seamus O'Kane, Billy Shannon (all from Belfast), Seamus Brogan and Pat Hegarty had joined them

[7] *Republican News*, No. 14, August 1943.

[8] There is an account, apparently by Jimmy Steele, of the end of the 1943 strip strike in *Resurgent Ulster*, March 1954. It is the basis of the story given here, alongside other sources as indicated. The account gives the sequence of O/C's and implies Steele was on the staff.

[9] This robbery also features in Laurie Green's novel, *Odd Man Out* (which implies the raid was led by Hugh McAteer or Rocky Burns). It is possible Harry White led the raid (and prompted his departure to Altaghoney). I.R.A. documents captured in William Burns house in June 1944 (see *Belfast Newsletter*, 7th March 1945) included requests to take action against warders. An undated robbery to be carried out by Frank Duffy and Louis Duffin is also mentioned in the memo (it must predate Duffin's arrest in June 1943). A week before the Clonard Mill robbery, James Kettle was shot in the thigh in Leeson Street. The R.U.C. arrested eighteen men but there was no public claim made of I.R.A. involvement.

Rocky

Rocky Burns, who had escaped from Derry, recaptured and then interned in the Curragh, was now persuaded to resign from the I.R.A., sign out of the Curragh and rejoin the I.R.A. He returned to Belfast in May and became Belfast O/C after Steele's arrest.[1] While there was still some semblance of a Battalion left after the raids of 1942 and the first half of 1943, the Battalion was now no longer in a position to mount operations of any significance. Burns himself had several narrow shaves. On one occasion, he was sat on a trolley bus when an R.U.C. man told him there was a problem with his identity card. As Burns gripped his revolver he asked the R.U.C. man what he thought he should do with it. He advised him to get it changed and let Burns go on his way.

In early February 1944 he was using safe houses in Ballymacarrett and Ardoyne. He left Albert Price in Ardoyne on the morning of the 11th February en route to meeting Liam Perry, Harry O'Rawe and Harry White in a bar on Francis Street that evening. He was stopped by two R.U.C. detectives leaving the Continental Café on Castle Street, although initially it didn't appear that they recognised him. As they were walking along Chapel Lane on the way to Queen Street barracks, Burns broke away from the two detectives and, drawing a revolver, tried to make good his escape. He hadn't known that a third policeman had been walking behind him the whole time. This R.U.C. man shot him four times in the stomach and chest and he died the next day. Burns was such a larger than life figure that his death was keenly felt. Harry White again went underground to Altaghoney in March. Harry O'Rawe appears to have taken over as Belfast O/C.[2]

With the R.U.C. observing proceedings, the lead at Burns' funeral was largely taken by Eamonn Donnelly and the former Belfast O/C Hugh Corvin. Donnelly and Corvin were both prominent in the Green Cross which supported internees dependents and raised and spent over £10,000 in 1943 alone. Later that year, Corvin and others were actively criticising the I.R.A. over its past treatment of Dan Turley and agitating for his case to be reconsidered. Jimmy Steele wrote out to Harry White from Crumlin Road advising that he and Joe McGurk would be happy to provide evidence and that it should happen as soon as they got out.[3]

Among the imprisoned I.R.A. volunteers, Liam Burke had taken over as O/C in A wing. He didn't have the same reservations as John Graham about hunger striking for political status despite the experience of the Armagh women a few months beforehand. Unlike the women, though, who started en masse, the men would join in smaller groups at intervals. In theory, this would spread the crisis periods out and allow pressure to build on the authorities. It placed a lot of strain on those in the first group but, as with the 1981 hunger strike, it meant that, even in the event of deaths, the authorities would face repeated crises over months instead of one big crisis over a couple of weeks. The flaw in a mass hunger strike is that it reaches crisis point once the first hunger striker's health has eroded to the point where death was likely. If the authorities could weather that initial storm, all of the hunger strikers would either die or have to pull back from the brink over a short period of time.

Having decided on joining in stages, the first group began refusing food on the 22nd February. The prison authorities delivered food and milk to their cells every day. The will power required to continue a hunger strike in the cold cells of Crumlin Road must have been formidable. The prison authorities also refused to supply the hunger strikers with warm water, which was the common practice elsewhere in Britain and India during hunger strikes. Indeed, the prison staff subjected the prisoners to a punishment regime and removed all water from their cells except between 7.30 am and 10.30 am, 12 pm to 2.30 pm and 3.45 pm to 5 pm. The prison staff also subjected the strikers to two to three searches a week, including strip searches, despite the fact they were no longer allowed out of their cells.

The first of the hunger strikers had already been moved to the prison hospital by 16th March (by then eighteen men were on hunger strike). On the 16th March, William Lowry, now the Unionist Home Affairs Minister, reported that the "...condition of these men is only what could be expected after such a prolonged period without food. The Government cannot accept any responsibility for the actions of these men..".[4]

On 16th March, Nationalist M.P. T.J. Campbell presented inaccurate information on the hunger strike in Stormont, without being contradicted, illustrating how the authorities were keeping a firm lid on news of the strike to stop it gaining publicity.[5] By 22nd March, the *Irish Times* was reporting that Liam Burke, Pat McCotter, Hugh McAteer and Jimmy Steele were all weak after 30 days on hunger strike and had abandoned the strike. That story was not true but it was becoming painfully obvious to the I.R.A. prisoners that censorship was preventing the strike having any impact on public opinion.

When the forty day mark was passed, the I.R.A. staff debated the futility of continuing when the chance of fatalities was now growing ever higher. On the forty-fourth day, it seems the I.R.A., rather than the hunger strikers, called for an end to the strike (Joe Cahill states that the decision was "...taken to bring them off.") The absence of media reporting or any meaningful public support campaign on the outside is crucial to the success of a hunger strike and, like the hunger strike in Armagh and strip strike the previous year, the I.R.A. staff were decisive once it was clear that they would only be continuing the protest needlessly.

The day the strike ended was the 6th April, which was Holy Thursday that year. The Easter weekend ended equally grimly. On the Bank Holiday Monday, the 10th April, a 16 year old Fianna member, Sean Doyle, was killed by a bullet discharged during a weapons lecture in the kitchen of his family home in Britton's Drive.[6] His older brother, Liam, was in A wing. In a follow up search of the house, seven Mills bombs, one hundred and thirty rounds of rifle ammunition and thirty assorted rounds were found concealed in a cavity wall. Sean and Liam's father James was arrested and charged with possession.

Sean Doyle's death showed that the I.R.A. had kept sufficient structures and arms dumps in place to continue training. It was also still capable of carrying out other actions. In the aftermath of Doyle's death, five youths were held at gun point in a recreation club at the bottom of the Whiterock Road and had tar and feathers poured over them. The R.U.C. followed up by raiding hundreds of houses. Jack McNally, who had reached his limit during internment and decided to sign out, immediately sought out the Battalion O/C and asked for the practice to stop.[7]

In the south, de Valera had tried to steamroller the I.R.A. out of existence. Charlie Kerins, the I.R.A. Chief of Staff, was arrested in Dublin in mid-June. He was swiftly tried and later hanged on 1st December. Harry White took over as Acting Chief of Staff after Kerins' arrest although White was uncertain as to whether he needed to convene an Army Convention to be formally recognised since he had little contact with Dublin.[8]

In Crumlin Road, the prisoners continued to receive 'rough treatment'. An incident, a couple of months after the end of the hunger strike, gives a graphic example of what that rough treatment could be.[9] On Thursday 15th June, a group of prisoners were at the receiving end of beatings from the prison staff, including Gerry Adams and David Fleming. Adams was punched and kicked to and from the doctor and then again to and from the governor's office. Fleming was batoned until he collapsed, bleeding heavily from a head wound then dragged into Hugh McAteer's (empty) cell on A1 and beaten by a group of warders. McAteer returned to his cell to find that "...the west wall of my cell was spattered with blood over a space of 42 square feet...". Adams and Fleming received three days' bread and water punishment.

Harry White, now both O/C Northern Command and Acting Chief of Staff, maintained communications in and out of the prison and returned to Belfast from Altaghoney that August. As word got out about the continued beatings, the I.R.A. prisoners demanded some support from outside.[10] White started monitoring the movements of prison officers. But a friendly warder advised the I.R.A. prisoners that White had been spotted. White retorted that he had to do it himself as he had no-one else to help him. So a number of internees, including Johnny Murphy, signed out from Crumlin Road during the autumn to replenish the Northern Command and Belfast staff. A small dump containing two revolvers and ten incendiary bombs was found in Ardoyne and led to Thomas McGlinchey being sentenced to five years in November.

Republican News was still appearing, produced by White and Dan Turley's son, also called Dan, in Turley's home in Drew Street. According to White they issued 7,000 copies of each edition. During 1945, rather than waiting until Steele and McGurk were released, White went ahead and reconsidered Dan Turley senior's case. As part of his inquiries he had Frank Moyna detained and interrogated him in Dan Turley Jr's house in Drew Street. While White seems to have effectively acknowledged Turley's innocence, he doesn't seem to have formally done so perhaps as he was uncertain as to the legality of his position as Chief of Staff. As it was, unable to decide whether Moyna had only been passing on what he thought was sound intelligence in good faith or was actively conspiring with the

R.U.C., White let him go. As a precaution, an arms dump in Turley's house was immediately moved by White and his brothers.

At the start of March, in an attempt to resolve the confusion over the role of Chief of Staff an attempt was made to rebuild Dublin G.H.Q. with Paddy Fleming installed as Chief of Staff in Dublin (brother of David Fleming). Harry O'Rawe was then captured on 6th March 1945 and Johnny Murphy appears to have taken over as Battalion O/C.[11] An I.R.A. organiser from G.H.Q. in Dublin, Gerry McCarthy, visited Belfast and strengthened the link to G.H.Q.. So White returned to hiding with the O'Kanes in Altaghoney. In Belfast, Murphy, Barney Boswell and John Bradley formed the Belfast staff.

---

[1] Harry White had previously signed out the same way (see his memoir *Harry*).

[2] It is implied by White in *Harry* that O'Rawe took over from him – I am suggesting it happened in April 1944.

[3] Memo, O/C 2nd Battalion, No. 4 Area, to O/C Northern Command, 20th November 1944 (P.R.O.N.I., Belf/1/1/2/139/5).

[4] This was an answer given in response to a question about the hunger strike by T.J. Campbell. Stormont *Hansard*, 16th March 1944.

[5] Campbell's figures are unreliable as he also states that the strike had been going on for 15 or 16 days, when it had begun 23 days earlier (this was stated during the same session in Stormont by Jack Beattie).

[6] *Irish Times*, 11th April, 1944.

[7] See McNally 1989, p113 and press on 27th April 1944. An 18 year old, John McNally (unrelated), was shot by four men with revolvers on 8th June. Whether this incident was also related to the tarring and feathering or the I.R.A. at all, is unclear.

[8] Memo, O/C 2nd Battalion, No. 4 Area, to O/C Northern Command, 20th November 1944 (P.R.O.N.I., Belf/1/1/2/139/5).

[9] Stormont *Hansard* 21st May, 1946.

[10] A letter to White was captured in Dan Turley Jr's Drew Street home in August 1945 (*Irish Press*, 21st September 1945).

[11] Information from Niall Ó Murchú.

preserving the spirit

In 1945, the winding down of the world war had seen a rise in the hope that the internees would be released and the political prisoners in A wing would have the terms of their imprisonment reduced. There was also sense of a challenge to unionist hegemony in Belfast. This included notable victories by various Labour candidates in Belfast in the Stormont election in July. The first batches of internees were released in the same month, and the women prisoners in Armagh were also released, with the last eight finally released in July 1945.

When one batch of internees was released on Monday 30th July, the tensions boiled over inside D wing. After the releases, the authorities claimed the remaining 184 internees had tried to hold a demonstration and order had to be restored by 100 warders. By the end of August, there were only fifty internees left inside D wing and they too were shortly released.

By the time internment was over, as least twelve men had been released early only to die shortly after their release. Six ended up in lunatic asylums, a number had tuberculosis. Many others spent spells in sanatoria or trying to get back to good health. The Unionists also perpetuated the internment through denying entitlements such as pension rights for their period in prison. Ex-internees typically found it difficult to source work and had 'internee' stamped on their Labour Exchange papers. The R.U.C. also stalked released internees warning them to emigrate. Some, like Chris McLoughlin, eventually left for America. Others went to Dublin or London. According to John McGuffin, 80% of interned republicans dropped out of the movement on their release.[1]

At the end of August, Dan Turley's house in Drew Street was raided. Turley was arrested as copies of *Republican News* and other documents, including letters from his father, were found in the house. That marked the end of production of *Republican News*. At Turley's trial, in September, it was noted that there had been no incidents in Belfast involving the I.R.A. for the past twelve months. By now, the Belfast I.R.A. was simply in a holding pattern. Seamus Twomey seemingly took over as Battalion O/C in late 1945 after his release, with the likes of Johnny Murphy now filling roles on the token Northern Command staff.[2]

After the last internees had been released, only sentenced prisoners remained in Crumlin Road. David Fleming was on the receiving end of another beating and then petitioned for his release in February 1946. He even sent the I.R.A. Chief of Staff his resignation so he could write to the authorities and demand his own release.[3] At least the lines of communication from the Belfast I.R.A. to the Chief of Staff in Dublin were functioning again. Later in 1946, Michael McCann and Jimmy McCorry from the Battalion were arrested in Dublin trying to secure some weapons. They got six months in prison. Fleming's response was to decide to go on hunger strike again. He started to refuse food on the 22nd March 1946. Statements by the Nationalist and socialist M.P.s in Stormont imply that some of the I.R.A. prisoners in A wing felt the conditions in A wing, and in his case, the beatings and forty days on hunger strike in 1944 had taken a psychological toll on Fleming. Twenty days into his hunger strike he was assaulted by prison staff.[4]

A week later, on the 19th April, Sean McCaughey decided to put de Valera's government to the test, demanding his release from Portlaoise. According to Liam Rice, McCaughey's decision to go on hunger strike came out of the blue. On the 16th April McCaughey informed his colleagues and handed a letter to the prison governor stating that he would go on hunger strike that Friday (19th), unless he was released. Another prisoner shouted at McCaughey, "What have you done, they will let you die".[5]

For the next few weeks, the two hunger strikes unfolded in tandem.[6] Externally the two protests were linked together in the public eye, yet in both cases McCaughey and Fleming were even, to a large extent, acting independently of their colleagues within the prison, never mind each other. How far McCaughey was aware of Fleming's protest, and vice-versa, isn't clear but there was no outside direction of their protests by the I.R.A..

In Belfast, the prison authorities began to attempt to force feed Fleming on 19th April, the same day McCaughey's hunger strike was to start. In the prison hospital, Fleming was badly manhandled and force fed (as Joe Malone had previously experienced).[7] The I.R.A. prisoners threatened to go on hunger strike en masse if Fleming died. The Unionists claimed, since he had been force fed, Fleming's protest only started on 23rd April (although admitting the last date it attempted to force feed him was 25th April, the thirty-fourth day of his protest).[8] As the press reported that Fleming was weak on 24th April, McCaughey suddenly announced that he was now also going on thirst strike. Clearly he was being kept informed of Fleming's condition by Portlaoise prison staff as the thirst strike would ratchet up the pressure since both prisoners were now at risk of dying within the next two weeks.

That Sunday (28th), a demonstration was held in Clonard calling for prisoner releases, and specifically Fleming's. It was addressed by various Stormont M.P.s and a cable of support from 2,000 Irishmen at an Easter week ceremony in New York was read out.[9] The two prison protests were also starting to be seen as reflections of each other, each casting shadows across both the Unionist and Fianna Fáil governments. The following Friday night, a meeting was organised by Ailtirí na hAiserige in O'Connell Street in Dublin demanding the release of both Fleming and McCaughey.

By the next day, despite the force feeding episode, Fleming had been on his protest for forty-four days and was very weak.[10] Two days later the Unionists erroneously claimed he had given up the hunger strike. Then, on the 11th May, having been on hunger strike since the 19th April and thirst strike since 24th, Sean McCaughey died at 1.10 am. Liam Rice saw him three days before he died. He said "His eyes were dried holes, his sight gone. His tongue was no more than a shrivelled piece of skin between his jaws, while his body and his hands, from what I could discern, were those of a skeleton."[11] De Valera had been receiving daily updates on his condition at least since 2nd May and knew exactly how he was dying. The Fianna Fáil government tried to quickly and quietly hurry through the inquest into his death by holding it in the governor's office in the prison on the same day. Sean McBride was ready for them and despite the attempts by the Deputy Coroner, used the inquest to ask questions about the regime inside the prison.

During the inquest, McBride exposed the government's treatment of the republican prisoners. For a week, newspapers carried accounts of the inquest and verbatim transcripts of the limited questioning McBride was permitted to undertake. To many, the episode is seen as a factor in the rise of McBride's new political project, the Clann na Poblachta party which precipitated de Valera's defeat in the 1948 general election. A prisoner release campaign and a ground swell of support for those still imprisoned on both sides of the border also grew in the town and county councils. This, in turn, prompted a debate within the I.R.A. over future directions.

McCaughey's coffin was brought to Belfast for a funeral in Holy Cross and burial at Milltown. The R.U.C., of course, removed the tricolour from his coffin at the border. By the time of McCaughey's funeral, David Fleming had been on hunger strike for fifty-one days. By late May, though, even the Unionists couldn't avoid a Stormont debate on the conditions in the prisons and the experiences of republican prisoners. Having gone to the brink, Fleming finally quit his hunger strike on 10th June. However, he went back on hunger strike again on 12th October.

Then, on Sunday 20th October, out of the blue, the R.U.C. raided O'Kane's shop in Altaghoney where Harry White had been living as Harry McHugh. An arms dump of twelve revolvers, various gun parts, three grenades, republican literature and several thousand rounds of ammunition was uncovered. White was arrested by the R.U.C. and rapidly bundled over the border, assuming the Free State government would quickly hang him. Apart from his trips up and down to Belfast, White was also visited by his sisters in Altaghoney. He used the O'Kane's as an occasional barber shop and also played in local dance bands. What seems to have drawn attention to him was the fact that he put signs up in Irish saying 'Fáilte' (welcome).[12] Johnny Murphy took over as O/C Northern Command.

David Fleming's hunger strike, which had begun on 12th October, continued for a total of forty-five days until 25th November. He was then unconditionally released by the Unionists on the 29th November. He had spent forty days on hunger strike in 1944, then eighty-one days and forty-five days in 1946.

The Belfast I.R.A. was barely visible by the late 1940s. It is not even clear how long Seamus Twomey remained as Belfast O/C. Even after Sean McCaughey's death, and with the internees released, I.R.A. volunteers were serving out sentences in Belfast, the south and Britain. In July 1946, Clann na Poblachta was formed by Sean McBride and others in Dublin. While not explicitly recognised as such, this was a further split in the wider community around the I.R.A..

The Belfast-based leadership of the 1930s and early 1940s was now scattered or gone. McAteer, Burke, Steele and Graham were still imprisoned in Crumlin Road. Other former Belfast I.R.A. staff officers, like Harry White, Mick Traynor, Charlie McGlade, Liam Rice, Pearse Kelly, Eoin McNamee and Dominic Adams, were either imprisoned in the south or living in Dublin. Sean McCaughey lay in a grave in Milltown, Tom Williams in an unmarked grave in the yard of Crumlin Road. Others had simply left the I.R.A.. Now, the Battalion kept as low a profile as possible.

David Fleming, still suffering the ravages of his hunger strikes and Crumlin Road experience, was arrested getting off a plane at Nutts Corner in September 1947. He had designs on re-invigorating the Battalion and starting a new campaign. The R.U.C. brought him back to Crumlin Road. As the Unionists grappled with what to do with him, he immediately went on hunger and thirst strike. At the end of the week he was brought to court despite being already unsteady on his feet and, after twenty-five days, assessed as to his state of mind. Even to the Unionists, the tragic legacy of Fleming's prison experience clearly weighed too heavily on him and his brother, Paddy, the former I.R.A. Chief of Staff, was allowed to collect him and return with him to a hospital in Dublin.

With the one hundred and fiftieth anniversary of the United Irishmen's 1798 campaign looming in 1948, the low point the Belfast Battalion had reached was illustrated by the 1948 Easter Rising commemoration. The Unionists were now so untroubled by the I.R.A. that they didn't bother banning the Easter commemorations. To rub salt in the wounds, the main event was held under a Labour banner. Early the same year, Sean McBride's latest political project, Clann na Poblachta managed to win enough seats to participate in forming a government, albeit with a disparate range of parties. One objective was to declare a republic in the twenty-six counties, while enshrining a territorial claim over the whole island in the constitution. For the I.R.A.'s part, the 1948 Army Convention issued General Order No 8 prohibiting any armed action against the forces of the southern government.[13] Whether the I.R.A. could bring itself to admit it or not, it was de facto recognition of the southern parliament. As with the constitutional change in 1937, the 1948 declaration was to usher in a renewed campaign by the I.R.A..

However, there was republican involvement in the Belfast 1798 committee which was chaired by Cathal McCrystal with former Battalion O/C Sean McArdle as vice chair, Joe Deighan as secretary and included Nora McKearney (of Cumann na mBan) and Leo Martin.[14] There were also socialists, republican socialists, communists and some non-Catholics involved giving a hint of the direction I.R.A. strategy needed to take.

---

[1] McGuffin, J. 1973, *Internment,* p75.
[2] This is implied by a profile of Twomey in *Irish Press,* 15th July 1972. The sequence of Battalion O/Cs after Rocky Burns isn't totally clear (until Jimmy Steele took over again in 1950).

[3] Joe Cahill and James Cahill also offered their resignation to the I.R.A. at the same time (the letters were captured on the I.R.A. Chief of Staff, Fleming's brother Paddy, later that year).

[4] *Irish Times*, 12th April 1946.

[5] Based on Liam Rice's account (eg in MacEoin 1997).

[6] The two hunger strikes, the north-south aspects to them, and the background, were being reported as far away as, eg *The Milwaukee Journal* (see 11th May 1946).

[7] *Irish Times*, 24th April 1946.

[8] *Irish Times*, 22nd November 1946.

[9] *Irish Times*, 29th April, 1946.

[10] *Irish Times* 7th May, 1946.

[11] MacEoin 1997, p538 (this account of the events inside Portlaoise on 11th May is largely based on Liam Rice's account).

[12] My father, then in his teens, lived a couple of miles away and knew White. He thinks the Fáilte signs also attracted the attention of the local R.U.C. He also believes White wasn't the first person the O'Kanes had sheltered in this way. White (in *Harry*) reckoned Altaghoney was given away by 'Killarney Pat'.

[13] See Bowyer Bell 1970, p266.

[14] Collins, P. 2004 *Who Fears to Speak of '98: Commemoration and the Continuing Impact of the United Irishmen*. UHF.

Top left: John Graham (P.R.O.N.I.); top right: Turlach Ó hUid (Ó hUid 1960); bottom left: Madge Burns (McVeigh 1999); bottom right: David Fleming (Kerryman, 4th May 1946).

RESURGENCE, 1947-61

rebuilding

In the midst of the problems for the Belfast I.R.A. in the late 1940s, there were some small hints of the future. Recruitment and training were still taking place, with Seamus McCallum and then Frank McKearney taking over the role of Battalion O/C.[1] McCallum, McKearney, and others that were prominent like Henry Cordner and Joe Quinn were all left-wing in outlook (McKearney's brother was a Socialist Labour councillor in Belfast).[2] It was not just on the political front that the I.R.A. was facing competition. Brendan O'Boyle, formerly of the Belfast and Northern Command staff, who had escaped from Derry in 1943 (only to end up in the Curragh) had set up his own organisation, called Laochra Uladh. After his release he had moved to Dublin and began a jewellery business. On a business trip to New York in 1949 he made contact with Clann na Gael, the republican support group in the United States. O'Boyle suggested he had support at home in Ireland and asked for funding and arms for a new campaign. As Clann was still officially affiliated to the I.R.A. while O'Boyle was not, he ultimately only received qualified support from within the organisation.

O'Boyle hadn't initially wanted to start his own organisation. He reportedly tried, unsuccessfully, to pressurise younger I.R.A. members into supporting him to be installed as I.R.A. Chief of Staff.[3] Before his visit to New York, Clann na Poblachta had been instrumental in the formal declaration of a republic in the south in 1949. The creation of the vague non-party Anti-Partition League was further sharpening the focus on the north and away from directly challenging the legitimacy and authority of the southern government.

O'Boyle was also making his pitch against a wider global backdrop of anti-colonial campaigns against Britain, including Palestine, Malaysia, Suez and others. These were taken as evidence that the small-scale guerilla methodology advocated by O'Boyle and others could bring success.

In August 1949, O'Boyle spelled out his requirements to those willing to listen in Clann na Gael. He would need $10,000, five hundred Thompsons, rifles, grenades and ammunition and the necessary intelligence and support structures for a campaign against the Unionists. The same month a Northern Action Committee was formed in New York to raise funds and procure the arms. The committee included the likes of Paddy Thornbury, the former 3rd Northern Division O/C. O'Boyle had the right contacts and flair to smuggle weapons into Ireland, despite being under surveillance from the I.R.A. to whom he lost the occasional shipment.

The renewing of connections between the I.R.A. and Sinn Féin in the late 1940s saw Jimmy Steele, still imprisoned in Crumlin Road, standing as a Sinn Féin candidate in West Belfast for the February 1950 Westminster elections against a Unionist and Jack Beattie the sitting M.P. for Irish Labour. Hugh McAteer also stood, in Derry, but as a 'Republican' rather than as a Sinn Féin candidate and was the sole candidate on the nationalist side. While McAteer benefitted from that, Steele did not impact much on the vote.

In reality, the aim of the I.R.A. was to use Sinn Féin as a platform to wrest control of the fragmented opposition to Stormont. Certainly, in the 1940s, there seemed to be a feeling that the prison struggles of the 1940s had generated political capital that had actually converted into votes for various left wing candidates as there was no current I.R.A. political project. In January 1950 the Labour party in the twenty-six counties had even amalgamated with 'Anti-Partition' Labour in the six counties to become a thirty-two county 'Irish Labour Party'. There was also the 'Northern Ireland' Labour Party to which the communists had affiliated in 1942. All of this posed an existential threat to the I.R.A. in Belfast, symbolised by Labour leading the 1948 Easter Rising commemorations.

In that regard, Beattie's loss was perhaps then seen as an acceptable outcome. In the 1940s, while the I.R.A. and Sinn Féin stubbornly remained aloof from the political stage, considerable ground had been conceded to the likes of the Nationalist Party, the A.P.L., Irish Labour party and other left wing candidates. This was to slowly change as, over the course of 1950, Liam Burke, Hugh McAteer and Jimmy Steele were all released from prison. While they (and others) remained in prison, a campaign for their release continued into the first half of 1950.

Prisoner release campaigns had attracted some support in the south and in the Irish diaspora through the 1920s, 1930s and 1940s. This also generated some awareness of the continuing abuses by the Unionists that had been criticised by the National Council for Civil Liberties in 1936 (their report continued to be referenced regularly in the press in the late 1940s).

In numerical terms, the Battalion was now down to a handful of active volunteers and kept a low profile. In Belfast, a number of attacks had been made on the R.U.C., such as Springfield Road Barracks (8th March), Roden Street Barracks (10th March), Kane Street at the Bombay Street/Cupar Street junction (30th March) and the Cupar Street/Falls Road junction (2nd April) in 1950, none of which appear to have been authorised by the I.R.A..[4]

The contemporary press did point the finger at the I.R.A., though, saying the bombings were to embarrass Basil Brooke on the eve of his official visit to the United States. Paradoxically, Harry Diamond claimed they were false flag attacks intended to provoke sympathy for Brooke prior to the same visit. Either way, the bombings allowed the Unionists to use the Special Powers Act to re-activate measures that had lapsed. An Ireland versus Wales rugby international took place in Ravenhill in Belfast on 11th March and saw the R.U.C. confiscating the tricolours of bemused fans at the border and arresting fans with tricolours at the game itself.

The fragmented landscape of republican politics in Belfast was evident at the Easter Rising commemorations on Easter Sunday 1950. There were at least three separate events held, each apparently attended by up to five hundred people. The Unionists did not ban the commemorations outright (although they were confined to Milltown), perhaps to try and gauge the way the various winds were blowing within republicanism.[5]

The first was at 12 noon, when the National Graves Association commemoration heard a statement issued by I.R.A. G.H.Q., which was read out by Joe McGurk (in his capacity as N.G.A. secretary). It called upon the people of Ireland to train and equip the young men to strike the final blow for freedom. The 1916 proclamation was also read out and a decade of the rosary was recited in Irish.

Next, Irish Labour staged a commemoration. They carried the tricolour and Starry Plough flags to the republican plot where Councillor Seamus McKearney recited a decade of the rosary in Irish, Victor Halley read the proclamation and Harry Diamond gave the main oration. Lastly, members of the Pre-Truce I.R.A. Association held their own, separate, commemoration at which the A.P.L. was officially represented by Jack McNally. Despite the fragmentation, all three ceremonies had the same format. The personal links are also startling. For instance, Seamus McKearney, an ex-prisoner himself, was a brother of the Belfast I.R.A. O/C, Frank McKearney (their sister Nora, who had been interned in Armagh, married Hugh McAteer, whose own brother Eddie was a Nationalist Party M.P.). Jack McNally was joint secretary of the A.P.L. and a senator in Stormont. Formerly on the I.R.A. Executive and Battalion staff, he had been imprisoned north and south. He had spent many of those years imprisoned with Joe McGurk, secretary of the National Graves Association's Belfast branch.

Harry Diamond made reference in his speech to the sanctity of homes being broken, alluding to two men who had been arrested and held over the Easter period for questioning about the bomb attacks in March and April.[6] One of the two men, Jim McIlvenny, was detained again during a British royal visit to Belfast that summer.[7] Another home-made canister bomb exploded outside a house in Gibson Street on 10th April but was discounted by police as a practical joke.[8] And at the end of August, McIlvenny was arrested with Billy McMillan after a confrontation with R.U.C. men on the Falls Road.

It is evident from events held after the release of Burke, McAteer and Steele over the course of the summer of 1950 that all three had some involvement in re-organising the I.R.A. in the north. Among those attending one ceilí celebrating their release was Sinn Féin Vice-President Christy O'Neill who had been central to the re-organisation of both the I.R.A. and Sinn Féin in Dublin in the late 1940s.[9] O'Neill spoke, saying that republicans had been charged with disruptive tactics and retarding progress by not co-operating with the A.P.L. and others. They denied the accusation, O'Neill said, and would never allow the national movement to swell on petty dimensions which they were able to control.

At a release ceili in Dublin, Hugh McAteer spoke of the need for rallying all republican elements into one great movement to complete the task of freeing Ireland. He said that the prisoners' aid committees and release committees had received great help from unexpected sources and this help could be availed of now to rebuild the movement. At the same event Steele emphasised how: "The British army which occupies the six northern counties and dominates the Twenty-Six, is the first obstacle in our path and we should rally all forces to make one great united effort to clear every British soldier out of Ireland, North and South."

After his release, Steele took over from Frank McKearney as O/C of the Battalion.[10] Slowly, he, McKearney, Cahill, Billy McKee, and other I.R.A. volunteers continued to recruit, train and collect intelligence and weapons. Eamon Boyce, talking about 1952, states that there was no more than about half a dozen active I.R.A. members in Belfast.[11] According to Joe Cahill, much of the I.R.A.'s activity in the early 1950s concentrated on gathering intelligence. Having spent the last few years very much in the shadows, the I.R.A. now needed to re-establish its hegemony in Belfast.

In February 1951, long after the spate of grenade attacks in 1950 had ended, graffiti in Belfast called for recruits for the I.R.A. for a rising that would take place by Easter that year.[12] In the first week of March 1951, the I.R.A. issued a statement denying the involvement of any I.R.A. unit in the bombings in 1950 or graffiti. It said, "The policy of the I.R.A. does not include sporadic outbursts of bomb-throwing or the intimidation of individuals."[13] The delay in commenting hints at uncertainty within the Battalion as to whether those who carried out the various attacks that had taken place in 1950 were acting on the I.R.A.'s authority or acting alone. Ultimately, it was decided that the 1950 attacks weren't authorised. Seemingly, only one army of the republic would be tolerated. There is an interesting footnote to this story, though. Dessie O'Hagan implies that left wing sympathies of some Battalion members, like Seamus McCallum, Frank McKearney and O'Hagan himself were also a cause of tension around this time.[14] But O'Hagan is the only apparent source for this and there is no evidence to suggest that there was a dispute with anyone other than O'Hagan. That was not over left wing politics. To accept a civil service post O'Hagan had taken a royal oath, but by doing so, he was deemed to have breached I.R.A. Standing Orders and was dismissed from the I.R.A. (O'Hagan held his dismissal against the Battalion O/C Jimmy Steele).

At the end of March 1951, the Unionists again permitted the Easter commemorations to take place at Milltown. This gave the Battalion an opportunity to show that it was re-establishing some form of hegemony in Belfast. While three commemorations had been held in Milltown on Easter Sunday in 1950 only two were held in 1951. The first, which was well attended, was held under the auspices of the National Graves Association. The tricolour and Starry Plough flags were carried from the gates of Milltown to the republican plot where the main oration was given by Jimmy Steele. The Pre-Truce I.R.A. Association and A.P.L. both were represented at this commemoration. The Irish Labour Party, with Seamus McKearney as the main speaker, held a separate commemoration. The same weekend, Sean McBride, the south's Minister for External Affairs claimed at a press conference in the United States that he believed partition would soon be a thing of the past.

In December of 1950, Geoffrey Bing, a Belfast-born British Labour MP (for Hornchurch in London) released a pamphlet entitled "John Bull's Other Ireland" which drew attention to the ways in which the Tories facilitated the Unionist government to curtail civil rights and suppress political opposition. Several million copies of Bing's pamphlet circulated and it displaced the National Council for Civil Liberties report as the main reference point for the abuses of the Unionist government.

During May 1951, the I.R.A. held an extraordinary army convention to resolve internal wrangling and confirm the leadership of Tony Magan, Paddy McLogan and Tomás MacCurtain. The result saw some, like Dominic Adams, leave the I.R.A. G.H.Q. staff.[15] The re-organised I.R.A. immediately began to issue directives on organisation. A call for subscriptions to purchase arms for the I.R.A. went out in Belfast just before the end of May (which obviously flagged an intent to renew its campaign).[16]

This prompted immediate action from rival republican groups. On 28th May, the R.U.C. found a home-made bomb alongside the wall of Cullingtree Road barracks. The nature of the operation suggests this was the work of O'Boyle's Laochra Uladh. An 'Irish Republican Brotherhood' had also thrown a bomb at the British Embassy in Dublin the previous week.[17]

An immediate unionist response to the Cullingtree Road bomb came on the 30th May. Under the pretext of a British royal visit, the R.U.C. interned thirteen leading republicans for seven days under the Special Powers Act as a 'security precaution'.[18] Those arrested included the Battalion O/C Jimmy Steele, his Adjutant Joe Cahill, Joe McGurk, Liam Burke, Paddy Doyle and Jack McCaffrey. Sinn Féin had organised public protests against the royal visit, but to make it clear it hadn't left the stage, a statement was issued (and reported in the press) under the by-line of the Adjutant, Belfast H.Q., I.R.A.: "In connection with the forthcoming visits of the King and Queen, we wish to make our position clear. We resent this visit but we are not prepared to take any action at the moment. If the police carry out any further raids and arrests and give unnecessary provocation to the nationally-minded people, we shall be forced to take action to stop these raids. We call upon all Irish-minded people to boycott this proposed visit and to support us in any action we deem fit."

The thirteen were interned in Crumlin Road in isolation from each other until the next Monday, 4th June, when they were released.[19] The next day, the I.R.A. began a new phase of official operations with a raid on Ebrington Barracks in Derry. Significantly, the first arms raids undertaken by the I.R.A. under Magan's leadership took place in the north, not the south. Publication of *An tÓglach* also re-started in July 1951. In R.U.C. raids after the Ebrington Barracks operation, an apprentice electrician, Patrick Fagan, was arrested with three pistols, ammunition and documents that showed the Battalion was indeed re-organising and re-arming.[20] The Unionists did not apparently take the threat from the I.R.A. to be that serious and Fagan was bound over for three years.

Following on from the re-launch of *An tÓglach*, a Belfast newspaper was launched in November 1951. Called *Resurgent Ulster*, its content was similar to *An Síol*. The R.U.C. still made the occasional arms find but none belonged to the I.R.A. as those arrested were not listed in the likes of *Resurgent Ulster* as republican prisoners.[21]

In another challenge to the I.R.A., a Tyrone I.R.A. volunteer, Liam Kelly, was dismissed by G.H.Q. over an unofficial operation in Derry City. He took most of the East Tyrone and Derry units with him to form the Fianna Uladh political party and a clandestine military group called Saor Uladh. Kelly was backed by Sean McBride and others in Clann na Poblachta (and the A.P.L. to which it was close). The key here, as with Laochra Uladh, is evident in the names. The 'Uladh' (Irish for 'Ulster') signified that these groups opposed the Unionists, not the southern government. The I.R.A., though, still rejected the legitimacy of both. This possibility of tacit Clann na Poblachta and A.P.L. support partly explains the apparent constitutionalism of Fianna Uladh.

While Saor Uladh was largely rural, Laochra Uladh's presence was in Belfast. It was the probable focus of the public criticism by the I.R.A. in March 1951. In Dublin, Cathal Goulding dissolved the group calling itself the Irish Republican Brotherhood while other Dublin-based groups, like Raymond Ó Cianáin's Arm na Saoirse and Gerry Lawless' Irish National Brotherhood (later known as the Irish Volunteers) were to be absorbed into the I.R.A. and Fianna Éireann over the next few years.[22]

There were other arms finds made in Belfast that do not appear to have been I.R.A. dumps. On 22nd October 1952, Frank McKenna of Cullingtree Road was arrested and charged with illegal possession of two Thompsons and ten rounds of ammunition. McKenna doesn't feature in a 1954 list of I.R.A. prisoners in the *United Irishman*.[23] Clearly, the Battalion still hadn't managed to re-organise all Belfast republicans under its banner. That was still a concern. The first birthday issue of *Resurgent Ulster*, in November 1952, outlined the position and attitude of the Battalion with explicit references to a need for unity. A statement on objectives said "..that the Freedom we seek is the Freedom envisioned by Pearse, Connolly and Mellows – not merely a change of masters – not a freedom tainted with Fascism, Communism or Imperialism – but a Freedom that will be political, Economic and Cultural to the last letter." Notably, the term 'Communism' is being used to describe the totalitarian Stalin regime here.

On the 7th December, the Battalion completed what it saw as unfinished business. In the early morning a colour party paraded in the cemetery and fired three volleys of shots over the graves of the republicans interred in Milltown over the previous few years. Six I.R.A. men had been buried there since 1940 in ceremonies subject to close R.U.C. surveillance. Later, a ceremony was held in Milltown to honour Liam Mellows, Rory O'Connor, Dick Barrett and Joe McKelvey. Wreaths were laid by the National Graves Association, the Four Courts Garrison Association and an oration was given by Tomás Ó hÉanáin (at that time chair of Conradh na Gaeilge in Belfast). The January 1953 issue of *Resurgent Ulster* noted that there were 16 members of R.U.C. C.I.D. mingled in with crowd, representing the various policing districts in Belfast.[24] The same issue of *Resurgent Ulster* explored some wider parallels, with a front page piece looking at the shared colonial experiences of Ireland and Kenya. There was also an article by a Welsh republican detailing the recent history of the Welsh separatist movement.

By early 1953, it was decided to upgrade the printing of *Resurgent Ulster* to a more professional layout. This coincided with preparations for the one hundred and fiftieth anniversary of Robert Emmet's rebellion. In Belfast, the commemoration committee encompassed a wide breadth of nationalist organisations, including the G.A.A., National Graves Association, the Pre-Truce I.R.A. Association and Conradh na Gaeilge. The prominence of Jimmy Steele and others in the Robert Emmett commemorations (later that year, in October) and the 1953 Easter Commemoration implies that the Battalion had established some form of primacy among republican and nationalist groups.

The 1953 Easter Commemoration was planned for 5th April. The return of a ban on Easter commemorations in Belfast by the Minister for Home Affairs was expected but when it wasn't forthcoming, the parade went ahead with a tricolour carried at the front and a statement from the I.R.A. Army Council read out. When the May issue of *Resurgent Ulster* reported that the I.R.A. was formally represented at the ceremony the Unionists carried out a series of raids against republicans on the night of 22nd May and morning of 23rd May 1953.[25] Billy McMillan confronted an R.U.C. constable over ill-treatment of his mother during one raid (McMillan was out). He was arrested, charged with using threatening and abusive language towards a policeman, and remanded to Crumlin Road.[26] Sean Kearney and Billy McBurney also ended up in Crumlin Road on various charges. Kearney and Frank McGlade had both been visited at work, with Kearney subsequently losing his job.[27] The I.R.A. had planned to execute a series of operations to coincide with coronation of the new British queen, Elizabeth, in London at the start of June. McMillan believed those operations had been deliberately sabotaged, presumably by an informer.

Then, on the night of 19th June a loud explosion rocked Cullingtree Road R.U.C. barracks between 12.30 and 1 am. R.U.C. Constables on duty rushed out to find a hole in the wall of the barracks facing onto Murdoch Street. The bomb had been placed in a ventilator beneath a window.[28] It was probably the work of Laochra Uladh.[29] The timing of the bomb was again inconvenient as two I.R.A. volunteers were due in court on the 21st June. When their case started, Billy McMillan would only address the court in Irish. He and Billy McBurney were bound over to keep the peace for twelve months.[30]

By the summer of 1953, *Resurgent Ulster* began to heavily promote Sinn Féin's projected participation in the upcoming Westminster elections, which were two years away. It was described as "..a bold, courageous step, especially when one considers the difficulties with which they will have to contend..".[31] Notably there was no appetite to contest Stormont elections, unlike Liam Kelly's Fianna Uladh for which Kelly himself intended to stand as a candidate (officially he stood as an A.P.L. candidate, effectively with the backing of Clann na Poblachta).

Despite McMillan's allegations of an informer, other clandestine groups like Laochra Uladh carrying out attacks and political competition from nationalist, labour and anti-partition groups, the Battalion still appears to have been relatively unruffled. During that summer, the I.R.A. also carried out the Felstead arms raid. Over 1953 and 1954, Joe

Cahill relates that the Battalion carried out successful arms raids at Palace Barracks in Holywood and Territorial Army huts. Intelligence gathering and training were ongoing. In February 1954, former Belfast O/C Seamus McCallum, now back in his home city of Liverpool where he was I.R.A. O/C, was arrested transporting five hundred rounds of ammunition and sentenced to six years in prison in April.[32]

On his release from the sentence he served in the summer of 1953, Billy McMillan confronted Jimmy Steele claiming he wasn't doing enough to weed out the informer McMillan suspected had given away the operations. A tense staff meeting saw a row between the two which led to McMillan resigning from the I.R.A.. A number of volunteers also left with McMillan. Collectively, they eventually hooked up with Saor Uladh, as did Dessie O'Hagan, providing it with a small Belfast unit. An apparent improvement in the security around operations suggested that the informer had departed with McMillan, according to Joe Cahill.[33] In Dessie O'Hagan's view the Battalion staff regarded Saor Uladh as little more than a 'bunch of mavericks'.[34]

At the 22nd October 1953 Stormont election Liam Kelly was returned for Mid-Tyrone. During an election meeting in Carrickmore, Kelly had stated that "I will not give allegiance to the foreign queen of a bastard nation. Do I believe in force? The answer is yes. The more the better, the sooner the better." He was arrested and, on 4th December, sentenced to twelve months.[35] Kelly refused to recognise the court. There was a huge outcry south of the border over Kelly's arrest. The I.R.A. was scathing though. Jimmy Steele wrote to the newspapers criticising how much "…indignation has been aroused by the imprisonment of Mr Liam Kelly, M.P., …" while other republican prisoners (including Cathal Goulding and Sean MacStiofain) were ignored despite having "… the letters PS after their name instead of M.P. …".[36]

---

[1] See English 2008, p402. Dessie O'Hagan records he was recruited to I.R.A. at this time and took part in weapons training.

[2] See Dillon, M. 1999 *God and the Gun*, p131-134. It is hard to assess O'Hagan's reliability as a source. His interview with Dillon, decades later, is clearly coloured by O'Hagan's own role in later events.

[3] For more on O'Boyle and his attempts to push for a military campaign inside and outside the I.R.A. see Tim Pat Coogan's *The I.R.A.* (on which this is largely based).

[4] See Anderson 2002, p105 and *Irish Times,* 9th March, 11th March, 31st March and 3rd April, 1950.

[5] The commemorations were reported in the *Irish News*, *Irish Press*, *Irish Independent* etc on 10th and 11th April 1950.

[6] James McIlvenny (41, from Carrickhill Place) and James Murphy (28, from Garnet Street who had been dismissed from the I.R.A. several years previously: see page 131).

[7] *Irish Times,* 1st September, 1950.

[8] *Irish News*, 12th April, 1950.

[9] Coogan 1970, p266-7 (see also Bowyer Bell).

[10] Anderson 2002, p111.

[11] Bryson 2007, p431.

[12] On 17th February two men brought Thomas Dwyer to Servia Street where he had shots fired over his head and was tarred and feathered. The response of the R.U.C. suggests it was the I.R.A. although they weren't blamed in the press.

[13] *Irish Times,* 6th March, 1951.

[14] Dillon 1998, p133.

[15] See the accounts of this period in Bowyer Bell (1970) and Coogan (1970).

[16] *Irish Times,* 26th July, 1951.

[17] *Irish Times,* 29th July, 1951.

[18] See press, eg *Irish News,* for 31st May, 1951.

[19] *Irish Press,* 5th June, 1951.

[20] See press, such as *Irish News* and *Irish Times* on 9th June, 1951 and 26th July, 1951.

[21] Such as Patrick Cunningham of Conway Street who got four years after weapons were found in house in December 1951.

[22] Bowyer Bell 1970, p302-3.

[23] *Irish Times,* 24th October, 1952.

[24] *Resurgent Ulster,* January, 1953.

[25] *Resurgent Ulster,* May, 1953.

[26] See *Irish Independent,* 22nd-23rd July, 1953.

[27] *Resurgent Ulster,* June, 1953.

[28] *Irish Times* 20th June, 1953. The same day, two incendiary bombs were thrown through the windows of the United States Information Service in Dublin (on College Green). No-one was injured in the attack which took place around midnight (there is nothing to indicate that these attacks were linked and the timings may merely have been coincidental).

[29] I've ascribed this to Laochra Uladh since it follows the modus operandi of its other attacks.

[30] *Irish Independent* 23rd July, 1953.

[31] *Resurgent Ulster,* July, 1953.

[32] McCallum was picked up on 28th January in Lime Street Station with the ammunition, some I.R.A. memos in code and an address in Dublin. The reference to him serving a period as the Belfast O/C is given by Dessie O'Hagan (see Dillon 1998, p130). That this is the same Seamus McCallum is indicated by the April 1954 issue of *Resurgent Ulster* where an item on republican prisoners lists him as J.P. McCallum, Belfast. He was sentenced, as James Patrick McCallum, to six years in prison the same month.

[33] See Anderson 2002.

[34] Dillon 1998, p134.

[35] See the December 2003 issue of *Saoirse* for more.

[36] The letter is dated 13th December, 1953, and appeared in various newspapers the next week. 'PS' stood for 'penal servitude'.

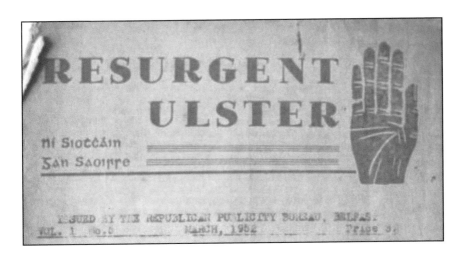

Republican newspapers: *Resurgent Ulster* (1951-1955), occasionally as *Ulaidh Ag Aiséirghe*, *Glór Uladh* (1955-56).

hegemony

The Battalion continued to strive for primacy among the broader nationalist and republican community in Belfast. Steele used the February 1954 issue of *Resurgent Ulster* to reflect on the 1943 strip strike, clearly trying to heal rifts among former prisoners. When the 1954 Easter commemoration was permitted to parade from the Whiterock to Milltown, it was led by a full colour party and the Wolfe Tone Pipe Band. Steele, as chair of the Easter Week Commemoration Committee, gave the oration and some 500 people participated in the parade, while over 5,000 attended the event. The Army Council statement read "The Irish Republican Army will not be led astray from its clear path of duty - to train, arm and organise the young men of Ireland for a full scale campaign against the British army of occupation." The commemoration now included Sinn Féin, the I.R.A., Fianna Éireann, Cumann na mBan, the Pre-Truce I.R.A., G.A.A. clubs, Conradh na Gaeilge and 1798 clubs. The colour party that led the parade was in defiance of the recently passed Flags and Emblems Act that deemed that it could never be illegal to fly the Union Jack but displaying other flags or emblems could be deemed as constituting a breach of the peace.

The contrast between the fragmented Easter commemorations that took place in 1950 and the 1954 event are significant. In 1950, the holding of separate events by multiple organisations was against a backdrop in which republicans, outside the control of the I.R.A., were carrying out attacks against the Unionists. By 1954, not only had the I.R.A. in Belfast established hegemony in organising and presiding over the sole commemoration, it also managed to involve both Conradh na Gaeilge and the G.A.A.. The A.P.L. had also fallen apart in March. It wasn't only republicanism that was fragmented as the republican groups overlapped into the scattered organisations of the left/labour/communists who stood under six separate banners in the 1953 election to Stormont.

Inevitably, the Catholic church clearly wasn't part of that I.R.A. consensus and some parish priests banned the sale of *Resurgent Ulster*. The June 1954 issue also advised subscribers that some copies sent through the post had been confiscated and that "...all correspondence coming to this office is censored by the Stormont authorities". Steele and Cahill were also organising re-unions of former prisoners to rebuild the networks that had fallen away since the early 1940s. It is probably not coincidental that these were taking place while the I.R.A. successfully raided Gough barracks in Armagh on 12th June. That summer, Sean McBride organised Liam Kelly's election to the southern Seanad, anointing Kelly and Fianna Uladh as his newest project following the demise of the A.P.L.. Brendan O'Boyle also issued a reminder that Laochra Uladh was still around. On Wednesday 18th August, a caller to the *Evening Herald*'s office in Dublin claimed that members of Laochra Uladh had exploded a bomb at the headquarters of the Royal Artillery on the Antrim Road during the previous night ('to avoid loss of innocent life'). The bomb was to protest a visit by Queen Elizabeth to Belfast. The R.U.C. said it could find no trace of the explosion."[1]

In the autumn of 1954, anticipating a ban, *Resurgent Ulster* began to be published as *Ulaidh ag Aiséirighe*.[2] It now contained extracts from memoirs that look like thinly disguised training for I.R.A. volunteers (the Dublin I.R.A. had resumed training camps that summer). These extracts had text like: "The details of a future action should always be strictly confined to those actually concerned. Others cannot disclose anything they don't know .. any known I.R.A. man never to be seen on the streets where he was known in the company of an unknown I.R.A. man, as he was unconsciously pointing out the unknown to the RIC.".

That autumn *Resurgent Ulster* also criticised comments made in Kerry about northern republicans by Liam Kelly of Fianna Uladh.[3] There was also an explosion in the grounds of Cloona House in Dunmurry occupied by Lt-Gen Sir John Woodall the British Army O/C in the north. Laochra Uladh telephoned a statement to the *Irish Independent*: "A further step in our campaign against the British occupying forces of Northern Ireland on Monday morning, October 11, at approximately 1 a.m. five members of Laochra Uladh entered the H.Q. of the General Officer in Command of all British Forces in Northern Ireland… where they succeeded in placing a powerful land mine containing over 50 lbs of high explosives… News of this operation and the damage caused was purposely withheld from the public by the military and R.U.C. H.Q…".[4]

A week after the Cloona House bombing, on 17th October, I.R.A. volunteers (mainly from Dublin and Cork), mounted an arms raid in Omagh in which eight of those involved were captured. Seven of the men received sentences of ten years for treason felony, while the eighth, Eamon Boyce, received a twelve year sentence. Their arrest, remand and trial ran through the news in November and December of 1954, along with their proposed candidacies in the upcoming Westminster elections in May 1955. The public disclosure of arms raids by the I.R.A. went some way to undermining the perception being promoted by Fianna Uladh and Laochra Uladh that the I.R.A. was inactive and, more so, hinted at preparations for a forthcoming offensive. As prisoners, Boyce and the others remained in the public eye as they became a significant focus of attention in 1955, ironically, drawing out electoral support through Sinn Féin.

Meanwhile, the Laochra Uladh campaign also continued. A report given to the press in Dublin on 8th November from the 'Executive of Laochra Uladh' claimed that the organisation had planted another timer-bomb on the night before. On this occasion, the target was stated to have been the British Ordnance Depot in the former airfield at Long

Kesh.[5] The British Army dismissed the report and denied that this incident ever took place. The same day the I.R.A. issued a statement denying in the media that it was involved in procuring arms or ammunition from military barracks in the south. In November 1954, Liam Kelly also now publicly claimed to be building up an army of his own to be used "when the time came".[6]

Laochra Uladh then mounted another attack on 14th December, 1954, when two loud explosions were heard during the night, at 1.30 am and 1.45 am. The source of the first wasn't clear but the latter was in Jackson's Road alongside Palace Barracks in Holywood. In the morning it was found that gelignite had been placed against the barrack railings and a grass bank. When they exploded there was little significant damage.[7]

With McMillan and others apparently linking up with Saor Uladh, the Battalion believed that the suspected informer in Belfast had been one of those who had left. Then, on 22nd December, the R.U.C. mounted a targeted search in which they found a box containing a .45 Colt revolver, a .38 revolver and a .38 Browning automatic pistol, two Mills hand grenades and a 350 rounds of miscellaneous ammunition in an entry to the rear of Oakman Street in the Beechmount area off the Falls Road.[8]

During 1955, having reviewed the incident, Joe Cahill decided that someone at a senior level in Belfast must have given the information to the R.U.C.. Sean Kearney has subsequently claimed the suspected informer was the then Intelligence Officer of the Belfast Battalion, while Cahill's description and other information implies the informer was Kearney.[9]

According to Bowyer Bell the Battalion along with several other northern units were deliberately allowed to decline in 1954.[10] Presumably some of that was, in part, down to defections to Saor Uladh. It is possible that there may also have been some drift into Laochra Uladh although it continued to bear the hallmarks of a lone campaign being waged by Brendan O'Boyle. Given Cahill's suspicions, recruitment and training in Belfast were being consciously slowed while the threat of an informer hung over the Battalion. Based on the increasing focus of *Resurgent Ulster* on electoral politics, though, the Battalion may simply have been placing more emphasis on political campaigning through 1955. Another issue may have been an awareness that, without an outlet, volunteers in an enlarged Battalion could become bored and either carry out unauthorised actions or demand other outlets such as armed robbery as a substitute for a military campaign. A smaller Battalion was easier to control.

In 1955, there was again a single Belfast Easter commemoration, with other organisations participating under the leadership of the I.R.A.. A parade was permitted from Beechmount Avenue to Milltown led by a colour party many wearing tricolour emblems. The parade even sang 'A Soldier's Song' before commencing. Around 200 took part in the parade itself led by a large tricolour and two bands, while 2,000 attended. Again, Steele gave the oration, saying: "The hour of decision was at hand for all who believed in Republican ideals and they look forward with quiet confidence to being able to make Ireland free from British aggression. In no circumstances must there be any deviation from the objective of organising the people of Ireland in a full-scale campaign against the

British forces of occupation." Plainclothes and uniformed R.U.C. men observed both the parade and ceremony.

The I.R.A. still wasn't meekly giving ground to either Saor Uladh or Laochra Uladh. On 24th April, 1955, an attempted raid at the Eglington Naval Base led to an exchange of shots. In the Westminster elections at the end of May, two of the I.R.A. volunteers arrested at Omagh, Philip Clarke (Fermanagh-South Tyrone) and Tom Mitchell (Mid-Ulster), won seats for Sinn Féin (which took 23.5% of the overall vote). Both Clarke and Mitchell were disqualified as they were in prison. Oddly, the runner up to Clarke, in Fermanagh-South Tyrone, was deemed elected but in Mid-Ulster a by-election was required. The Sinn Féin candidates in Belfast improved on Steele's performance in 1950 and, notably, the Labour vote significantly declined.[11]

On Saturday 2nd July, Laochra Uladh mounted yet another attack. This time the intended target was the telephone exchange at Stormont and was carried out by Brendan O'Boyle himself. When he reached the Belmont Road, O'Boyle had explosives and a detonator on the floor in front of the passenger seat. He appears to have bent over to prime the explosive device when it detonated prematurely blowing off the car roof and passenger side doors and scattering debris over a 30 m radius. The blast blew off O'Boyle's right hand and right foot and reduced his face to a pulp.

His wife Carmel and another man had accompanied him. They had left the vehicle but were only yards away when the bomb detonated. Carmel received minor injuries in the blast. Bystanders noticed her, bleeding from the face and heard the other man tell her, "Come on now, you will be alright. Don't look back." He managed to return to Dublin whereas Carmel went to hospital where she was arrested, although she was later released without charge.[12]

The Laochra Uladh campaign died with O'Boyle.[13] The main beneficiary seems to have been Liam Kelly's Saor Uladh to whom the U.S.-based Northern Action Committee switched allegiance after O'Boyle's death. Saor Uladh received around $5,000 and gained access to the arms received by Laochra Uladh. More publicly, though, on 13th August the I.R.A. raided Arborfield barracks in Berkshire and got a considerable haul, although it was all recaptured within a few days. Again the capture of three volunteers and subsequent trial prolonged the story in the public eye.

It wasn't just in the north that the I.R.A. had issues with fragmentation. In October 1955, Joe Christle and others defected from the Dublin I.R.A. unit and began to call themselves Óglaigh na hÉireann. Gerry Lawless and some of those who had been in his Irish National Brotherhood/Irish Volunteers group left to link up with Christle. The breakaway groups, north and south, wanted immediate action, no doubt inspired by press reports on the anti-colonial success of the Viet Minh and the campaign by E.O.K.A.. The I.R.A., though, was building its capabilities for a new campaign that was growing closer.

On 12th December 1955, the Unionists decided to ban *The United Irishman*, *Resurgent Ulster* (which changed its name to *Glór Uladh*) and *Gair Uladh* (Fianna Uladh's paper). They remained banned until the end of 1962. *Glór Uladh* was added, belatedly in 1959 (bizarrely, after it ceased publication). The Battalion used *Glór Uladh* to criticise 'certain individuals' who were planning to carry out actions that would be blamed on republicans. The 1956

Easter commemoration under the National Commemoration Committee (effectively, the I.R.A.), was led by the Battalion and attended by around 6,000 people with the National Graves Association, G.A.A. and Pre-Truce I.R.A. all represented. A broadening of political support also became visible as the electricians union, E.T.C., passed a resolution protesting the treatment of republican prisoners. In so far as *Glór Uladh* reflected the opinions and attitudes of the Belfast staff, it implies there was support for a political strategy in Belfast.

---

[1] See reports in the press for 18th and 19th August, 1954.

[2] The Irish translation of the title.

[3] *Resurgent Ulster*, October, 1954.

[4] *Irish Independent*, 18th October, 1954.

[5] *Irish Times*, 8th November, 1954.

[6] *Irish Times*, 25th November, 1954.

[7] *Irish Times*, 15th December, 1954.

[8] *Irish News* and *Irish Times*, 23rd December, 1954.

[9] Kearney, S. 2003, 'Joe the 'Ra and me, *Fortnight,* p8-10. Cahill identifies the suspected informer as a senior Belfast I.R.A. man, who signed out very early from internment and was alive in the late 1990s. Kearney fits all those descriptions.

[10] Bowyer Bell 1970, p340.

[11] Liam Mulcahy took 7.3% in East Belfast, Frank McGlade took 8.5% in North Belfast, Patrick Kearney 3.9% in South Belfast and Eamon Boyce 14.4% in West Belfast.

[12] See *Irish Times* 4th July, 1955.

[13] There was no lasting enmity between O'Boyle and his former colleagues in Belfast. In 1966, the National Graves Association produced *Antrim's Patriot Dead* and O'Boyle was given an entry, although he was stated to have 'severed his connections' and was carrying out what it describes as 'unofficial operations'.

the border campaign

By 1956 preparations and training were under way for the upcoming campaign. There is a hint at trouble, though, in the May issue of *Glór Uladh*, where there is an oblique criticism of Sinn Féin as being controlled by a 'Dublin Group'. Given the overlap in the leadership of Sinn Féin and the I.R.A., this relatively open disapproval coincides with a number of other changes in the middle of 1956. Around August, G.H.Q. sent organisers to the north for the upcoming campaign. Jimmy Steele stood down as Belfast O/C and Paddy Doyle (one of the G.H.Q. organisers) took over, while Joe Cahill remained as Adjutant. Given the political success of Sinn Féin and the apparent decline of some northern units since around 1954, it is possible that this hints at northern disapproval of what was seen as a campaign directed from Dublin, presumably with less input than the north would have liked. According to Billy McKee, at the time, the Battalion was not in a position to handle a pogrom (the ever present fear if a campaign was to take place). Sinn Féin was also starting to get more organised in the city. The November issue of *Glór Uladh*, apparently still under Steele's editorship, discussed Paddy McLogan's Sinn Féin ardfheis address on providing a political alternative for republicans.

In October, Doyle had been unable to travel to a senior staff planning meeting but Cahill went instead and raised the issue of a possible informer in Belfast.[1] He told Anthony Magan (the Chief of Staff) but no further action was taken. This is generally taken as the point where problems arose with the role the Battalion might play in the upcoming campaign. The suspected presence of an informer, it is claimed, led to Belfast being left out of the campaign.

A directive for the campaign, dated November 7th 1956, called for three phases.[2] In phase one, to last one month, there was to be the destruction of listed targets. In phase two, over a three month period, the I.R.A. would build its forces and continue guerrilla attacks while maintaining itself (through captured arms, ammunition and supplies). Phase three of the campaign was to see a continuation of the struggle into higher levels where the I.R.A. would control territory and thus co-ordinate through better communications. There was also an outline of the I.R.A.'s aim: "Our mission is to maintain and strengthen our resistance centres throughout the occupied area and also to break down the enemy's administration in the occupied area until he is forced to withdraw his forces. Our method of doing this is use of guerrilla warfare within the occupied area and propaganda directed at inhabitants. In time as we build up our forces we hope to be in a position to liberate large areas and tie these in with other liberated areas - that is, areas where the enemy's writ no longer runs." In that regard, it also made reference to the need for propaganda: "The resistance of the people (nationalists) can be built up by clever propaganda on top of guerrilla successes. From the point of view of guerrilla warfare the co-operation of the people is essential. If this is lost - or never received the guerrilla cannot win." As part of the campaign it suggested that 50,000 leaflets should be printed and circulated.

The planning for the campaign required the selection of five training organisers for Derry, Tyrone-Fermanagh, Armagh, Down and Belfast-Antrim. An initial period of preparation for the campaign was to be three months, to include one month's intensive course on guerrilla warfare and organisation. It called for four columns of twenty-five men each to be organised and trained, although none were to operate out of Belfast (instead they were each allocated an area overlapping with the border). The required armament for a column was a Bren gun, ten rifles, thirteen submachine guns, grenades and explosives. All of that is consistent with Paddy Doyle being sent to Belfast as the organiser in August for a campaign that would begin at the end of October.

Another document, entitled 'Operation Harvest', identified the various operational areas north of the border as Derry City, Derry North, Derry South, Derry South-East, Omagh-Strabane, Fermanagh, East Tyrone, North Armagh, South Armagh, South Down, North Antrim and Belfast.[3] It described the objectives required by the I.R.A. units in each operational area: cut all communications, telephone, road and rail; destroy all petrol stations and enemy vehicles where found; hit enemy strategic strongpoints, where supplies could be found, or where the administration of the enemy could be disrupted. This included specific lists of targets in each operating area and the areas code name, although it included neither for Belfast and several areas had no assigned code name.[4] In Bowyer Bell's summary, the overall plan was to centre around flying columns made up of the volunteers, hand-picked from all over Ireland, while the local units in the north were to provide "...the basic web along which supplies, instructions, and reinforcements could be run in from the South." The campaign was to be tightly controlled from G.H.Q..[5]

Either intentionally, or otherwise, the plan reflected the 'foco' theory of revolutionary warfare where the initial phase involved establishing primacy in rural and remote areas prior to moving on the urban centres. This had been the strategy adopted by the communists in China and Vietnam and was to be used in Cuba in 1959.[6] This differed significantly to the likes of Irgun in Palestine or E.O.K.A. in Cyprus which tried to carry out high profile attacks against British occupation and administration and attract publicity and so exert political pressure rather than hold territory. This was also the tactic Laochra Uladh had adopted.

While the new campaign had been scheduled to start in October, it was delayed by the fall-out from the Joe Christle split in Dublin. When Christle linked up with Saor Uladh for operations along the border in mid-November, the I.R.A. was still delaying.[7]

In the run-up to the launch of the campaign, during the planning phase, the Battalion was re-organised into two companies, basically the volunteers already known to the R.U.C. and the unknown volunteers. Paddy Doyle, as a former G.H.Q. organiser, and now Belfast O/C, was fully aware of the plans for the campaign. According to a Belfast I.R.A. volunteer at the time, Sean McNally, they went through the training phase as described, aware that something was in the pipeline.[8] But Doyle was arrested getting on a Dublin train in Belfast on the 1st December, barely two weeks before the launch date. Among the incriminating evidence in his possession were copies of *Resistance*, a new publication that was to be issued by the Battalion. A copy of *An tÓglach* carried by Doyle got him three months in prison. At the end of his sentence, in February 1957, he was interned in D wing where he remained until 25th April 1961.

According to Joe Cahill (Doyle's Adjutant), the Battalion had been tasked with cutting the telephone cable to Britain on the night of 11th/12th December.[9] This contradicts the commonly held story that Belfast was left out of the plan. In reality, the Battalion simply wasn't able to re-organise in time after Doyle's arrest to carry out the action. It is implied that Doyle's arrest appears to have reinforced G.H.Q.'s opinion of security issues in Belfast, despite the fact that Doyle's planned movements were also known in Dublin and could just as easily been given away by an informer there (indeed Sean Cronin and the campaign plans were captured there only weeks later).[10] If G.H.Q. had security concerns about Belfast it also seems odd that they held a series of meetings there on 9th and 10th December just before the campaign started.[11]

Doyle's arrest also reinforced the cynical opinion in Belfast as to the quality of G.H.Q.'s planning. When asked about the Battalion staff attitude to the overall plan of operations for that December, Billy McKee just laughed and said "Plan? Anybody can draw up a plan."[12] Another notable contribution made by the Belfast I.R.A. was in moving its stores of weapons to the south (which surely aggravated the long-standing anxieties about the Battalion's capacity to defend districts in the city from attacks by unionists).[13]

There are clear hints of mutual animosity between the Battalion and G.H.Q. in the run up to the launch of the campaign. Despite limited electoral success, if *Glór Uladh* was anything to go by, it appears that the Battalion was becoming more politicised over the course of the mid-1950s. The last issue of *Glór Uladh* appears to have been published around the same time that a new Battalion news-sheet, *Resistance*, first appeared. Perhaps *Resistance* was intended to replace it (although it appears it was being sent to Belfast from Dublin). There was also the discontent about the influence of a 'Dublin group' voiced earlier in the year via *Glór Uladh*. The apathy and dismissive attitude voiced by Sean McNally and Billy McKee seems consistent with this and are mirrored in the antipathy of G.H.Q. towards the Battalion.

It is quite possible that, following Cahill's meeting with Magan in October, the Battalion was left out of the plan, or had question marks over the details of its participation. Hence Cronin left Belfast out of his 7th November draft. Between 7th November and Doyle's arrest, it appears Belfast had been assigned with cutting the cable to Britain on the night of 11th /12th December. This must have been agreed between Doyle and Cronin in the strictest secrecy. As Doyle had only relatively recently taken over in Belfast, he hadn't confided the details to anyone else, even Cahill.

---

[1] Anderson 2002, p133-134.

[2] *Irish Examiner, Irish Independent* and *Irish Press* for 18th January, 1957. The details of the campaign were captured in Dublin after the arrest of the plan's author, Sean Cronin, on 8th January 1957.

[3] This name is often given to the whole campaign but appears to refer only to the initial phase of operations to coincide with the start of the campaign.

[4] This suggests that the documents recovered were not the final drafts.

[5] Bowyer Bell 1970, p332.

[6] The theory was articulated by Che Guevara (*La Guerra de Guerillas*, 1961) and later Regis Debray (*La Révolution dans la Révolution*, 1967).

[7] Bowyer Bell 1970, p330.

[8] In an interview with the author.

[9] See account of this period in Anderson 2002.

[10] Bowyer Bell, 1970, p340.

[11] Mick Ryan 2018 *My Life in the IRA, The Border Campaign*, p68. As Bryson (2007, p205) notes, the explanation for Belfast's role has shifted from fear of sectarian violence to fear of an informer, mainly prompted by Cahill's account in *Joe Cahill: A Life in the IRA* (Anderson 2002).

[12] In an interview with Billy McKee.

[13] Quinn 1999, p131.

'Operation Harvest'

The launch of the campaign on the night of 11ᵗʰ/12ᵗʰ December prompted the Unionists to intern a large number of republicans (mainly in D wing in Crumlin Road prison). Joe Cahill escaped the first swoop and took over as Belfast O/C. Only a handful of operations were carried out in Belfast over the course of the campaign and the Battalion was to be largely concerned with prison issues until the early 1960s. It is clear from the likes of Mick Ryan and Danny Donnelly that the lack of operations in Belfast was balanced by the provision of safe houses for volunteers to rest and as a transit centre and this may have been part of the reason why it suited the I.R.A. to have so few operations mounted by the Battalion in the city.

On January 8th, as the Battalion must have wryly observed, first Sean Cronin was picked up by the Gardaí in Cavan, then the draft versions of the operational plans for the campaign were found in his flat in Dublin along with a review of the campaign to date. Cronin believed they had achieved some success in the early attacks but still had problems in terms of lack of training, collection of intelligence and "…lack of understanding on the part of some of our local volunteers and the people as to the purpose of the campaign."[1] By the end of the month, Cahill too had been arrested and interned (apparently replaced as O/C by Jimmy Steele).

In terms of offensive operations, Belfast's role in the campaign was minimal. On 5ᵗʰ March 1957, a caller phoned a bomb warning to the G.P.O. in Belfast. The same month eighteen-year-old James Corbett was arrested in Ardoyne with some weapons and Battalion documents. The documents showed that the Battalion was still systematically collecting intelligence on government buildings and communications infrastructure in the city (largely in line with Bowyer Bell's summary of the function of local units in the campaign).

In Crumlin Road there was a major protest by prisoners on the 2ⁿᵈ April. The 109 internees banged their cell doors and made noise to complain about the food and to demand the extension of lights out. In mid-April 1957, Saor Uladh's Dessie O'Hagan and Paddy McGrogan tried to rescue an internee from the hospital (Thomas Lennon from Lurgan). Lennon refused to go with them and O'Hagan and McGrogan were arrested and imprisoned.

That year's Easter Rising commemoration ceremony was confined to Milltown once again. Around 1,500 attended but there were a large number of R.U.C. present inside and outside the cemetery. The tricolour was paraded from the gates to the republican plot where an oration was given.[2] The oration, by Jimmy Steele, was visibly recorded by an R.U.C. stenographer and he said "…we are meeting under the shadow of the internment camp, the penal cell made possible by the infamous Special Powers Act. Whilst there is no attempt to prevent us from meeting here… the eyes of our enemies will be focussed here to-day picking out men and boys for future interrogation and probably internment." That summer de Valera returned to power in the south and introduced internment again. A number of republicans in Belfast were arrested over the 12th July, including Jimmy Steele. Most were only held for a short time, rather than interned. However, on October 9th and 10th the R.U.C. again raided homes across Belfast detaining and interning twenty more men (including Steele). The same day a car containing arms was found at Springfield Avenue. Other Belfast republicans, like Tommy O'Malley (a veteran of 1920-22) and Paddy Collins received lengthy sentences in October for having put up republican posters that summer. While some individuals remained at liberty, by autumn 1957 the core of the Battalion was now interned in Crumlin Road. The Belfast republican involvement in the 1956-62 campaign was largely to be a prison experience.

The Battalion operated lines into the prison, through the likes of Billy McKee and Joe Cahill, using messages secreted in the spine of books. Prison trustees carried messages between A wing and McKee and Cahill in D wing who used warders to communicate with the outside.[3] Inside D wing, the internees, now with Steele as O/C, challenged the prison authorities. A proposed minute's silence on Armistice Day, to be commemorated on 10th November, was to be disrupted. When it came to the appointed time, 11 am on the Sunday, internees in D wing shouted during the silence. From as early as November 1957 Eamonn Boyce records that there was talk that Operation Harvest would be called off and there were clearly tensions among the sentenced I.R.A. prisoners in A wing, as well as with the Saor Uladh prisoners.[4] That month saw further men from Belfast interned. A press release from the Unionists in January 1958 indicated it was holding one hundred and sixty-six internees in D wing, fifty-six sentenced men in A wing and twenty-two on remand.[5]

By February 1958, the press were labelling the combined Saor Uladh/Christle group as I.R.A. 2, and accurately flagging the support it was receiving from the U.S.A. (which had been transferred from Laochra Uladh on Brendan O'Boyle's death). It also claimed that this I.R.A. 2 was also now modelling itself on E.O.K.A.. This sounded good, but in reality they were trying to operate flying columns similar to the I.R.A., not E.O.K.A.'s tactic of clandestine cells carrying out attacks then merging back into the community (tactics actually inspired by the I.R.A.'s campaign in 1919-21).

Behind the scenes, there were meetings between I.R.A. G.H.Q., Saor Uladh and Joe Christles group, leading to exchanges of weapons, intelligence and co-operation. There remained a certain amount of unease. Belfast remained quiet with its attention largely centred on Crumlin Road prison. With two hundred or so men in the prison, Belfast's part of the 'basic web' was connecting those men back to G.H.Q. in Dublin.

Joe Cahill described the regime in D wing as significantly different from his experience in A wing during the 1940s: "We had the run of D wing. The cell doors were opened in the morning and you were left to your own devices all day. Lock-up was initially at seven o'clock, but was later extended to nine."[6] That time was filled with the usual activities under elected I.R.A. staff officers who looked after the morale and welfare of the internees. This included cooking and cleaning duties in D wing, organising sports, exercise, entertainment, crafts, political debates and education.

As well as the activities that passed the time there were also authorised escape attempts from D wing. Soil from an escape tunnel in Prionsias MacAirt's cell had been difficult to dispose of, being scattered by the internees in the exercise yard from their pockets. The tunnel itself had progressed beyond the wall into the prison garden from where it was intended to escape. On Tuesday 11th March, a warder discovered the entrance concealed behind a mirror and postcards. Joe Cahill recalls that MacAirt's cell door was locked to trap those working on the tunnel, so the internees dismantled part of handrail on the stairs to D3 and forced the door open. This allowed the tunnelers to merge back into the body of internees in the wing.

The response from the prison authorities and staff was predictable. All internees were immediately confined to their cells and their privileges withdrawn. Extra warders were on duty on the Wednesday morning but Thompson, the governor, only had the normal complement of staff that afternoon. Lock-up was 8.15 pm as usual. Then, after lock-up, warders came to Prionsias MacAirt's cell and searched it. They then demanded he strip. MacAirt refused. The warders left MacAirt's cell. Shortly afterwards, the members of the R.U.C.'s Special (Commando) Reserve entered his cell and beat him until he was semi-conscious, then stripped him. The R.U.C. paid similar visits to other cells that night with the same result, tossing the cells and destroying the internees' possessions.

All visits, letters and parcels were stopped and exercise was reduced to one hour per day. The already tense situation spilled over on the Wednesday evening as the internees decided to resist more searches, breaking up tables and chairs to defend themselves. Outnumbered and poorly armed, in Joe Cahill's words, the R.U.C. "…knocked the shit out of us". A large number of internees had to be treated in the prison hospital for their injuries.[7] The battered and bruised internees were again only permitted to leave their cells for one hour of exercise. Jimmy Steele, as O/C, famously used this time to raise morale of the internees, as he "…marched and drilled them up and down the prison yard for most of their exercise period, making them sing patriotic songs until their flagging spirits rose…".[8]

In an attempt to broker a deal and restore calm in D wing, Steele met with Fr McAllister, the senior prison chaplain. Fr McAllister told him that the governor was pretty sore about the escape attempt. Needless to say Steele and the internees were not impressed.

As tensions continued, on St Patricks Day (the following Monday), women and children tried to force their way into the prison and demanded that the internees be allowed to receive visits as normal. They managed to get past the outer doors of the prison and there were two hours of scuffles between the R.U.C., prison staff and the women before they were removed from the prison grounds.

That Saturday all those in D wing went on hunger strike for a week. The stress of internment was now beginning to tell and a sour atmosphere in D wing began to create tensions among the internees. On 2nd April (Easter Sunday) 1958 there was a vote which led to further trouble in D wing and again two weeks later, when the authorities disciplined Ciaran O'Kane for slopping out in the wrong place. All the internees again refused prison food on the 15th and 16th April. The time during internment was beginning to pass very slowly.

Then, on 2nd May 1958, some ten internees were released including Sean Kearney.[9] But some were just arriving into D wing with the likes of Liam Burke only being interned in May 1958. The issue of the prison diet was raised in Stormont at various times from June to October 1958, and with the Red Cross in D wing in June. A court case over the beatings in March rumbled on from May to July.

With all the disruption in D wing it wasn't until August that the Battalion and G.H.Q. again stabilised its secure line. But by mid-October, all of D wing was again on bread and water, arising from protests about over-crowding. By 21st October the authorities announced that twenty men would be transferred to Armagh prison. By the end of that month, six more internees were released on good behaviour bonds, reducing the number back to one hundred and sixty-five.[10]

As Mick Ryan notes, Belfast continued to be used as a staging point for volunteers travelling to join units and the lack of operations meant they could use safe houses there before moving on to the intended location. The Battalion also stored weapons for use by the units and one such dump was discovered by the R.U.C. in Ton Street on 2nd January 1959. The home owner, Tom O'Kane, got six years in Crumlin Road.

On 27th January 1959, though, tensions had again re-surfaced and the internees smashed up D wing. Trouble kept brewing through until April (1959) but G.H.Q. and the Army Council refused to permit a hunger strike to take place.

The physical toll of imprisonment was also being felt as both Tommy O'Malley and Jimmy Steele were reportedly in bad health by July 1959. O'Malley was moved under guard to a hospital, while another prisoner was removed to a mental institution. There was further trouble in D wing in October 1959. Then, on 10th December, Tommy O'Malley died amidst a dispute over whether he had been officially released from prison prior to his death. In November, Sean Garland from Dublin who had been active around the north was arrested getting off a train in Belfast, allegedly en route to receive gelignite from the Stranraer-Larne ferry.[11] Garland's period of time in Crumlin Road (he was released in July 1962) meant he was well known to some of the Belfast I.R.A. like John Kelly.

In January 1960, perhaps to forestall any significant reaction to O'Malley's death, there were rumours that unconditional releases of internees from D wing would begin soon (internment in the south had ended in 1959). On 16th January, Ciaran O'Kane and Tom Lennon became the first of the internees to be allowed to go free from D wing without signing some form of undertaking. For the remainder of January and into February, two or three internees were released every few days, with no prior notice. For the men in D wing, the pressure was intense. No-one knew who would be released, when or why.

All this time the Battalion had been involved in very little in the way of operations. The Battalion had raided an R.A.F. hut at Edenmore in Whiteabbey and an Air Training Corps hut in the Oldpark and four Bren guns and seventeen rifles were taken (all were for drilling). The R.U.C., though, recovered the items from a house in Ardoyne at the end of January and made six arrests, including several boys from St Malachy's College. Robert Murray and Tony Cosgrove received sentences of ten years, while James Campbell and three others were bound over. The Battalion received heavy criticism for the arrests as Murray was only 18 and the rest were 17 or younger. Later that year, a small explosion on the window of Cullingtree Road R.U.C. Barracks using a pipe bomb may not even have been the work of the Battalion.[12] However on Christmas Eve 1960 John Kelly arranged for the Battalion to have cars ready to pick up himself and Danny Donnelly, from Tyrone, after they sawed through bars ready to escape from A wing (both were sentenced prisoners). The escape attempt didn't go ahead, but two days later, Donnelly did manage to get beyond the outer wall (Kelly didn't as he got stuck inside the outer wall). The Battalion was put under so much scrutiny by the R.U.C. that it was unable to aid Donnelly although Belfast republicans helped him escape to the south.[13]

---

[1] *Irish Press,* 18th January 1957.

[2] See *Irish Times, Irish News* and *Irish Press* 22nd April, 1957.

[3] See Bryson, A. 2007 *The Insider: The Belfast Prison Diaries of Eamonn Boyce, 1956-62.*

[4] Much of this account of internment and A wing during 1957-61 is based on Eamon Boyce's diaries.

[5] See *Irish Examiner* 28th January, 1958.

[6] Anderson 2002, p147.

[7] Bryson, A. (2007, p152) notes that *The Irish Times* reported that there were 12 injuries while *The United Irishman* reported that there were 44 injured. Eamon Boyce, who was in A wing at the time gives a figure of 30 injured, stating that some internees had broken bones.

[8] *Republican News*, August 1970.

[9] Joe Cahill (in Anderson 2002) claims the suspected Battalion informer in the mid-1950s found a pretext to sign out early from internment. Rightly or wrongly (as explained elsewhere), this seems to imply that Cahill is trying to hint that it was Séan Kearney who was the most likely suspect to be the informer (see also Kearney 2003 in *Fortnight,* No. 411). Admittedly, my reading between the lines of Cahill's text here could (obviously) be completely wide of the mark.

[10] For instance, see *Irish News* for 21st and 23rd October 1958.

[11] Bryson 2007, p254.

[12] *Irish Independent* 29th August 1960.

[13] Donnelly, D. 2010 *Prisoner 1082: Escape from Crumlin Road, Europe's Alcatraz.* Collins Press. Donnelly stayed with the Kelly's (the family of John, Billy and Oliver in Adela

Street mentioned elsewhere in this book). He also stayed with other families in Belfast prior to his journey over the border. It is claimed (below) that the number of safe houses available to the I.R.A. in Belfast dramatically declined between 1961 and 1962. It is possible that, as happened immediately after previous escapes, R.U.C. raids following Donnelly's escape revealed the extent of R.U.C. knowledge of Belfast safe-houses and made some more cautious about offering the house as a safe house.

Top: 1962 picket of Crumlin Road over continued detention of political prisoners with Harry Diamond at the front followed by Sean Caughey, Jim O'Kane and Gerry Fitt (Baker 2010).

"NOT FASCISTS, NOR COMMUNISTS", 1961-69

rebuilding (again)

When he was released from internment, Billy McKee took over as O/C of what was left of the Battalion and started a process of rebuilding.[1] The condition of the Battalion that McKee took over after the border campaign was dire. Billy McMillan states that, when the last internee was released the total membership in Belfast was twenty-four men armed with two serviceable short-arms.[2]

A salutary lesson came on the first Easter Sunday at the start of April 1961. In the mid-1950s, just before the border campaign began, the primacy of the National Graves Association (and the I.R.A.) in leading the commemoration, had been established. A tricolour-carrying colour party had led parades, in front of thousands, along the Falls Road from Beechmount to Milltown. In 1961, only the National Graves Association held an Easter commemoration and it was now once again confined to Milltown cemetery, harking back to the 1930s and 1940s. The only parade permitted was from the gates of the cemetery to the republican plot. There Tomás Ó hÉanáin read the proclamation and gave an oration. Two buglers also sounded the Last Post. Jimmy Steele led the recitation of a decade of the rosary. The attendance was reported as several hundred people. If the submission of the I.R.A. wasn't clear enough from the restrictions placed on the ceremony, R.U.C. detectives visibly mingled with the crowd, some openly photographing those in attendance.[3]

Of the various republican factions that were active in Belfast before internment, Laochra Uladh had ceased to exist when Brendan O'Boyle died. Others, like McMillan and Dessie O'Hagan had coalesced around Saor Uladh. After the releases from internment and prison sentences in Crumlin Road, members of Saor Uladh drifted back into the I.R.A. and, after spending a year working in Britain, McMillan also returned. The I.R.A./Saor Uladh rift was healed and McMillan took up the role as Adjutant to McKee.

It has become convention to dismiss I.R.A. critics of the politicising strategy of the new Chief of Staff Cathal Goulding as vehemently anti-communist. In reality, Billy McKee maintains that Belfast was wary and critical of involvement with Soviet-aligned communists. This clearly harked back to the Battalion's experience of the failed Republican Club of 1940-41 and subsequent rumours of the Communists collaborating with the Unionists. And many of those on the left were significantly discomfited by the Soviet Union's suppression of the Hungarian revolution of 1956 (and later again in 1968 during the Prague spring). The Soviets were seen as no less totalitarian or imperialistic than the British Empire.

McKee also insists that typical I.R.A. volunteers were left-wing (indeed he describes himself as a socialist). John Kelly probably described it best when talking about his own (republican) parents as "… unconscious socialists, without being conscious of terms like social justice or anything, the struggle they had simply to rear a family would make them socialist."[4] In Jimmy Steele's case, Gerry O'Hare maintains that he had sufficient traction within the unions to get O'Hare elected as a shop steward in Hughes Bakery in the 1960s.[5] At the same time as McKee began to rebuild the Battalion, a distinct dynamic was emerging at I.R.A. G.H.Q. in Dublin. Cathal Goulding was emphasising politics and rethinking the I.R.A.'s militancy and looking beyond physical force towards evolving a strategy that was openly left-wing. That dynamic wasn't particularly visible in the early 1960s, as both Belfast and Dublin participated in the same, broad, political initiatives. But, as events impacted and personalities began to assert themselves, the I.R.A.-Saor Uladh split in Belfast seems to have resurfaced and communication between Belfast and Dublin became heavily filtered by the individuals involved. However, none of this was apparent just yet.

As the internees were released on both sides of the border, tensions developed inside and outside the prisons began to surface. Clearly, the Border Campaign was not delivering success. Competing factions inside the Curragh carried on their disputes on the outside but the trio that had led the republican movement into the Border Campaign, Magan, McLogan and MacCurtain were displaced when Cathal Goulding was elected as Chief of Staff. Belfast had been a staging point for operations but as Eamon Boyce notes, the number of available safe houses dried up rapidly between 1961 and early 1962.[6] The I.R.A. officially declared an end to the Border Campaign on 26th February 1962.[7] The gradual easing out of the likes of McLogan over the course of 1962 coincided with vague suggestions about abandoning abstentionism (in the south, at any rate) and it was becoming clear by 1963 that Cathal Goulding was not interested in a further military campaign.[8]

Goulding had been exposed to potential alternative political strategies during his time in prison in England. One of those believed to have been influential in the evolution of Goulding's political formation was Klaus Fuchs (a renowned physicist who was jailed as a Soviet spy). The loss of electoral support from the mid-1950s to 1960 was blamed on the failure to develop a suitable political programme to evolve that support. With that in mind, Goulding wanted to shape a political programme which began to focus on utilising trade unions, political campaigns and community groups to draw support to the aims of the republican movement.

According to Billy McKee, the Battalion was encouraged by Goulding to seek to infiltrate those types of organisations. This was mostly done in a covert way. McKee says that he met regularly with Goulding at this time, as did Jimmy Steele, and the Battalion and Sinn Féin appear to have worked in tandem with Dublin to develop the infiltration strategy.

But McKee (as Battalion O/C) thought that Goulding was little different from previous members of the I.R.A.'s G.H.Q. and Army Council. It was felt that Goulding didn't understand that, for that approach to work in Belfast, they needed to infiltrate the likes of the Orange Order and that simply wasn't possible. In reality, the I.R.A. was infiltrating organisations that its members would be involved with in the normal course of events. But the value of it lay in creating a broader spectrum of sympathetic bodies to support I.R.A. strategy. For infiltration to be effective, though, it had to be particularly discreet or covert since an openly infiltrated body would be simply dismissed as acting as a mouthpiece.

But the strategy was neither discreet nor covert. Roy Garland reports that at this time unionists, preacher William McGrath and others, were publicly claiming that the I.R.A. had gone communist and was being directed in its activities by Moscow.[9] How much of that was standard rhetoric and how much was informed by an awareness of I.R.A. policy isn't clear. What the infiltration strategy does expose is a gulf in understanding between senior I.R.A. figures in Belfast and the Dublin leadership around Goulding.

This also characterised the eternally fractious relationship between Belfast and Dublin which was still coloured by the most recent perceived slighting of Belfast at the onset of the Border Campaign. Veterans, like Joe Cahill, drifted from the I.R.A. or were pushed to the margins as the decade progressed. In Belfast, Billy McKee and the likes of Jimmy Steele, Jimmy Drumm and Frank McGlade maintained a wide network involving former I.R.A. volunteers through the commemorative and fundraising activities of the National Graves Association or the Felons Club ex-prisoner organisation.

As part of the politicisation strategy it was decided to resume publishing a republican newspaper in Belfast which was launched at the end of 1962 and called *Tírghrá* which means 'Patriotism' (again with Steele as editor). It began in the low quality, cyclostyled newsletter format of the Republican News in the 1940s. By 1963 it had returned, in terms of production quality, to where *Glór Uladh* had left off. In other respects, it was very much a direct return to the same format that *Glór Uladh* and *Resurgent Ulster* had adopted prior to the 1956-62 I.R.A. campaign. According to Billy McKee, who was the Belfast O/C at the time, print runs sold out but production and distribution of the paper took up much of the Belfast I.R.A.'s energy and resources.

As part of the attempts to broaden its appeal, the I.R.A. was using the opportunity of the bicentenary of Wolfe Tone's birth (in June 1963) to emphasise Protestant and Presbyterian contributions to the United Irishmen programme. This included developing the Wolfe Tone Society from within the republican movement late in 1962, seemingly relying more on former I.R.A. volunteers more than current activists.[10] At Wolfe Tone Society meetings in May 1963 Belfast was represented by the former I.R.A. Adjutant-

General Liam Burke, Sean Caughey from Sinn Féin and trade unionists like Jack Bennett, Fred Heatley, Michael McKeown and John Irvine. Also present were Sean Cronin, Harry White, Cathal Goulding and Hugh McAteer, all of whom had served as I.R.A. Chief of Staff. They agreed on a programme of events including printed publications, a Wolfe Tone week in Casement Park in Belfast, as well as a ceremony on Cavehill.

In late 1962 and early months of 1963, the National Graves Association had held a funding drive to raise money to erect a plaque to Sean McCaughey at the Republican Plot. This included the National Graves Association publishing a 23 page pamphlet, entitled *Belfast Patriot Graves* and edited and largely written by Jimmy Steele, as part of the Wolfe Tone Society programme. Copies of the pamphlet were sold at 1 shilling. The emphasis was very much on the United Irishmen and Fenians in line with the emphasis on Wolfe Tone's bicentenary.

Enough was raised to fund the £42 cost of a square marble plaque measuring two foot square, with a red hand emblazoned on the surface.[11] On Sunday 12th May, the National Graves Association organised an unveiling of the plaque at Milltown. That morning, some of the members had gone up to do a final clean-up of the plot in preparation for the unveiling.[12] A couple of hours later, around two hundred republicans gathered in the cemetery with Jimmy Steele, as chair, presiding, Eamon MacThomais up from Dublin to give an oration and a nephew of McCaughey present to perform the actual unveiling. Three plainclothes R.U.C. detectives hovered on the edge of the crowd whilst ten more stood at the entrance to Milltown cemetery.

Before proceedings got underway, an inspection of the plot revealed that the plaque was missing. Word quickly spread and Steele had to step in and appeal for calm, asking those in attendance not to be provoked into any hasty response. MacThomais then spoke and told those present that those responsible could try and remove all traces of McCaughey's name from the cemetery, but they could never take away his spirit. McCaughey's nephew then placed a wreath at the Republican monument and the ceremony finished with a bugler playing the last post and prayers being recited in Irish. The R.U.C. found the plaque hidden close to the monument the next day.

Part of the intention of Goulding's broader strategy was to draw out a public debate engaging non-republicans that might help define a political way forward for the wider republican movement. The Wolfe Tone festival planned for Casement Park on 17th June had Irish dancers, singers and bands. Extracts of speeches by Wolfe Tone and Robert Emmet were to be read and there would be orations from Ciaran Mac An Fhaili and Jack Bennett representing Catholics and Dissenters. Bennett had been a member of the Communist Party and Connolly Association and, like Roy Johnstone and Tony Coughlan, supported Goulding's politicisation strategy. The event was to culminate with a salute to the flag and the United Irishmen to the music of 'Who fears to speak of 98'.

On the 20th June, Tone was to be commemorated at McArts Fort on Cavehill with a ceremony including a lone piper playing 'The Memory of the Dead' and orations by Roger McHugh from University College Dublin and Jack Bennett. Liam Burke was to preside. While the planned ceremonies more or less went to plan, behind the scenes the event created issues for the Battalion.

[1] Interview with Billy McKee.

[2] Details given in McMillan, L. 1972, *Lecture on The Role of the I.R.A. 1962-67* (see https://cedarlounge.files.wordpress.com/2008/10/bmcosf.pdf).

[3] *Irish Press,* 3rd April 1961.

[4] Sweetman, R. 1972 *On Our Knees, Ireland 1972*, p207.

[5] Interviews with Billy McKee and Gerry O'Hare.

[6] Bryson 2007, p425.

[7] McMillan 1972.

[8] Treacy, M. 2011 *The IRA, 1956-69: Rethinking the Republic*, p.17-21. McLogan had been an I.R.A. staff officer in Belfast in 1920-22, he died on 21st July 1964 in Dublin from an accidental gunshot wound although some dispute whether it was self-inflicted.

[9] Garland, R. 2008 Protestant Fears & Civil Rights: Self-Fulfilling Conspiracies? *History Ireland*, Vol.16, No.5, p30-33.

[10] The archives of the Wolfe Tone Society are summarised and quoted by Roy Johnston at www.rjtechne.org. The term 'Directory' deliberately echoes the United Irishmen (Ribbonmen and Fenians used the same administrative term for individual units).

[11] Two feet is the same as sixty centimetres.

[12] *Irish Independent*, 13th May 1963.

Top left: Joe Cahill; top right: Billy McKee (*An Phoblacht*, 29th October 1973); bottom left: Jim Sullivan; bottom right: Billy McMillan (*United Irishman*, May 1975).

Billy Mcmillan

As it transpired, a dispute arose from a request by the Wolfe Tone Directorate to the I.R.A. over providing a colour party for the parade before the Casement Park event on the Monday night.[1] The R.U.C. banned the display of the tricolour on the (pretty spurious) grounds that parading it from Beechmount Avenue to Casement Park could lead to a breach of the peace. A large R.U.C. force arrived at the junction of Beechmount Avenue where the parade was to form up and the organising committee hurriedly met to decide what to do. According to Billy McMillan, who was McKee's Adjutant, the I.R.A. volunteers who were on the committee wanted to display the tricolour but lost the vote. Billy McKee, as Battalion O/C, agreed to proceed without the tricolour.

The parade went ahead, without the tricolour, but rather than stay at Casement for the entertainment, McKee, McMillan and other members of the Battalion staff, returned to a hall used by the I.R.A. off Leeson Street. There, McKee and McMillan had a heated argument which culminated in McKee resigning from the I.R.A. His replacement was McMillan, whose staff now included the likes of Jim Sullivan, Bobby McKnight, Denis Toner and Leo Martin.[2]

That the I.R.A. was again training volunteers was revealed fairly quickly, as McKnight was arrested at a Waterford training camp in July, along with George O'Hara and Paddy Maguire. The Dublin Brigade O/C Phil O'Donoghue was also present. All received two months in prison. After the three were released and returned to Belfast, the R.U.C. carried out a series of raids and searches on their homes and the homes of other members of the Belfast staff on 30th October. They also issued a statement warning against a possible I.R.A. offensive that coming winter.

With disaffection and division growing within Belfast, Jimmy Steele tried to keep a wider network of republicans together through the likes of the National Graves Association and the Felons. In 1964 he got Joe Cahill, who had resigned from the I.R.A. back in 1962, to get himself involved in the National Graves Association. At that time, it was seeking to erect a monument on the plot purchased for Tom Williams in Milltown (the authorities didn't release Williams' remains for burial until 2000). Cahill didn't need any convincing to get involved and felt that, shrewdly, Steele did this with him and others to keep them in close touch with developments in the republican movement.[3]

Conscious of the events of the previous year, McMillan later wrote that the Battalion's own 1964 Easter parade intentionally sought a confrontation with the R.U.C. by carrying the tricolour openly along the route. It passed off without incident, though.

In May 1964 Dessie O'Hagan, formerly of Saor Uladh, briefly re-surfaced at a meeting of Irish left wing groups in London to perpetuate the rift with the Belfast communists. He heckled the speaker from the Northern Ireland Communist Party, shouting "…where were you when my comrades were in the Crumlin Road Jail in 1942?".[4]

That July a Cork-born soldier, Denis Murphy, was arrested in Ballymena barracks and charged with trying to '…pass information to the enemy'. R.U.C. officers, posing as republicans, had induced him to give them information about security at St Patrick's barracks in Ballymena. He received a two year sentence. It is known though that the I.R.A. had tried to import some small caches of weapons from the United States during 1964.[5]

The October 1964 General Election saw I.R.A. candidates stand in all four Belfast constituencies (as 'Republicans' since Sinn Féin was banned). Billy McMillan stood in West Belfast, Frank McGlade in North Belfast, Daithi O Conaill in East Belfast and Bobby McKnight in South Belfast. With the value now being placed on political action, significant effort was invested in mounting a campaign. McMillan had his election headquarters on Divis Street where he displayed tricolour and starry plough flags in the window. These were ignored until Ian Paisley threatened to march to Divis Street with his supporters and remove them.[6]

The R.U.C. subsequently broke into the office and removed the tricolour. When new flags were put up, the R.U.C. returned and removed the tricolour. A riot then broke out that was to continue over a couple of days. A few days later, the I.R.A. paraded up the Falls behind a tricolour without any R.U.C. interference. The publicity drew in several dozen new recruits but no significant electoral advantage. Indeed, only McMillan didn't improve on the previous performance of I.R.A. candidates in 1959 although all were well below the vote for Sinn Féin candidates in the four Belfast constituencies in 1955. The widespread media coverage, now including television, did draw attention to the repressive nature of the Unionist government. This struck a chord with the civil rights groups and began to identify the intersectionality of their activities with the long running theme of political repression as highlighted by the National Council for Civil Liberties back in 1936, Geoffrey Bing in 1950 and the recurrent prisoner welfare and release campaigns (as mentioned elsewhere in this book).

Earlier in 1964, an ongoing campaign to expose religious discrimination in the allocation of housing by the local councils had led to the formation of the Campaign for Social Justice in Dungannon. It embarked on a campaign of writing letters, mainly to M.P.s. The Irish emigrant Connolly Association, in Britain, believed that Section 75 of the Government of Ireland Act 1920 gave Westminster the power to end the discriminatory and repressive measures used by the Unionists such as the Civil Authorities (Special Powers) Act. It hoped that equality would create the circumstances in which support would emerge for a united Irish (socialist) republic. The Connolly Association helped form the Campaign for Democracy in Ulster with support from (mainly Labour) backbench M.P.s in January 1965.

Just before then, a motion had been passed at the Sinn Féin Ardhfeis in December, to found Republican Clubs in the north as an organisational basis for electoral campaigns. This would circumvent the Unionists's ban on Sinn Féin. The Wolfe Tone Societies now were amalgamated into a single group and were heavily influenced by Desmond Greaves through involvement of former Connolly Association members like Roy Johnston (who had been involved with the communist Irish Workers League since its foundation in 1948) and Anthony Coughlan. They promoted Greaves' analysis through the Wolfe Tone Society, insisting that votes were being lost due to abstentionism and refusing to enter the legislatures (in Belfast, Dublin and London) to implement policies. The Wolfe Tone Society presented this analysis to Sinn Féin in March 1965, four months after the Republican Clubs motion. A proposal to abandon abstentionism had also been put to an I.R.A. Convention in November 1964 then deferred. Early in 1965, Bobby McKnight was transferred from his role as Battalion Training Officer to a G.H.Q. role as an Education Officer strengthening the links between Goulding and Belfast. G.H.Q. also embarked on a process for inventorying the I.R.A.'s weapon stocks and centralising dumps.

The Battalion was slowly relinquishing control to I.R.A. G.H.Q. in Dublin. This became evident early in 1965 when it stopped publishing its own newspaper, *Tírghrá*, with a northern edition of the *United Irishman* appearing instead under the title of the *Ulsterman*. This northern edition of *United Irishman* only lasted from March to December 1965 and was then discontinued. Despite the fact that *Ulsterman* was discontinued, *Tírghrá* wasn't revived to replace it, though.

---

[1] McMillan 1972.
[2] Quinn 1999, p136. John Kelly claims that this roughly coincides with the later split in the Battalion (see https://www.pbs.org/wgbh/pages/frontline/shows/ira/inside/ kelly.html).
[3] Anderson 2002, p160.
[4] See http://www.rjtechne.org/century130703/1960s/polrj60.htm
[5] Treacy 2011, p22.
[6] See Chapter 11 in Andrew Boyd 1969 *Holy War in Belfast*.

1966

The next political project of the I.R.A. was to promote a 'one man, one vote' campaign. This was signalled by Tomás MacGiolla at the 1965 Easter commemorations just as Cathal Goulding had been ruling out a new armed campaign.[1] While the debate around political methods was much more intense in the south, when the Sinn Féin Ard Fheis in June 1965 rejected proposals to end abstentionism it prompted the resignation of Seán Caughey from Belfast, the Sinn Féin Vice President. As an incentive to get approval for his political strategies, including an end to abstentionism, Goulding now shifted to floating the idea of a future military offensive.

Regardless, the Battalion was now to form 'one man, one vote' committees as well as Republican Clubs. Much of the year was also absorbed by preparations for the fiftieth anniversary of the 1916 Easter Rising. As part of the planning for the 1966 commemorations, a meeting was held in the Felons at the end of August 1965.[2] MacGiolla attended and explained that Sinn Féin was now developing social consciousness as part of its political programme. He encouraged the assembled Belfast republicans to widen the appeal of republicanism and talked of finding common cause with trade unions and local pressure groups to develop a broad base for a political programme.

At that stage there were already three 1916 commemoration committees in Belfast. A follow-up meeting was organised so that the three committees could co-ordinate their activities through a central committee. Republican, nationalist, cultural and labour organisations were invited to attend and all agreed to a Central Committee. Billy McMillan was elected organising secretary, to some extent establishing I.R.A. primacy on the committee. In Dublin, the 1916 commemorations were organised by the state with the intention of keeping the I.R.A. on the sidelines. Given that there was no state involvement in 1916 commemorations in the north, it offered potential for the I.R.A. to dominate in a way that wouldn't be possible in Dublin. Notably, James Clarke and Kevin McMahon, the two northerners on the state-sponsored National Committee in Dublin, were not directly involved with the I.R.A. or Sinn Féin.

With the development of the Republican Clubs, Denis Foley, the editor of the *United Irishman*, began to push for an end to abstentionism by the summer of 1965 in line with the analysis being provided by Johnston and Coughlan. It is probably not coincidental that the same month the Belfast I.R.A. briefly surfaced to disrupt a British Army recruitment event in the city. Ten volunteers raided St Gabriel's School as a British army recruiting film was being shown. The projectionist and army youth liaison officer were slightly injured during the incident and the film projector was destroyed.

In 1965 the Army Council approved armed robberies to raise funds although they had to be in the north. Matt Treacy records that the Battalion took £1,300 from a Belfast bookmaker on 30th October 1965. This appears to be bookie Des McGranaghan who reported £3,500 stolen from his car outside his mother's house in Andersonstown Crescent in January 1966.[3] The Battalion sent £1,000 of the takings to G.H.Q. and retained the balance.

But keeping the lid on discontent was becoming more difficult. That November five men were arrested in a parked car and charged with possession of bayonets and documents detailing R.U.C. movements. The five men, including Joe McCann, Seanie Watson, Harry O'Neill, Michael Kieran and Sean Murphy, each got twelve months in jail. All were aged between seventeen and nineteen. When they were first charged, three were wearing combat gear. The five were apparently part of a group of younger, militant, republicans operating under the name Irish Freedom Fighters. The Unionists's Minister of Home Affairs, Brian McConnell started to make very public calls for the I.R.A. to have the 'good sense' not to get involved in violence.[4]

The organisational structure of the 1916 Commemoration Committee hardened in early 1966. To coincide with the new year, a Directorate was appointed with Frank McGlade in the chair, Liam McDonagh responsible for publicity, Kevin Murphy as treasurer and D. Moore secretary. In February, Jimmy Steele was made President of the Directorate. Frank McGlade was also urging northerners to commemorate the 1916 rising in the north and not simply travel over the border to attend events in the south.

While that was happening, there were a number of attacks in February. A petrol bomb was thrown at an R.U.C. Landrover in Andersonstown and another was thrown at Unionist Party headquarters. Again these attacks were by the Irish Freedom Fighters and some of the press did report that this was the work of a republican splinter group. The I.R.A. vehemently denied any connection to the incidents and issued a statement of denial from the 'Republican Movement' to the press through the Irish Republican Publicity Bureau on 22nd February. Three nights beforehand there were attacks on Catholic Church properties including St Gerard's, St John's and St Joseph's primary school in Crumlin. On the night of 24th February, two petrol bombs were thrown at the Broadway Presbyterian Church.[5]

It wasn't clear exactly who was doing all this but, in March, Billy McMillan and Denis Toner were arrested and held over Easter (to the public this associated the attacks with the I.R.A.). This seems to have ended the Battalion's patience with the Irish Freedom Fighters and senior I.R.A. members visited the homes of some of those involved, including one who ended up being beaten with a brush handle. While some more members were arrested over Easter, there were no further attacks by the group.

As the 1916 commemorative programme was to include a concert, the Ulster Hall had been booked with Belfast Corporation for the 13th April. But in March, the Corporation informed the organisers that it was cancelling the booking in case it led to a breach of the peace (it had similarly cancelled a 1798 commemoration in 1948). Instead, the Corporation rented the hall to Ian Paisley who held a celebration of the defeat of the 1916 rising. The concert took place in St Mary's Hall. In the days before the commemorations, a petrol bomb was thrown at Holy Cross Girls School on the Crumlin Road. That same March, the I.R.A. didn't field candidates in the general election and Gerry Fitt took the Westminster seat of West Belfast for Republican Labour. He was the first non-unionist to hold the seat since Jack Beattie in 1951. Non-unionists took 58.8% of the vote.

The first of the 1916 events was the conventional Easter Sunday commemoration on the 10th April 1966. On the day, 5,000 marched in the parade itself and some 20,000 turned out to watch. The parade began at Beechmount and ended at the new County Antrim Memorial plot in Milltown. The main events were then to take place the next weekend.

On the Saturday night, 16th April, there were screenings of Mise Éire and Saoirse in St Mary's Hall. The following Sunday the fiftieth anniversary Easter Rising Commemoration took place. That morning, unionists detonated a bomb at Milltown in the republican plot but it did little damage. A second bomb was exploded at Ligoniel. The R.U.C. mounted armed checkpoints across Belfast. Ian Paisley also organised marches to try and disrupt the republican commemorations (Paisley's marchers paraded behind a banner saying 'Ireland belongs to Christ'). A number of people heading for the republican commemorations were assaulted, including one man almost beaten to death for trying to cross a road through Paisley's marchers.

The republican march formed up in Hamill Street, Institution Place, John Street and Barrack Street. Again some 5,000 took part in the parade, but an estimated 70,000 people came out to watch. Stormont had banned rail travel from the south over the weekend (as had the southern government). The parade included the likes of the G.A.A. and Belfast District Trades Council with Mount Street Bridge veteran Joe Clarke as the guest of honour. Since the parade terminated in Casement Park, the G.A.A. insisted on vetting speakers and managed to veto the Communist Party's Betty Sinclair.[6]

Leo Martin had chaired the commemoration committee, while Dublin attendees included Tomás MacGiolla, Eamonn MacThomais and Eamon Ó Driscoill (from Cork). Malachy McBurney read the Easter Proclamation, while Seamus Costello spoke about unemployment, poverty and the social agenda. The presence of so many senior republican figures, like MacGiolla, MacThomais, Ó Driscoill, McBurney and Costello underscored the emphasis the I.R.A. placed on the Belfast commemoration in 1966. One veteran I.R.A. volunteer who joined the march, Chris McGouran, collapsed and died while walking during the parade.

The Unionists, discomforted by the scale and enthusiasm of the commemorations, had the Battalion Adjutant, Jim Sullivan, Malachy McBurney and Leo Martin charged with failing to give sufficient notice for the commemoration and for conducting an 'illegal procession'. In Dublin, Bobby McKnight was arrested for assaulting a Garda.

While Nelson's Pillar in Dublin had been blown up by republicans in March, despite all the unionist claims to the contrary, no violent action had been planned by the Battalion. Yet in April, an additional battalion of the British Army had been sent to the north. In the weekend after the main 1966 commemorations, a Catholic owned shop off the Shankill Road, O'Hara's Self-Service Stores, was petrol bombed although little damage was done. The same night, a family in Hopewell Street had three shots fired into their house from a moving car.

That unionists were behind the attacks was apparent at the start of May, as the newly reorganised Ulster Volunteer Force publicly threatened that "…known I.R.A. men will be executed mercilessly and without hesitation." On the 7th May, it tried to firebomb a Catholic owned bar in Upper Charleville Street (in the Shankill Road area of Belfast), but instead set fire to the adjoining home of Matilda Gould, who subsequently died from her injuries (on 27th June). The same night, a petrol bomb was thrown at the home of Josephine MacMahon on Northumberland Street and two petrol bombs were thrown at St Marys Training College on the Falls Road. At a debate that followed in Stormont, the Home Affairs Minister, Brian McConnell revealed there had now been eight such petrol bomb attacks in March, April and May.

The I.R.A. had been debating how to become an open and legal (but still revolutionary) organisation that could move beyond the 'emotional appeal of arms'. At the same time, the 'Garland Plan' was being developed. It recommended that a campaign would be fought in the north although the "structure, organisation and control of the army in that area is unsound for campaign conditions the nature of which is envisaged." If the Battalion had access to the plan, this might have reignited its concerns over earlier campaigns. But one key difference was that this did signal a tactical shift away from the foco strategy of Operation Harvest to E.O.K.A.-style revolutionary cells and operations. It was even agreed that the Battalion could mount retaliatory operations if a repetition of the Divis Street riots occurred. This was called the 'Garland' plan as it was captured on Sean Garland by the Gardaí on 7th May 1966 (they passed it to the R.U.C. who had some knowledge of it already). The I.R.A. plans were to be referred to by Unionists to underscore militant unionist policy during 1966.[7] After Garland's arrest Sean MacStiofáin took over the tentative planning for a military campaign and began to secure arms dumps. The previous year had seen an increase in I.R.A. training camps (none in the north) but any vague sense of momentum towards a campaign was illusory.

A couple of weeks later, on 27th May, U.V.F. members shot John Scullion in Oranmore Street having originally been trying to find and kill an I.R.A. volunteer, Francis McGuigan.[8] The R.U.C. reported to the press that Scullion had been stabbed and that they believed he knew the name of his attackers (yet they had already been given a bullet that had hit Scullion).

At the start of June, a unionist crowd, led by Ian Paisley, was permitted to march through Cromac Square in the Markets even though Unionist marches had been discouraged from passing through there since 1935. Paisley was en route to protest at the Presbyterian General Assembly. The resultant riot in Cromac Square restarted the next night and two petrol bombs were thrown at the R.U.C. by the I.R.A. in Lagan Street. A few days later, on 11th June, John Scullion died of his wounds. The R.U.C. stuck to the stabbing story and reported that he had passed away 'without divulging the name of his attacker' even though the U.V.F. had already claimed responsibility. A few days after Scullion's death, the U.V.F. fired shots into William Gamble's shop on the Shankill Road. A brick had been thrown through the window some days previously.

Due to the ongoing controversy, the State Pathologist in Belfast then ordered that John Scullion's remains be exhumed (he had been buried a week earlier). On the 20th June, Jim Sullivan, Malachy McBurney and Leo Martin failed to turn up for a scheduled court appearance for the Easter commemoration. They had fines imposed by the court in absentia.

The next day, Terence O'Neill, the Unionist Prime Minister, claimed there was no reason to use the Special Powers Act against the U.V.F.. Then, during the night of 24th-25th June, three U.V.F. men broke into Leo Martin's house in Baden-Powell Street in the Oldpark district. They tried to set fire to the house with little success. That night, two U.V.F. men also entered the house of Thomas Maguire on Canmore Street, between the Falls Road and Shankill Road. Maguire was disabled but still had a gun put to his stomach and was told to leave his home. Several hours earlier a friend, who had been visiting Maguire's house, was stabbed after leaving the house. There were a number of other attacks involving minor vandalism and bomb hoaxes at the houses of prominent Catholics on the same night. There were also attacks on six houses in Ardmoulin Avenue.

That same night, the U.V.F. unit that had failed to find Leo Martin encountered four Catholic barmen drinking in the Malvern Arms off the Shankill Road. The U.V.F. shot the barmen outside, wounding two and killing Peter Ward. Just two days later, Martha Gould died from the injuries she had sustained in May.

The Belfast I.R.A. issued a statement on the day after Matilda Gould died, stating that "The Republican movement condemns in the strongest possible terms the recent outrages in Belfast, and expresses deepest sympathy with the relatives of all those killed and wounded in these incidents. We would reiterate that Republicans are utterly opposed to sectarian bitterness and strife and would remind our members that their duty is to resist all efforts to provoke them into acts of retaliation. Discipline and self-restraint must be exercised by all."

The cumulative effect of the deaths of Scullion, Ward and Gould was that the Unionist government was forced to declare the U.V.F. an illegal organisation and various U.V.F. figures now were arrested and charged.

A British royal visit at the start of July now coincided with more confrontations and protests. There were further attacks over the weekend of the Twelfth with a Catholic couple assaulted in their home in Frenchpark Street. A mob also attacked houses in Rockview Street and three people received serious head injuries. The same night windows were broken in Charles O'Hara's shop on the Newtownards Road. His window had been smashed during the election earlier that year and a petrol bomb also thrown at the shop. There were further attacks in late July on Catholics in Alloa Street between Manor Street and Clifton Park Avenue.

Having failed to turn up for their court appearance in June, Jim Sullivan and Malachy McBurney were now arrested and given three months in jail. The trial of the U.V.F. members also dragged on through August and September. It was late August before the R.U.C. finally admitted that John Scullion had been shot rather than stabbed.

In the middle of August the Wolfe Tone Societies had met in Maghera to discuss the wider political context. The Dublin branch brought a proposal to develop a convention on civil rights with a view to drawing up a civil rights charter. The proposal showed little comprehension of differences in the trade unions in the north and south. Billy McMillan was critical of the proposal but it was endorsed and discussions were initiated with interested parties in Belfast.

The cumulative effect of the U.V.F. attacks had prompted many in the nationalist community to fear more widespread violence. However, perhaps focusing on the Republican Clubs and civil rights campaign, the Battalion didn't move to either increase its available armaments or train sufficient members in weapons in anticipation of another major campaign of unionist violence. This conformed to the view the I.R.A. had articulated in its June statement, emphatically rejecting any idea of the I.R.A. defending Catholics on the basis that doing so, in itself, identified the I.R.A. with a sectarian role. Instead, the Battalion continued to concentrate on its political activities. As it was, Cathal Goulding had used the pretext of a putative northern campaign to concentrate the weaponry available to the I.R.A. under people loyal to him.[9]

In November, a public meeting agreed on the need for a new organisation to campaign for civil rights. On 29th January 1967, then, the Northern Ireland Civil Rights Association was founded in Belfast with various Battalion members present. It identified its objectives as: (1) To defend the basic freedoms of all citizens. (2) To protect the rights of the individual. (3) To highlight all possible abuses of power. (4) To demand guarantees for freedom of speech, assembly and association. (5) To inform the public of their lawful rights.[10] The argument presented by Johnston and Coughlan and accepted and promoted by the likes of Goulding was that through achieving these objectives people would come to support the republican perspective and a united Irish republic would follow.

The unionist response to the political initiatives of the I.R.A. was to ban the Republican Clubs. In March (1967), the Republican Clubs announced they would defy the ban and that Jimmy Steele, Chair of the Northern Directory of Republican Clubs would host a public meeting of Republican Clubs, civil liberty and trade union organisations and Labour politicians in Divis Street "...to protest against this flagrant abuse of civil liberties and democratic freedom which this action entails."[11]

At this time the Battalion had mounted few recent offensive operations. One of the few incidents in which it was involved was in the tarring and feather of Patrick Joseph Magennis who was found tied to a lampost in Leeson Street on the 13th February. A caller rang the Irish News and said the attack had been carried out by the 'First Division' of the I.R.A. and claimed Magennis was an R.U.C. informant.[12] But the Battalion then suddenly carried out two bomb attacks on the night of the 24th May. One was at the Territorial Army Centre at Firmount on the Antrim Road and the other was at another Territorial Army Hall at Wallace Avenue, Lisburn. At Firmount, there was substantial damage done to the ground and lower floors. The I.R.A. unit involved had broken in and used gelignite to set petrol alight inside the building. There was only slight damage done at the hall in Wallace Avenue.

￼i

On the Thursday, the I.R.A. issued a statement from Dublin under the name of the Irish Republican Publicity Bureau and signed by J.J. McGarrity. It said that "We have been asked to state that the Republican Movement was responsible for the action carried out against British military installations in Belfast and Lisburn on Wednesday, May 24th. The operations were carried out as a protest against the visits of British Royalty to our country and as a demonstration of the hostility towards the British Occupation Forces." This was followed by a second letter claiming responsibility, this time issued by the 'Publicity Department, Irish Citizen Army' to the office of the Belfast Newsletter. It stated that "As a protest against members of British Monarchy on Irish soil, the 'I.C.A.' Northern Command issued instructions to volunteers in Belfast and Lisburn, to put to fire and destroy selected property used by the British forces, namely, 'Firmount' and 'Wallace' TA centres. Signed: O/C Field Operations, T. Higgins."[13]

A few years later, Billy McMillan wrote that while the "…rest of the country was striving towards reality, Belfast dragged its feet. The Belfast Battalion Staff impressed on Headquarters the necessity for a happy blend of political agitation and military activity."[14] Attacks on British Army recruiting centres were clearly a compromise target and for much of the rest of 1967 and early 1968, the Battalion encouraged its volunteers to actively involve themselves in the newly-formed civil rights movement.

There was still a heightened sense of violence, though, partly perpetuated by numerous bomb hoaxes and scares throughout the year. In June 1967 there was a petrol bomb attack on a public house in Upper Charleville Street where Matilda Gould had been killed. The I.R.A. did attempt another bomb attack on the Territorial Army headquarters on the Malone Road in January 1968, coming back eight days later to try again (in the end £1,500 worth of damage was done). The Battalion was now mainly using incendiary bombs as its explosive stocks were non-existent. Fifty pounds of gelignite was in such poor (and dangerous) condition it had had to be dumped in the brickworks in the Upper Falls in October 1967.

---

[1] Treacy 2011, p48.

[2] See Daly, M. and O'Callaghan, M. 2007 *1916 in 1966: commemorating the Easter Rising*, P99-107; *Irish News* 30th August 1965.

[3] Treacy 2011, p56. And see *Evening Herald* 6th January 1966 for McGranaghan robbery. This may be the robbery involved and Treacy's date of 30th October is when it was sanctioned. McGranaghan may have been pressured into it and over-declared the loss as £3,500.

[4] *Irish Times* 21st January 1966.

[5] See *Irish News* and *Irish Times* for coverage at the relevant dates in February. Some sources refer to a hand grenade thrown (by the I.R.A.) at the R.U.C. in McDonnell Street in 1966 but I've not found a clear reference to it in the press.

[6] This is presented as an example of conservative and/or Catholic forces in the G.A.A. opposing Sinclair as she was a Communist but some of it may have been personal. Twenty years previously she, along with other Communists like Billy McCullough, had been rumoured of supplying information on the I.R.A. that led to arrests and imprisonment.

[7] Treacy 2011, p53-56.

[8] This is referred to in the trial of various U.V.F. members in late August (see contemporary press on, eg. 30th August) where he is named as an 'I.R.A. man called McGuigan', I assume it is Francis McGuigan.

[9] Treacy 2011, p108.

[10] Purdie 1990, p133 lists the 5 objectives of N.I.C.R.A..

[11] See *Irish News* and *Irish Times* on 18th March 1967.

[12] *Irish News*, 14th February 1967. The designation 'First Division' wasn't typically used by the Battalion.

[13] The 'I.C.A.' statement was issued to the Belfast Newsletter during the night of 26th-27th May 1967. It contained an error naming Firmount as Fairmount, the same typo had been made in *The Irish Times* on the Friday (26th).

[14] McMillan 1972.

the new departure

One internal Battalion critic was veteran Jimmy Steele, who was also Chair of the Northern Directory of Republican Clubs. In England for a centenary commemoration for the Manchester Martyrs, Steele was the main speaker and he used the opportunity to critique current I.R.A. strategy, alluding to the 'New Departure' of Davitt and Devoy in 1878-79. The 'New Departure' was a campaign to work with the Home Rulers and take parliamentary seats in Westminster. Clearly, Steele was referring to the debates within the I.R.A. about ending abstentionism and taking seats in Leinster House, Stormont and Westminster.

The early N.I.C.R.A. didn't have a clear plan of action but by the spring of 1968 republicans were pressing for a campaign of protest marches.[1] The marching campaign was aimed in part at pushing back against state limitations on protest and asserting the right to protest. Globally, the news was dominated by revolution. In January and February the Vietnamese Tet Offensive had shocked an American establishment and public opinion that had been repeatedly told that the war was won. Domestically the United States was divided over the civil rights and anti-war protests and saw the assassinations of Martin Luther King Jr in April and Robert Kennedy in June. There was the Prague Spring, with Czechoslovakia threatening to break free from the Soviet bloc and institute democratic reforms. Polish students had protested in March, left-wing protests in West Germany were ongoing and in mid-May France almost exploded with revolutionary intent. The year 1968 had been designated by UNESCO as International Human Rights Year.

Against this backdrop, the N.I.C.R.A. protested against the ban on an Easter commemoration in April. More street protests followed in June at Caledon and August saw the first fully-fledged civil rights marches in the north.

But how this could be politically developed by the republican movement was unclear as Cathal Goulding had consistently failed to push through a motion on ending the abstentionist policy at either I.R.A. or Sinn Féin conventions. As the civil rights campaign grew in strength throughout 1968, it was heavily supported by the I.R.A. and Sinn Féin. The ground swell of opinion was clearly going to lead to some political gains for whoever could harness the involvement of those in the civil rights groups. Still, occasional attacks took place such as a grenade thrown at the R.U.C. between Leeson Street and Cyprus

Street in July 1968. The grenade was an old Mills bomb and appears to have come from an old I.R.A. arms dump (there was no statement admitting responsibility though).

As had happened following the violent defeat of the Hungarian uprising in 1956, the Czech nationalist Prague Spring was brutally suppressed by the Russians in August 1968. The September edition of *Irish Democrat* (the Connolly Association newspaper) struggled to defend the Soviet actions stating that UK criticism of the Soviet invasion should make people hesitate to have 'sympathy for the Czechs'.

In September 1968, Goulding took a different approach and had changes made to the structure of the I.R.A., expanding membership of the Army Council from seven to twenty. Constitutionally, an Army Council was to be elected by an Army Convention and so would reflect the broader attitudes of the membership of the I.R.A. Now, albeit temporarily, Goulding could install his supporters and push through abstentionism before a convention formally elected a new Army Council that might not be dominated by Goulding's supporters.

But then the civil rights campaign suddenly took centre stage as the Unionists violently attacked a march in Derry in October 1968. The Nationalists even withdrew as the 'official opposition' at Stormont in protest and violence followed at further civil rights marches over the winter including, famously, at Burntollet in Derry and then subsequently in Derry city. The 'Long March' which was attacked at Burntollet was organised by People's Democracy which had emerged as a student grouping at Queens and took shape as a Marxist-Leninist revolutionary party which caused friction with N.I.C.R.A., the main civil rights body. As N.I.C.R.A. debated the need for stewards to manage and protect the marches, People's Democracy openly sought confrontation with the Unionists who were more than willing to give it to them. As it was, there was a split within N.I.C.R.A. involving some former Wolfe Tone Society members like Fred Heatley (who had been instrumental in creating N.I.C.R.A.) and People's Democracy representatives over a proposed march along what would be an exceedingly hostile route through East Belfast to protest at Stormont. After an emergency meeting Heatley and others resigned but the proposed march was postponed.[2]

Despite the obvious parallels with the mid-1930s, the Battalion was happy to assist in stewarding or protecting marches but made no attempt to address the now overt threat of another violent pogrom. This should have become even more obvious when a series of bomb explosion took place outside Belfast starting at Castlereagh on 30th March, barely a week after the internal N.I.C.R.A. dispute ended in resignations. More bombs were then detonated at a series of targets including Dunadry (4th April), Silent Valley and Kilmore (20th April), Lough Neagh pipeline (24th April) and Belfast pipeline (26th April). The explosions coincided with the Unionists agreeing to some reforms including 'one man, one vote'. Unionist politicians repeatedly indicated that they believed the I.R.A. was responsible but, as in the past, the more revealing admission was the failure of the R.U.C. to carry out any raids or arrests (the bombs were the work of the U.V.F.). Quietly, British soldiers were deployed to guard key installations.

Very publicly, the civil rights marches had come up against repressive violence from the R.U.C. and B Specials. Some I.R.A. veterans, like Jimmy Steele, and the former volunteers scattered around organisations like the National Graves Association and Felons Club, were concerned both by the failure of the Battalion to procure arms and the increasing emphasis on politics when unionism was clearly intent on resorting to violence.[3] Clearly, as with the Irish Freedom Fighters there were younger republicans also looking for more militant action. When violence took place in Derry, in April 1969, the response of the Battalion was to burn nine Post Offices and a bus depot on 20th April to try and draw off R.U.C. and B Specials from Derry. Their return to Belfast, in theory, would give those in Derry some respite. Instead, it really highlighted the I.R.A.'s lack of weaponry.

In May and then again in July, Goulding told meetings of I.R.A. G.H.Q. staff that there were plans in place to defend northern nationalists in the event of unionist violence. However, he told a meeting of local I.R.A. O/Cs that, in a crisis, it would be the British government who would have to step in and disband the B Specials and bring in reforms. In May the northern O/Cs had met and had a request for weapons approved but they never got them.[4] Roy Johnston, then on the Army Council, claims Goulding intended to leave Belfast undefended as he hoped that a backlash to any sustained violence against Catholics would lead to the disbanding of the B Specials.[5] Goulding himself admits that G.H.Q. had arms but they withheld them from the north as they had not believed what they had been told about the threat of violence.[6] Billy McMillen states that the Battalion staff was under pressure to supply weapons in May and June but that they were reluctant to use weapons as they feared the meagre amount of weapons available would be hopelessly inadequate. He and Goulding also believed that the use of firearms would only serve to justify the use of greater force against the community and increase the risk of a sectarian pogrom.[7]

When McMillen was asked about the number of weapons available to the Battalion at the May meeting he admitted the Battalion had a single Thompson and one revolver. Meanwhile, Seán McStiofáin began to allow some weapons to reach the Battalion via the Intelligence Officer, Leo Martin. McMillen's admission in May also prompted some to try and source weapons from dumps in the south. Liam Burke, who had been O/C of the Eastern Command for a while in the 1940s, tried to locate some old dumps and recover weapons to be available in Belfast if needed.[8]

The conflict between some of the Battalion and G.H.Q. then surfaced publicly at the reinternment of Peter Barnes and James McCormick at Ballyglass cemetery in Mullingar in July. Barnes and McCormick had been executed in England in 1940 and the final return of their remains for reburial meant that a sizeable crowd of 1930s and 1940s veterans would congregate for the ceremony. Their former unit commander, Jim O'Regan, was asked to speak on behalf of the I.R.A. by Goulding who refused to let Jimmy Steele speak. Instead, the repatriation committee asked Steele to speak on it's behalf and he got to speak before O'Regan.

Steele's speech deconstructed the Goulding leadership and accused it of having been infiltrated by individuals wishing to dominate, re-direct, then use the republican movement as a platform for their own agenda. At one point he stated that "There comes a time in every generation when men try to re-direct the republican movement along a different road to that upon which our freedom fighters trod… And Connolly's words on this matter should give us all food for thought when he said, "Unity is a word used by many with ulterior motives, to achieve political ambition, or ultimately, to seek power and control in a united movement." Therefore in striving for genuine unity we must be careful that such efforts may not lead to that seizure of power and control by the wrong people as defined by Connolly."[9]

Some of the Belfast I.R.A. volunteers and former volunteers like Leo Martin, Billy McKee, Jimmy Drumm and Joe Cahill had known the speech was coming (Martin even taped the speech). Others had been waiting for someone to put themselves forward and voice opposition to current I.R.A. strategy. According to Billy McKee, the speech was what people had been waiting to hear. As another Belfast republican, John Kelly immediately recognised, the speech was going to lead to trouble. Up on the podium, Sinn Féin President, Tomás Mac Giolla, claimed he could feel the tension, while in the crowd, Goulding loyalists from Dublin felt the criticism sharply. An army council member present, Roy Johnston, was appalled by the speech. Another, Mick Ryan, said you could feel the ground move under the feet of the current I.R.A. leadership. Séan Dunne, one of the colour party drawn from Goulding's supporters in the Dublin Brigade, wondered melodramatically if he should shoot Steele on the spot.[10]

Steele's speech wasn't reported in the official account given of the reburial in the next issue of *The United Irishman*. According to Roy Johnston Goulding's standing committee met on the next Monday and Goulding had a cryptic motion delisting Steele as a speaker for republican events approved.[11] By the Wednesday, he had Jim Sullivan and Malachy McGurran pay Steele a visit to tell him he was immediately expelled from the I.R.A. without even a court-martial (which was actually contrary to I.R.A. rules).

In reality, Steele's speech created a talking point among I.R.A. volunteers and veterans that seems to have articulated concerns about the current direction the I.R.A. was taking. When events overtook the I.R.A. the next month, particularly in Belfast, those who questioned what the I.R.A. had been doing already knew they weren't alone.

There wasn't much time to dwell on Steele's speech. Serious violent clashes occurred on the 12th July in Derry, Belfast and Dungiven and didn't die down straight away. In Dungiven, Francis McCloskey was beaten by the R.U.C. and subsequently died as did Samuel Deveney who had been beaten in Derry. There was then a bombing by U.V.F. in Dublin at R.T.É. on 5th August.

---

[1] Hanley, B. 2013 'The needs of the people: the IRA considers its future 1967-68' in *Saothar* 38.

[2] See the series of articles by Heatley in *Fortnight*, issues 80 to 84 from March to June 1974.

[3] By the summer of 1969, the Battalion had around one hundred and twenty men and twenty-three handguns.

[4] Sean MacStiofáin in Rosita Sweetman 1972 *On Our Knees,* p155.

[5] Treacy 2011, p165.

[6] Cathal Goulding quoted in Tony Geraghty 2000 *The Irish War: The Military History of a Domestic Conflict*, p10.

[7] McMillen, L. 1975 Lecture – The Role of the I.R.A. 1962-67. *Repsol Pamphlet*, No. 21.

[8] See Swan 2008.

[9] Peter Taylor's book *Provos* (1998) contains quotes from the speech but the published text doesn't match the surviving audio of the speech, now held by the Irish Republican Museum in Conway Mill. Subsequent references to the speech, such as in Patrick Ryan's *The Birth of the Provisionals*, Robert White's biography of Ruairí Ó Brádaigh, and, Sean Swan's *Official Irish Republicanism 1962-72* all base their analysis of the ideological basis of the I.R.A. split on the text quoted by Taylor.

[10] See Treacy, M. 2011 *The I.R.A. 1956-69: Rethinking the Republic.*

[11] Johnston, R. 2004 *Century of Endeavour*, p261.

August 1969

When an Apprentice Boys march ended in the battle of the Bogside on 12th August, the Battalion was put under pressure to draw off the R.U.C. and B Specials from Derry. To that end, and perhaps embarrassed by the very limited resources left to him, the Battalion O/C Billy McMillan ordered a number of operations to be carried out against the R.U.C. and B Specials over the evening and night of 13-14th August after a demonstration at Springfield Road R.U.C. station and then in Hastings Street. On the night of the 13th August, shots were fired at a police patrol in the Leeson Street area. A hand grenade was also thrown but failed to explode. Police also confirmed that six shots were fired from a passing car at Andersonstown Police Station but no damage was done. These occurred in the midst of more widespread violence where petrol bombs were thrown at the R.U.C. across much of Belfast.

In contrast to the limited security response to the wave of bombings in the spring the Unionist cabinet met that afternoon and decided to intern 'I.R.A. agitators'. Immediately, Billy McMillan and twenty-three others were arrested (Malachy McGurran and Prionsias MacAirt were to be interned until the end of the year).[1] Despite that, the pitiful condition of the Battalion on 15th August was blamed both on McMillan and the I.R.A. leadership. However, that was not to be an issue until a month after the violence of mid-August.

By this time, the Battalion consisted of around eighty volunteers and an auxiliary of around two hundred.[2] In reality, though, it could only mobilise around thirty volunteers, supported by Cumann na mBan, Cumann na gCailíní and Fianna Éireann. This was a far cry from the days in the late 1930s or 1922 when it could almost match the R.U.C. for numbers (not including the Special Constabulary).

The Battalion had now managed to scrape together twenty-three handguns and some grenade casings. With the Battalion O/C and many of his staff arrested, from the night of 14th-15th August unionists mounted concerted attacks across Belfast, openly involving B Specials and some Unionist MPs. Catholic residents were burned out in many districts, with Bombay Street becoming the most famous. Seven people were killed, six of them in Belfast. At least 133 were wounded.

The Unionists had asked for further deployment of the British army on the 14th in Derry and by midday on the 15th for Belfast too and had decided to start closing border roads to prevent 'infiltration'.[3] The Unionist cabinet also considered imposing a curfew but doubted it could actually be enforced until troops had been deployed.

In the absence of most of the Battalion staff, ad hoc defensive units had formed including I.R.A. volunteers still at liberty, former volunteers and some Catholic ex-servicemen (technically the Battalion organised them into volunteer companies and auxiliary units).[4] A handful of weapons were dug out from half-forgotten caches containing odd revolvers and some badly stored ammunition. The long term and recurring anxieties of the Battalion were writ large. Belfast republicans now were minimally armed and under fire in a unionist assault that they had regularly warned against. At the same time, Goulding's main supporters among the Battalion staff were largely absent (albeit interned by the Unionists).

Two deeply contrasting images starkly illustrate the failure of the I.R.A. on the night of 14th-15th August and the depth of the antagonism that followed in its wake. At Broadway, where gunfire continued until past 3 am, the residents were defended by Joe Cullen, who had commanded the Engineering Battalion of the Belfast Brigade in 1922, and Jimmy Steele, who had been summarily expelled from the I.R.A. in July having been continuously active since 1920. Both were now in their sixties. While Belfast burned, the I.R.A. Chief of Staff, Cathal Goulding and other Army Council members like Mick Ryan were dressed in combat fatigues in the Dublin Mountains accompanied by a British television crew. They were staging an I.R.A. training camp for the cameras for which they had negotiated a £200 fee.

Steele and Joe Cahill walked down the Falls Road the next day. There was a mood of despair and anger directed at the I.R.A. for its failure to be prepared to defend the population. Both were called deserters and traitors and Cahill claims they were even spat upon.[5] But that day, more and more former volunteers, including those who had resigned or been dismissed from the I.R.A., sought out the Battalion and reported back for active duty. As Billy McMillan and others were still detained by the Unionists, Steele, Cahill, Billy McKee and others threw themselves into organising defensive groups alongside what was left of the Battalion. Internationally, there were unprecedented calls for the United Nations to send in a peace-keeping force. The southern government also called up its First Line Reserve and even proposed to the British government that they would jointly form a peace-keeping force (they were quickly rebuffed).

On the Friday afternoon (15th August) the Battalion took over Broadway Cinema for use as a temporary refugee centre. Some people had already fled over the border to family and friends and 150-200 were now in the care of the southern defence forces (the southern government had to initiate 'Operation Assist' in the border areas to provide help). In Dublin an angry public meeting at the G.P.O. was told by Sinn Féin President Tomás MacGiolla that the I.R.A. were the only people in a position to defend the people of Belfast but that their weapons and ammunition were much weaker than the B Specials and Unionists.

Meanwhile, besieged by northern I.R.A. officers looking for G.H.Q. to open its dumps and distribute arms and ammunition, Goulding retreated to an upstairs office with Mick Ryan and said "This is terrible, Jesus Christ, this is terrible. What am I going to do? Living

Jesus, what are we going to do?" Goulding hadn't been able to locate the I.R.A.'s Quartermaster General, Pat Reagan, so he replaced him, on the spot, with Ryan. The depth of disorganisation around Goulding is shown by the fact that Ryan didn't know Reagan had been Quartermaster and thought Goulding was filling the role himself.[6]

A Citizens Action Committee was formed in Dublin to provide support to those under attack in Belfast and make provision for those fleeing the violence. A crowd of 2,000 then marched on Collins Barracks demanding guns to defend the north. Many individuals volunteered for service in Belfast and transport was organised to Dundalk by the Committee. There had already been a similar response in Dundalk where a crowd of 2,000 had gone to the military barracks and asked for the officer in charge to obtain permission to send help and weapons into the north. By 1 am, 100 men had arrived in Dundalk from Dublin intent on making their way north. The I.R.A. in Dundalk was completely overwhelmed and neither had weapons for the men, or the capability to get them to where they were needed. Even in New York, following a public meeting, Peter Finnegan, of a newly formed United Ireland Committee, said that twenty men had already been dispatched to Belfast.

The next day, at another public meeting in Dublin, people who wished to apply to join the I.R.A. were told to present themselves at the Sinn Féin office in Gardiner Street. A meeting of I.R.A. O/Cs and the Army Council that day was told by Goulding that they should not respond with armed action.[7] Meanwhile, the Unionist Prime Minister, Chichester-Clarke, blamed Catholics, the I.R.A., civil rights movement and Irish government for trying to discredit and subvert Stormont.

Amid the chaos, on the Monday (18th August) Cathal Goulding issued a statement in Dublin claiming that northern units of the I.R.A. had been in action in Derry and Belfast and that the Army Council had placed "...all volunteers on full alert and has already sent a number of fully equipped units to the aid of their comrades in the Six Counties and to assist the local Defence Committees, Citizen Action Groups and other popular organisations...". The statement noted, somewhat paradoxically, that "The people of the Falls Road area have gratefully acknowledged this assistance in the past few days and have contrasted it bitterly with the failure of the Dublin Government to act in their defence."

While official Unionist sources refused to comment on the statement, the likes of Ian Paisley and Ronald Bunting made predictably belligerent responses. The Citizens Defence Association in Derry rapidly denied that there were any I.R.A. units operating in the city. Various civil rights groups also criticised the statement and the next day, an I.R.A. spokesman in Dublin tried to downplay the claims. Oddly the reference to volunteers being sent to the north was true, they had just never made it past Dundalk.

Over the same few days, Joe Cahill, Jimmy Drumm and Leo Martin had been dispatched in three teams to make contact with I.R.A. units south of the border and retrieve any dumped weapons they could find. They drove non-stop across the south for twenty-four hours then regrouped in Dundalk before bringing the weapons to Belfast. This included a few Thompsons, some Sten guns, .303 and .22 rifles (including M1 carbines, Garand semi-automatics, bolt-action Springfields and Lee-Enfields) and revolvers. Ammunition calibres varied widely as the Thompson fired a .45 bullet, M1s and Garands a .300 and the Lee-Enfield a .303. Many younger volunteers had little expertise in using the weapons. Notably, older volunteers from the 1940s (and earlier) were required to maintain and oversee their use.[8]

Meantime, Steele had remained in Belfast and organised a meeting to be held a couple of days later, on the return of Cahill, Martin and Drumm. The meeting was held in the social club at Casement Park on 22nd August. It was attended by the likes of Daithi O Conaill, Jimmy Drumm, Joe Cahill, Billy McKee, John Kelly, Billy Kelly, Leo Martin and Seamus Twomey. Cahill, Drumm and Martin were able to report on the attitude of the I.R.A. units, members and supporters they had encountered on their whistle-stop tours. According to Billy McKee, John Kelly and Joe Cahill, those in attendance agreed that the Battalion staff prior to August 15th had to take responsibility for the failures of mid-August and lack of preparedness of the I.R.A. in Belfast. This failure had been compounded and confused by the direction being given by G.H.Q. in Dublin. This included both the emphasis being placed on politicisation and the unwillingness to listen to those in Belfast who had reported that the risk of significant violence against Catholic communities was getting critical.

Those present appear to have decided to allow the current Belfast leadership and G.H.Q. time to respond to events. In the meantime, they could do their best to distribute the arms and ammunition recovered by Cahill, Drumm and Martin and provide other supports to the threatened districts across the city. As it was, they were going to have to await Billy McMillan's release to involve him in discussions. Although it is not described in any detail, clearly those present on August 22nd appear to have already decided to adapt to circumstances and channel the emotional response to the pogrom into a new military campaign. According to Seán MacStiofáin, this was the opposite of what G.H.Q. wanted since it still believed it could significantly grow the political opposition to the Unionists through a continuation of the civil rights campaigns.[9] In the context of what just had happened in Belfast, this must have seemed absurd to those in the city.

The same evening an edited interview with Cathal Goulding (described as I.R.A. Chief of Staff) was broadcast on R.T.E. and I.T.V. in which he claimed that, if it came to it, the I.R.A. was prepared to kill the B Specials and Paisley supporters who were attacking people's homes. Both R.T.E. and Goulding were criticised for the broadcast. Behind the barricades in Belfast, the Falls Radio Free Belfast was transmitting programmes and airing the demands of the Citizens Defence Committees, which were: (1) disarm and disband the B Specials, (2) disarm the R.U.C. and dismiss the senior officers, (3) release all internees and repeal the Special Powers Act, and (4) suspend Stormont. Inside the barricaded areas newssheets were also produced and circulated.

Over the next few weeks, McKee, Steele, Cahill and the others threw themselves into re-organising and supplying I.R.A. units across the city alongside the Defence Committees and the remaining Battalion staff under Jim Sullivan, McMillan's Adjutant. Joe Cahill gives accounts of the negative reaction in areas like Turf Lodge, Ardoyne and the Short Strand over the failure of the I.R.A. to provide sufficient defensive cover in mid-August as he toured around each, effectively sounding them out for the group that had met on

22nd August. Local ad hoc defensive committees had been set-up and were slowly brought under the umbrella of the Citizens Defence Committee whose central organising committee was chaired by Jim Sullivan (thus keeping them within the orbit of the Battalion).

---

1 Those arrested were Frank Campbell, Denis Cassidy, Denis Casson, M. Darity, J.J. Davey, Frank Donnelly, P. Duffy, R. Fitzpatrick, Jimmie Hargey, L. Johnston, D. Loy, H. Mallon, Prionsias MacAirt, Joe McCann, P.J. McCusker, John McEldowney, F. McGlennon, John McGuigan, Malachy McGurran, Liam McIlvenna, Billy McMillan, L. Savage, M. Toal and F. White. Not all were from Belfast.

2 McMillan gives a figure of one hundred and twenty volunteers (in Rosita Sweetman 1972 *One Our Knees: Ireland 1972*, p188-189).

3 P.R.O.N.I., CAB/4/1461/12.

4 MacStiofáin 1975.

5 It is repeatedly reported that 'I Ran Away' was written up on the walls, but no-one has ever identified a photograph showing the actual graffiti and the story may be apocryphal (although it was no doubt said to republicans, if not actually written on a wall).

6 This is mainly based on Mick Ryan's interviews included in Swan 2008, p297.

7 Treacy 2011, p167.

8 Quinn 1999, p148.

9 MacStiofáin 1975, p124-129.

Map showing location of barricades in Falls Road, August 1969 (*United Irishman*, September 1969).

split

When the British Army was deployed in mid-August 1969, it also brought into play its own well-established counter-insurgency strategy as well as its best known advocate and practitioner in Brigadier Frank Kitson. This included creating its own intelligence gathering capabilities in the absence of any effective intelligence held or shared by the R.U.C., Special Branch or the Unionist government.

On 30th August, MacAirt, McMillan and McGurran were all charged with possession of weapons, while MacAirt and McGurran were charged with possession of literature. The remainder detained under Special Powers Act were released. This meant that, for the time being, Jim Sullivan would be in charge of the Battalion and the Defence Committees.

Attempts to start negotiating the removal of barricades from districts that had been attacked in mid-August now provided a pretext for British Army officers to meet and profile the Citizens Defence Committee (and effectively I.R.A.) leadership from close-in. On 6th September, Jim Sullivan, as chair of the C.D.C. and acting Battalion O/C, met with the Major General Tony Dyball, the British Army's deputy director of operations in the north (revealed in that weekends Sunday papers).[1] This happened alongside meetings with Catholic clergy and others over defence of the districts that had come under attack. Sullivan and Dyball agreed that the barricades would now be guarded by British soldiers alongside the Defence Committees.

That weekend, three barricades in Albert Street were taken down and replaced with British Army barriers. British soldiers maintained a presence at them, as had been agreed. The press was rife with rumours that the discussion where this was agreed wasn't between the British Army and local clergy as publicly claimed, but between the I.R.A. and British Army. The British Army tried to quell the rumours by releasing a press statement on 8th September claiming that while Dyball and Sullivan had been present in the same house at the same time, they had not met or negotiated. The Unionists were outraged, claiming they were being bypassed and again demanded that the British Army forcibly remove all the barricades.

Given the decline of the Battalion (in particular) since the early 1940s, for it now to be negotiating directly with British Army commanders, with a sense that this was being done without the explicit consent of the Unionists, must have dramatically increased its sense of importance and relevance.[2] While only on a specific issue, for the I.R.A. as a whole, and Cathal Goulding, this level of recognition may have felt like dealing directly with the British government and, as such, a broad affirmation of current strategy.

But the agreement reached in Albert Street wasn't replicated elsewhere as almost nightly attacks on isolated Catholic families continued. Around 300 barricades had been erected across the city but the example of Albert Street didn't lead to further exchanges of hastily erected barricades for British Army barriers. Within a couple of days, Sullivan was threatening to re-erect barricades if the British Army removed them without agreement. He, along with Stormont M.P.s Paddy Devlin and Paddy Kennedy then travelled to London to try and meet senior British government figures for discussions.

On Sullivan's return, the Battalion staff met with Mick Mills, acting as an intermediary for Charlie Haughey and Neil Blaney. The staff then met Haughey and Blaney in Dundalk on Thursday 12th September. It was agreed to open a bank account and that money would be funnelled into the account for the Battalion to buy weapons.[3]

Meanwhile, a demarcation line was being erected by the British Army along the boundary of the most threatened areas (described as a 'peace line'). This was continuing over the course of the next week and was mostly completed by 16th September. Pressure was growing to have the other barricades removed and the C.D.C. organised meetings of delegates from the various districts to gauge the mood. Assurances were given by the British G.O.C. that the army would provide adequate security and that the Special Powers Act would not be applied. Again, Jim Sullivan pushed for the barricades to come down but often agreements had to be made on a street-by-street basis indicating a high level of discomfort over the proposed arrangement. This was not misplaced.

An agreement to jointly guard barricades with the C.D.C. now provided the British Army with a pretext to engage with the I.R.A. and profile leading figures for itself. Frank Kitson himself had requested a meeting with the I.R.A. leadership (which was turned down), but John Kelly has recounted that the depth of contact between the I.R.A. and British Army extended as far as a British officer providing a class on machine guns.[4] Kelly suspected that this was to evaluate the level of the technical capacity of the I.R.A. (and presumably to identify the relevant personnel). The contacts with the British Army and apparent Unionist discomfort at their presence maintained hopes in the Battalion that their deployment was the precursor to a British withdrawal. But it was just as likely that initial British Army contacts were part of a strategic phase of intelligence gathering by the British Army (in an absence of any meaningful intelligence passed to them by the R.U.C.). The Central Committee of the C.D.C. now laid down six conditions to the British: (1) disarm and disband the B Specials, (2) disarm and reorganise the R.U.C., (3) repeal the Special Powers Act and release of all political prisoners, (4) implementation of the civil rights covenant, (5) an amnesty for those who defended their homes against attack in the Falls, and (6) Westminster legislation over the head of Stormont if Stormont fails to introduce the necessary reforms. This only differed from the demands of the I.R.A. as listed in the September issue of *United Irishman* in that (6) was replaced by a demand that any settlement should be in the context of moving towards a united Ireland and that the

British government should allocate money to address issues such as housing and unemployment.

Jim Sullivan (as chair of the C.D.C.) said he would not say what would happen if the troops used force when they moved in (to remove barricades) but only that plans had been prepared. One barricade that was slow to come down was the one that had been erected at the top of the New Lodge Road, at its junction with the Antrim Road. This too was taken down on Tuesday 17th September. As with elsewhere, it was then replaced with a British Army barrier which was one of those jointly guarded by the C.D.C. and 2nd Light Infantry. That Antrim road barricade gives a sense of the complex issues around their removal that was being replicated nightly across Belfast in September 1969. On the Saturday night, unionists opened fire at the barricade, wounding a soldier and four young men. Following the shooting a local taxi firm was also attacked. As crowds gathered at either side of the barricade, hundreds of soldiers were rushed into the area and found a weapon and made four arrests in the adjoining (unionist) Tigers Bay district (leading to one conviction). At their remand hearing, on the Monday morning, R.U.C. Head Constable Thomas McCluney explained to the court that those arrested for the shooting had only fired the shots as 'feelings had been running high'.

On the Sunday, the C.D.C. for the New Lodge and Docks had met and agreed further security measures with a graduated curfew for children (8 pm) and others not involved in patrols and defence (10 pm). The C.D.C. then put in place a rota and schedule of patrols for the defence of the area. Oliver Kelly (vice-chairman of the C.D.C. and brother of John Kelly) said the shooting had been a salutary lesson for all those involved. The Major in charge of the 2nd Light Infantry in the district admitted that he hadn't believed that they would be fired upon by unionists.

Later that night unionists left a 2lb gelignite bomb in Exchange Street in the Half Bap area (immediately to the south of the New Lodge and North Queen Street). It exploded in the middle of the street, shattering windows in thirty houses although no-one was badly injured. Immediately a barricade was re-erected at the end of Exchange Street. The same pattern was to follow over the next week as local violence prompted the return of barricades.

That weekend Billy McMillan was released from internment. Against the backdrop of the New Lodge Road shooting and the bombing of Exchange Street, McMillan called a meeting of the Belfast I.R.A. staff in Cyprus Street on the Monday to have his position as Battalion O/C reconfirmed. Famously, he was confronted about the rapidly changed political landscape in a meeting later regarded as critical to the fragmentation of the republican movement (this was to accelerate over the next few months).

The group that had met on 22nd August had reconvened in North Queen Street that day and reviewed what had happened over the previous month. Their organisational efforts meant that they had sounded out pretty much the whole city. After a discussion they left for the Battalion council meeting chaired by McMillan. According to Joe Cahill, it had been decided "...to challenge the existing Battalion staff of the Belfast I.R.A. as to where their loyalties lay, whether to the people or Dublin...".[5] There are a number of relatively dramatic accounts of the meeting. McMillan claims that, after half an hour, only three staff members had turned up and he decided to postpone the meeting when Jimmy Steele and the others burst in.[6] John Kelly believed that McMillan actually knew they were coming. Kelly states that he was armed as was Billy McKee and that the main issue discussed was the failure of G.H.Q. to supply adequate resources to the northern units.[7] According to Billy McKee, Cahill and Kelly's versions are correct.[8] He states that, contrary to McMillan's version, when he, Steele, John Kelly and the others arrived they found Jim Sullivan there and Billy McMillan missing. According to Joe Cahill (and McKee), Sullivan "…couldn't do anything without shouting…" but McMillan soon arrived and Billy McKee and John Kelly led the discussion with him.

McKee says that it was just that, a discussion. He and Kelly outlined the concerns of the Belfast units and put three proposals to McMillan. The first was that they asked for co-options onto the Battalion staff for the likes of McKee, Leo Martin, Seamus Twomey and Sean McNally (six co-options were made in the end).

The second was that Belfast was to break with G.H.Q. until it acknowledged its responsibility for the failures of August. In that regard, it wanted four named members - Cathal Goulding, Mick Ryan, Roy Johnston and Seamus Costello - to step down and be replaced. The proposed replacement for Goulding was Sean Garland.[9] Garland had overseen the development of the plan for a northern campaign that had been captured by the Gardaí in May 1966. As he was known to be a committed Marxist this seems to further indicate that left wing politics was simply not a factor in the issues between Belfast and Dublin.

McMillan accepted the first and extended the Battalion staff accordingly and, on the second point, agreed to break with G.H.Q. and the Army Council for three months to allow the necessary changes to happen.

McMillan notes a third issue that was agreed but has generally been overlooked – a demand that the money donated to the Northern Defence Fund for the purchase of arms was to be spent on arms. Goulding was already known to be diverting this it into his political projects (supposedly he insisted that the first £10,000 raised would go to fund political activity).[10]

Having discussed and agreed the various points, the meeting broke up.

Seán MacStiofáin, the I.R.A. Director of Intelligence, had been in Belfast and called to McMillan's house that evening. McMillan advised him of the decision and asked him to inform the Chief of Staff, Cathal Goulding. MacStiofáin did so. It was 22nd September 1969.

The Belfast Battalion had now split from G.H.Q. in Dublin.

---

[1] This all happened in the public eye – the account here is based on the press accounts of these events in September 1969.

[2] Within three years representatives of the republican leadership would be flown to London to negotiate government ministers – all of these events must helped form the I.R.A.'s sense of its political power and what it could achieve.

[3] Official Sinn Féin 1972 *Fianna Fáil and the I.R.A.*

[4] See text of the interview with John Kelly here: https://www.pbs.org/wgbh/pages/frontline/shows/ira/inside/kelly.html.

[5] See Cahill's account in Anderson 2002. In Sweetman 1972 (p189), despite claiming that the division was over politics, Billy McMillan emphasises that Steele was unhappy with 'Dublin' quoting Steele directly.

[6] Billy McMillan in Rosita Sweetman 1972, p190.

[7] https://www.pbs.org/wgbh/pages/frontline/shows/ira/inside/kelly.html

[8] Interview with the author.

[9] Swan 2008, p312.

[10] Billy McMillan in Rosita Sweetman 1972, p191 and MacStiofáin 1975, p128-129.

epilogue

The very next day, McStiofáin returned to tell McMillan that Cathal Goulding wanted to meet. Contrary to what had been agreed the previous day, McMillan then consented to it going ahead, apparently without the knowledge of Billy McKee, John Kelly, Jimmy Steele and the others (although they soon found out). All the old anxieties within the Battalion over its autonomy and influence on overall I.R.A. strategy and the balancing of political initiatives and military action, remained on the surface. Everything was also deeply coloured by the experiences of that August. At the same time, much of the dramatic, demagogic characterisation of the split that developed in the Battalion was only really attached to it much later, in mutual attempts to delegitimise the two main factions that emerged (what became known as the 'Official' and 'Provisional' wings of the I.R.A.).

Much of what now happened unfolded quite slowly and over a number of months. Organisationally, the Irish Republican Army was no different to the likes of the Irish Republican Brotherhood and United Irishmen in being a network of local republican organisations, each grafted onto the particular circumstances of its own peculiar social and economic geography. Overall strategy was delegated to a central headquarters, usually but not always Dublin-based. That a local structure, like the Belfast Battalion, might derogate from the Dublin-based G.H.Q. wasn't unusual as, for instance, both Cork and Kerry had histories of temperamental on-off relationships with G.H.Q. in Dublin.

What now came to the fore in the Battalion was decades of frustration at the limited appreciation in Dublin of the realities of intercommunal violence in Belfast. The Belfast I.R.A. for long tolerated a subordinate role in directing overall I.R.A. policy towards partition and away from challenging the southern government. In many ways, the I.R.A. had recognised the limitations of its own capabilities in deferring its hopes to, firstly, the Boundary Commission, then de Valera, then more and more vaguely to the possibility of exerting pressure through Irish-American influence. The civil rights movement, with significant I.R.A. involvement, offered vistas of popular opposition to the Unionists only witnessed previously in the merest of glimpses, such as the Outdoor Relief Riots. At the intersection of Dublin-Belfast friction over strategic direction, many of those who had been around the Battalion for all those previous dramas and dilemmas, now believed they were witnessing an opportunity to support or lead a popular and existential challenge to the Unionists and simply were no longer willing to give Dublin a deciding say over it. Not only that, but in the space of weeks the Battalion had rapidly gone from insignificance to negotiating directly with British Army commanders in the full glare of the media and against the wishes of the Unionists.

But the unfolding dramas split the Battalion across various planes. Some retained a loyalty to I.R.A. G.H.Q. or found a deeper resonance in the increasing emphasis on the political direction that was being propounded by Goulding. Others could not escape the human roots of the organisation in communities which were now under violent attacks. Despite the forewarnings from the episodic recurrence of violence since 1964, it was clear by the months leading up to August 1969 that the I.R.A. had not made any contingency plans in the event that there was a return to the street violence of the 1920s and 1930s. The analysis being offered in Dublin to the I.R.A. leadership may have intended to address the socio-economic needs of the community but simply wasn't calibrated against the capacity of Unionism to mobilise significant street violence.

Some intricate theories weave conspiracies into the splits that occurred in the I.R.A. in 1969 and 1970, between Belfast and Dublin, between modernisers and traditionalists, between its left wing and not-so left wing. Belfast appears to have split along a web demarcated by personalities and personal histories, loyalty to Dublin and G.H.Q., distrust of Dublin and G.H.Q. and the impact of events over the summer of 1969. Much of it coloured events into the future.

The I.R.A.'s Belfast Battalion in 1969 was merely it's most recent incarnation. The Irish Republican Army structures created in Belfast after 1919 had continuously expanded up to the 1921 truce, after which it had gone through a short period of rapid expansion just prior to the chaos of 1922. It then shrank dramatically before stabilising as a small, tight-knit organisation until 1929. An expansive Fianna Éireann programme from 1929 onwards saw a dramatic increase in numbers in the early to mid-1930s while much of the 1920s old guard melted away. For a decade, a more muscular Battalion had some significance that was only finally eclipsed in late 1942. By then the Battalion was mainly cooped up in the prison camps and, by 1943, confined to staging publicity coups on the outside. Only a shrunken organisation, smaller even than that of the late 1920s, survived through the late 1940s, 1950s and 1960s.

By 1969, though, the decades of I.R.A. activity had created sizeable communities of former I.R.A., Cumann na mBan and Fianna Éireann volunteers, ex-prisoners and ex-internees. Just as the Battalion orbited the organisational centre of G.H.Q. in Dublin, so too did many individual former members and republican-minded groups swim in the same sea as the current I.R.A. volunteers. This provided a substantial pool of militant know-how and craft from which the Battalion now dramatically expanded after 1969. What happened over the next years and decades is a story for another day, though.

sources and bibliography

A handful of I.R.A. memoirs cover this period, from Jack McNally, Turlach Ó hUid, Vincent McDowell, Harry White and Joe Cahill as well as Ray Quinn's invaluable *A Rebel Voice, A History of Belfast Republicanism 1925-72* (published in 1999) which was largely put together from oral histories collected by Quinn from a number of key figures from that period. Others, like Uinseann MacEoin, Ronnie Munck and Bill Rolston, also gathered and published oral histories from I.R.A. volunteers covering the 1920s through to the 1940s. There is also a brief account of the Belfast Brigade by Jim Lane which was published by the Cork Workers Club in 1972. All of these works are cited throughout the text. There are some fragmentary archival records from the I.R.A. itself, its own publications, in newspapers like *An Síol*, *Republican News* and *Resurgent Ulster*, and a handful of memoirs written by, or at least with the assistance of, former activists. I have detailed as many of these as possible in the bibliography, even where not specifically referred to. There are also a number of historical treatments that are presented as fiction but are deeply rooted in actual events and provide rich contextual material (e.g. *Ulster Idyll* by Vincent McDowell and Laurie Green's *Odd Man Out*).

In terms of official records, the I.R.A., even though a clandestine organisation, did keep minutes and reports, send communications and memos and publish statements and newspapers. Surviving records are more abundant for the 1920s and 1930s (in the likes of the Moss Twomey archive in U.C.D.) and have been picked apart by Brian Hanley. For other periods there are small groups of documents dispersed among collections in the N.L.I. and P.R.O.N.I. (among others). Similarly, the Military Archives in Dublin hold a range of useful documents, particularly for the 1920s. As well as the mainstream I.R.A. publications like *An Phoblacht*, *War News*, *Republican News* and *The United Irishman* the Belfast I.R.A. issued a series of its own publications or Belfast/northern version of the Dublin edition. This included *An Síol*, *War News*, *Republican News*, *Resurgent Ulster*, *Glór Uladh*, *Resistance* and *Tírghrá*. Some of these survive in partial runs in N.L.I. but there is still a bit of work to be done to collate them.

Archival sources:
National Library of Ireland, Public Records Office Northern Ireland, Eileen Hickey Republican History Museum Conway Mill, Military Archives, Bureau of Military History, Moss Twomey Archive (UCD), Hansard (Stormont), CAIN.

Print media:
An Phoblacht, An Síol, An tÓglách/An tÓglach, Arm Luchta Oibre na hÉireann Newsletter, Belfast Gazette, Belfast Newsletter, Belfast Telegraph, Donegal News, Evening Herald, History Ireland, Irish Echo, Irish Examiner, Irish Freedom, Irish Independent, Irish News, Irish People,

Irish Press, Irish Times, Kerryman, Kildare Observer, Milwaukee Journal, Nacht-Ausgabe, Northern Whig, Red Hand, Republican News, Resurgent Ulster, Saoirse, Strabane Chronicle, Sunday Independent, Time, Tírghrá Ulster Herald, United Irishman, War News

Books and articles:
Adams, G. 1982 *Falls Memories*. Dingle.
Anderson, B. 2002 *Joe Cahill: A Life in the I.R.A*. O'Brien Press.
Baker, J. 2010 *Belfast in the 1960s*. Glenravel Local History Project.
Behan, B. 1958 *Borstal Boy*.
Bowyer Bell, J. 1970 *The Secret Army, A History of the I.R.A. 1916-70*. Sphere.
Boyd, A. 1969 *Holy War in Belfast*.
Bryson, A. 2007 *The Insider: The Belfast Prison Diaries of Eamonn Boyce, 1956-62*. Lilliput Press.
Collins, P. 2004 *Who Fears to Speak of '98: Commemoration and the Continuing Impact of the United Irishmen*. UHF.
Coogan, T. 1970 *The I.R.A*. Pall Mall.
Dillon, M. 1988 *God and the Gun*. Routledge.
Donnelly, D. 2010 *Prisoner 1082, Escape from Crumlin Road, Europe's Alcatraz*. Collins.
Donohoe, L. 1998 'Regulating Northern Ireland: The Special Powers acts, 1922-1972', *The Historical Journal*, Vol. 41, No. 4, p1089-1120.
Debray, R. 1967 *La Révolution dans la Révolution*.
English, R. 2003 *Armed Struggle: The History of the I.R.A*. Macmillan.
Garland, R. 2008 Protestant Fears and Civil Rights: Self-Fulfilling Conspiracies? *History Ireland*, Vol.16, No.5, pp. 30-33.
Glennon, K. 2013 *From Pogrom to Civil War: Tom Glennon and the Belfast I.R.A*.. Mercier Press.
Green, F.L. 1945 *Odd Man Out*. Michael Joseph.
Guevara, E. 1961 *La Guerra de Guerillas*.
Hanley, B. 2002 *The I.R.A., 1926-1936*. Four Courts Press.
Hanley, B. 2010 *The I.R.A. – A Documentary History*.
Hanley, B. 2013 'The needs of the people: the IRA considers its future 1967-68' in *Saothar* 38.
Hastings, M. 2011 *All Hell Let Loose*.
Heatley, F. 1974a The Beginning 1964-Feb. 1968. *Fortnight*, No. 80, 10-11.
Heatley, F. 1974b The Early Marches. *Fortnight*, No. 81, 9-11.
Heatley, F. 1974c The PD and Burntollet. *Fortnight*, No. 82, 8-9.
Heatley, F. 1974d The N.I.C.R.A. Split. *Fortnight*, No. 83, 13-14.
Johnson, R. 2004 *Century of Endeavour*. Lilliput Press.
Kearney, S. 2003, Joe the 'Ra and me. *Fortnight*, 8-10.
Kleinrichert, D. 2001 *Republican Internment and the Prison Ship Argenta, 1922*. Irish Academic Press.
Lane, J. 1972 *On the IRA: Belfast Brigade Area*. Cork Workers Club.
Lynch, R. 2009 The Northern I.R.A. and the Early Years of Partition, 1920-22. (see https://dspace.stir.ac.uk/bitstream/1893/1517/3/robert%20john%20lynch-24072009.pdf.txt)
Mahon, T. and Gillogly, J. 2008 *Decoding the I.R.A*.. Mercier Press.
MacEoin, U. 1980 *Survivors*. Argenta.
MacEoin, U. 1985 *Harry*. Argenta.
MacEoin, U. 1997 *The I.R.A. in the Twilight Years, 1923-1948*. Argenta.
McDermot, J. 2001 *Northern Divisions: the old I.R.A. and the Belfast pogroms 1920-22*. Beyond the Pale.

McDowell, V. 1989 *An Ulster Idyll*. Annamount Press.
McGuffin, J. 1973 *Internment*. Anvil Books.
McMillan, L. 1975 Lecture on The Role of the I.R.A. 1962-67. *Repsol Pamphlet*, No. 21.
McNally, J. 1989 *Morally Good, Politically Bad*. Andersonstown News.
MacStiofáin, S. 1975 *Memoirs of Revolutionary*. Gordon and Cremonesi.
McVeigh, J. 1999 *Executed: Tom Williams and the I.R.A..* Beyond The Pale.
Milotte, M. 1984 *Communism in Modern Ireland*. Gill and Macmillan.
Mitchell, S. 2017 *Struggle or Starve: Working-Class Unity in Belfast's 1932 Outdoor Relief Riots*. Haymarket Books.
Munck, R. and Rolston, B. 1987 *Belfast in the 1930s, an oral history*. Blackstaff Press.
Daly, M. and O'Callaghan, M. 2007 *1916 in 1966: Commemorating the Easter Rising*. RIA.
O'Callaghan , S. 1956 *Easter Lily: the story of the I.R.A.*
Ó hUid, T. 1960 *Ar Thoir Mo Shealbha*. Foilseacháin Náisiunta Teoranta.
Ó hUid, T. 1985 *Faoi Ghlas*. Foilseacháin Náisiunta Teoranta.
Parkinson, A. and Phoenix, É. 2010 *Conflicts in the North of Ireland 1900-2000*. Four Courts Press.
Purdie, B. 1990 *Politics on the Streets: the origins of the civil rights movement in Northern Ireland*.
Quinn, R. 1999 *A Rebel Voice, A History of Belfast Republicanism 1925-72*. Belfast Cultural and Local History Group.
Ryan, M. 2018 *My Life in the I.R.A.: The Border Campaign.*
Ryan, P. 1994 *The Birth of the Provisionals*. (available on the CAIN archive at http://cain.ulst.ac.uk/othelem/organ/docs/ryan01.htm)
Steele, J. undated *Belfast Graves*. National Graves Association.
Steele, J. undated *Antrim's Patriot Dead*. National Graves Association.
Steele, J. 1966 *Belfast and nineteensixteen*. National Graves Association.
Stephani, E. 1965 *Spies in Ireland*. Four Square Books.
Swan, S. 2008 *Official Irish Republicanism, 1962 to 1972*. Lulu Books.
Sweetman, R. 1972 *On Our Knees, Ireland 1972*. Pan Books.
Taylor, P. 1998 *Provos: The I.R.A. and Sinn Féin*. Bloomsbury.
Treacy, M. 2011 *The I.R.A. 1956-69: Rethinking the Republic*. Manchester University Press.
Watt, J. 1981 *Na Fianna Éireann, Case Study of Political Youth Organisation*. PhD submitted to University of Glasgow.
White, R. 2006 *Ruairí Ó Brádaigh, The Life and Politics of an Irish Revoluntionary*. Indiana University Press.

Index

Adams, Dominic: 49, 61, 97, 101, 109-110, 172, 179.
Adams, Gerry: 146, 167.
Adams, Joseph: 98.
Adams, Paddy ('Maghera'): 61, 111, 154, 158.
Aiken, Frank: (as I.R.A. Chief of Staff) 21, 27, 34; as Fianna Fáil Minister 66, 115, 124.
Al Rawdah: 121, 123-4, 137, 161.
An Phoblacht: 20, 31-33, 37, 41-3, 45-6, 49-51, 61-2, 72, 102, 111, 127-9.
An Síol: 60, 66, 70, 72, 76, 78-9.
An tÓglach: 6 (as *An tÓglách*), 180, 193, 108, 111, 124, 180, 237-8.
Anderson, Charles: 57, 58, 61.
Andrews, J.M.: 96, 157.
Anti-Partition League: 63-4, 96, 100, 175-80, 182, 186-7.
Arbour Hill: 70-1, 81, 113.
Ardoyne: 5, 45, 86, 88, 91, 95, 97, 100, 114, 119, 121, 148-9, 153, 165, 167, 195, 199.
Argenta: 8, 10, 12-13, 15, 21.
Armagh: 66, 146, 187, 192.
Armagh (I.R.A.): 66, 145.
Armagh (prison): 22, 96, 162, 166, 177, 198; hunger-strike: 163; releases: 169.
Atkinson, Joe: 117, 121, 130-132.
Austin, John: 106, 119.
'B Specials': see R.U.C.
Bailey, John: 72.
Ballymacarrett: 5, 11, 14, 24, 28, 30, 68-70, 76, 96, 100-102, 112, 114, 119, 121, 153, 165.
Ballykinlar (prison): 21.
Ballykinlar (camp): 112, 114-5, 119, 123.
Bannon, James: 146, 164.
Barnes, Joe: 16.
Barnes, Peter: 110-2, 114; reburial: 221.
Barrett, William: 49, 121.
Barrett, Dick: 10, 181.
Barry, Tom: 56, 60; (as Chief of Staff): 87, 93-4, 110.
Baxter, Samuel: 48.
Beasant, Harry: 113.
Beattie, Jack 168, 176, 213.
Beattie, R.J.: 95.
Behan, Brendan: 78, 143.
Belfast (prison): see Crumlin Road.
Bell, John: 98.
Bennett, Jack: 205-6.

Benson, Terry: 128.
Bing, Geoffrey: 179, 209.
Blaney, Neil: 231.
Blythe, Ernest: 10.
Boland, Gerry: 2, 97, 113, 117-8.
Boswell, Barney: 39, 41, 106, 168.
Bowyer Bell, John: 2, 138, 188, 192, 195,
Boyce, Eamon: 178, 187, 190, 196, 200, 203.
Boyle, Leo: 78.
Boyle, Patrick: 70.
Brady, Des: 159.
Bradley, Dympna: 97.
Bradley, John: 168.
Bradley, Liam: 97, 105, 112, 124.
Bradley, Margaret: 97.
Bradshaw, Bob: 23, 41-2, 47-53, 60-1, 94.
Brady, Jack: 39, 41, 53, 68-9, 96, 100, 104, 122-3.
Brady, Josephine: 94-6.
Brady, Michael: 94.
Brennan, Hugh: 49.
Brennan, Walter: 49.
Brogan, Seamus: 164.
Brooke, Basil (Lord Brookeborough): 56.
Buckley, Margaret: 32.
Bunting, Matthew: 98.
Bunting, Ronald: 226.
Burke, Liam: 109, 141, 144, 158, 206, 221; prison escape: 126, 149; in Dublin: 146; as Adjutant-General: 128, 153-56; on hunger-strike: 166; in prison: 166, 179, 198; released: 176; involved in Wolfe Tone Society: 205.
Burke, Seamus: 116.
Burns, Brian: 49, 65, 87, 90.
Burns, Frank: 25.
Burns, James: 97 (also appears as Francis James Burns).
Burns, Madge: 150, 163, 174.
Burns, Seamus (Rocky): 109, 136, 158, 164-5, 173.
Byrne, James: 111.
Byrne, Richard: 149.
Byrne, Thomas: 121.
Cahill, James: 173.
Cahill, Joe: 42, 110, 200, 208; in prison: 126, 129, 152-3, 158, 195-7; resigns from I.R.A.: 173, 204; as Belfast Adjutant: 178-9, 182, 186, 188, 190-1, 193-

239

4; as Belfast O/C: 195; returned to I.R.A.: 222, 225, 227-8, 233-4.
Cahill, Joseph (Senior): 41.
Cahill, Thomas: 41.
Cairns, Thomas: 122.
Callaghan, Owen: 124-5, 129.
Callaghan, Sarah: 124-5.
Campbell, Frank: 228.
Campbell, James: 199.
Campbell, Michael: 97.
Campbell, Philip: 61.
Campbell, Rory: 61.
Campbell, Thomas (T.J.): 63, 136, 166, 168.
Campbell College: 74-7, 80-1, 85.
Campbell's Coffee House: 237.
Carleton, Paul: 34, 39.
Carleton, Peter: 33-4, 39, 47, 64.
Carlin, Joe: 155.
Carmichael, Sean: 58.
Carolan, Mick: 11, 23.
Carson, Hugh: 76.
Carson, Patrick: 76.
Casey, Leo: 97, 119.
Cassidy, Denis: 228.
Casson, Denis: 228.
Caughey, Sean: 201, 205, 211.
Cavanagh, Paddy: 66, 70, 81.
Chamberlain, Frank: 101.
Chichester-Clarke, Robert: 226.
Christle, Joe: 189, 193, 196.
Citizens Defence Committees: 226-8, 230.
Clann na Gael: 175-6.
Clann na Poblachta: 63, 171-2, 175, 180-2.
Clarke, James: 211.
Clarke, Jimmy: 154-5.
Clarke, Joe: 18, 213.
Clarke, Philip: 189.
Clarke, Tom: 80.
Clerkin, John: 66.
Clyde, George: 71.
Collins, James: 48.
Collins, Michael: 7.
Collins, Paddy: 196.
Collins, Tim: 114.
Collins, Tom: 146.
Comhairle na Poblachta: 33.
Comhairle na dTeachtaí: 21, 28-9, 33.
Communist party: Workers Revolutionary Party/Revolutionary Workers Group: 39, 56; Great Britain: 47, 58; Ireland: 57-60, 88, 149, 206; Irish Workers League: 210; Northern Ireland: 209, 213.
Connolly Association: 205, 209-10, 220.
Connolly, Charles: 25.
Connolly, Daniel: 126, 129.

Connolly, James (Bam): 32, 40, 58-59.
Connolly, James (1868-1916): 66, 122, 180, 222; James Connolly Workers Republican Club: 63.
Connolly, Joe: 65.
Connolly, John: 24.
Connolly, Roddy: 63.
Connolly, William: 61.
Conradh na Gaeilge: 181, 186.
Coogan, Billy: 123.
Coogan, Tim Pat: 2, 100, 115, 122-5, 129, 158.
Cooney, Andy: 32, 34, 56.
Cooper, John: 12.
Corbett, James: 195.
Cordner, Henry (Dixie): 150, 175.
Corr, Arthur: 76, 78, 81, 123, 125, 128, 145.
Corr, Bridget: 106.
Corrigan, Pat: 164.
Corvin, Hugh (Aodh Ó Coirbhin): 7, 12, 14, 18, 20-1, 24-7, 30, 63, 93, 165.
Cosgrove, Tony: 199.
Costello, Seamus: 203, 233.
Coughlan, Anthony: 210-11, 216.
Cox, John: 131.
Craig, James (Lord Craigavon): 33, 48, 80.
Craig, John: 12.
Crawford, James: 49.
Crawford-Browne, Alexander: 71.
Crean, John: 136.
Cremin, Denis: 144.
Cronin, Sean: 193-5, 199, 205.
Crosskerry, Jack: 52-3, 61.
Crumlin Road (prison): 14, 21-2, 47, 58, 80-1, 87, 89, 93-4, 96-7, 99, 106, 118, 121, 123-4, 133, 136-8, 145, 147-9, 153, 164-7, 170, 172, 176, 180-1, 195-202, 209, 212-3; escapes 126-7, 149, 152-4, 197, 199.
Cullen, Joe: 225.
Cullen, Patrick: 25.
Cumann na mBan: 4-6, 18, 19, 21, 27, 29, 31, 33, 35, 51, 55, 66, 94-5, 102, 104, 125, 152, 172, 186, 224, 236.
Cumann na gCailíní: 224.
Cumann Poblachta na hÉireann: 77.
Cunningham, Mary: 121.
Cunningham, Patrick (Etna Drive): 114, 119.
Cunningham, Patrick (Conway Street): 183.
Cunningham, Sean: 85.
Curragh (camp): 7-8, 10, 12.
Curragh (prison): 143, 156, 158, 165, 175, 203.
Curran, Bernard: 161, 164.
Cusack, Sean: 8.
Dartmoor: 115, 126, 137.
Daly, Arthur: 131.
Daly, George: 131.
Dalzell, Eddie: 128.

McCallum, Seamus: 178, 182; Belfast O/C: 175; Liverpool O/C: 182.
McCann, Arthur: 124.
McCann, Charles: 106.
McCann, Dan: 12.
McCann, Frank: 158.
McCann, Joe: 212, 228.
McCann, Michael: 170.
McCann, Patrick: 61.
McCann, Robert: 90, 97, 100.
McCarthy, Gerry: 168.
McCarthy, Patrick: 163.
McCartney, Eddie: 75, 77, 93, 97.
McCartney, Sarah Jane: 106.
McCaughey, Sean: 75, 80, 84-5, 104, 133, 172, 205; Ginger Group: 87; in prison: 110, 132, 170-; Northern Command O/C: 112, 118-9, 122-4, 130; Adjutant-General: 130; Stephen Hayes: 115, 130-2; acting Chief of Staff: 131; death sentence: 132; hunger-strike: 170-1.
McCloskey, Francis: 222.
McCloskey, Hugh: 87, 90, 100.
McCluney, Thomas: 232.
McCluskey, Jack: 109.
McComb, Sam: 63.
McCombe, Andy: 128.
MacConaill, Michael: 5.
McConnell, Brian: 212, 214.
McConnell, Willie John: 117.
McConville, Patrick: 106.
McCool, Sean: 30, 59, 94; Crown Entry: 79; hunger-strike: 82; Adjutant-General: 133; Chief of Staff: 133, 139, 142-3.
McCorley, Roger: 6.
McCormick, James: 110-2, 114, 221.
McCormick, John: 58, 61, 67.
McCorry, Billy: 119.
McCorry, Jimmy: 170.
McCotter, Charlie: 128.
McCotter, Pat: 110; Ginger Group: 87; hunger-strike: 166.
McCotter, Sam: 159.
McCoy, John: 120.
McCreevey, Seamus: 158.
McCrystal, Cathal: 172.
McCullough, Billy: 88, 122, 149, 218.
McCullough, Denis: 7-8, 10-11, 65.
McCullough, Philip: 106.
McCurry, Willie: 25, 41, 61.
MacCurtain, Tomás: 111, 179, 203; hunger-strike: 113, 117.
McCusker, Cathal (Chips): 155, 158.
McCusker, Frank: 98.
McCusker, James: 164.

McCusker, P.J.: 228.
McDermott, Jim: 1.
McDermot, John: 25.
McDonagh, Liam: 212.
McDonald, Alexander: 76, 81.
McDonnell, Arthur: 98.
McDowell, Charles: 145.
McDowell, Vincent: 154, 158, 237.
McEldowney, John: 228.
McEntee, Sean: 65.
MacEoin, Uinseann: 37.
McErlean, Mickey: 161.
McGahey, Sophia: 71.
McGeough, Eddie: 152.
McGeough, Frank: 15.
McGinley, John: 161.
MacGiolla, Tomás: 211, 213, 225.
McGivern, Art: 105.
McGlade, Charlie: 39, 41, 124, 172; Crown Entry: 79-82, 84, 86; Northern Command O/C: 100, 104, 111, 119, 127; Quartermaster-General: 130, 131; shot in Dublin: 133.
McGlade, Frank: 181, 190, 204, 209, 212.
McGlennon, F.: 228.
McGoldrick, Francis: 61.
McGouran, Chris: 213.
McGouran, George: 149.
McGouran, James: 12, 25.
McGowan, Peter: 49, 61.
McGranaghan, Des: 212, 218.
McGrath, Pat: 37, 70, 72.
McGrath, Paddy: 109.
McGrath, Tom: 59.
McGrath, William: 204.
McGrath, Paddy: 121.
McGrogan, Frank: 78.
McGrogan, Henry: 113.
McGrogan, Paddy: 195.
McGrogan, Thomas: 49.
McGuffin, John: 169.
McGuigan, Francis: 214, 218.
McGuigan, John: 228.
McGuinness, Bobby: 132.
McGuinness, David: 6, 9.
McGuinness, Patrick: 128.
McGuinness, Willie: 109.
McGurk, Harry: 98.
McGurk, Joe: 24, 36, 39, 59, 167; Adjutant: 41, 47, 57, 60: in prison: 56-7, 165, 179; National Graves Association: 177.
McGurran, Malachy: 222, 224, 228, 230.
McHenry, Sean: 96.
McHugh, Hugh (see Harry White): 171.
McHugh, Roger: 206.

White, F.: 228.
White, Harry: 40-1, 48, 60, 70, 86, 93, 141; Gyles Quay: 69; Ginger Group: 77, 87, 93, 97; in prison: 69, 89, 143, 168; England: 97, 106; Northern Command O/C: 143-6, 150, 152, 154-8, 163-5, 172; Acting Chief of Staff: 167: Altaghoney: 171; Wolfe Tone Society: 205.
White Cross: 27.
Wiggins, Billy: 85.

Williams, Tom: 138, 141, 142, 172; execution: 144-7, 149-50, 162, 208.
Wilson, Capt: 30.
Winston Green: 112.
Woodall, John: 187.
Woods, James: 95, 98.
Woods, Patrick: 13, 24-5, 27, 58, 100.
Woods, Seamus: 9; Divisional O/C: 6-7.
Wright, Teresa: 88.